NEW PERSPECTIVES IN EARLY EMOTIONAL DEVELOPMENT

i

Summary Publications in the Johnson & Johnson
Pediatric Round Table Series:

1. *New Perspectives in Early Emotional Development*
   Edited by John G. Warhol, PhD

Series includes continuing education programs
and patient education materials.

For additional information,
call 1-877-JNJ-LINK or fax 1-877-565-3299.

NEW PERSPECTIVES IN EARLY EMOTIONAL DEVELOPMENT

Edited by
John G. Warhol, PhD

Introduction by
Steven P. Shelov, MD

Sponsored by

Library of Congress Catalog Card Number: 98-67497

Main entry under title:

New Perspectives in Early Emotional Development

Johnson & Johnson Pediatric Institute, Ltd. Pediatric Round Table series: 1998

Includes bibliography

Summary of a pediatric conference held in February 1998.

ISBN 0-93-1562-19-8

Previously published in *Pediatrics* Vol.102, No.5, Supplement, P.1225-1331, November, 1998.

Cover photo: Elaine Siegel

Table of Contents

Table of Contents

Participants

Ronald G. Barr, PhD
Professor, Montreal Children's Hospital
2300 Rue Tupper
Child Development Program C-808
Montreal QC, CANADA H3H1P3

Lois Bloom, PhD
Edward Lee Thorndike Professor
of Psychology and Education
Box 5
Teacher's College
Columbia University
525 West 120th Street
New York, NY 10027

Nadia Bruschweiler Stern, MD
14 CH. De Clairejoie
1225 chene-Borg
Geneva, Switzerland

William B. Carey, MD
Clinical Professor of Pediatrics
(U of Penn)
Children's Hospital of Philadelphia
Department of Pediatrics
34th and Civic Center Boulevard
Philadelphia, PA 19104

Harry T. Chugani, MD
Professor, Pediatric Neurology at
Wayne State University
Children's Hospital
3901 Beaubien Boulevard
Detroit, MI 48201

Robert N. Emde, MD
Professor, University of Colorado
Health Sciences Center
University of Colorado Medical Center
4200 East 9th Avenue
C268-69
Denver, CO 80262-0001

Tiffany M. Field, PhD
Professor, Pediatrics, Psychology
and Psychiatry
University of Miami Medical School
Director, Touch Research Institutes
Nova Southeastern University
3301 College Avenue
Fort Lauderdale, FL 33314

Nathan A. Fox, PhD
University of Maryland
Human Development
Room 4304, Benjamin Building
College Park, MD 20742-1131

Julia Freedman
Pediatric Institute of
Johnson & Johnson
Grandview Road
Skillman, NJ 08558

Robert J. Haggerty, MD
Department of Pediatrics
(Room 4-8104)
University of Rochester School
of Medicine
601 Elmwood Avenue
Rochester, NY 14642-8777

Marshall Klaus, MD
Adjunct Professor, Pediatrics
University of California, San Francisco
657 Creston Road
Berkeley, CA 94708

Lewis A. Leavitt, MD
Professor of Pediatrics
University of Wisconsin
Medical Director, Clinical
Services Unit
Waisman Center 546
1500 Highland Avenue
Madison, WI 53705-2274

Participants

Lewis P. Lipsitt, PhD
Professor of Psychology and
Medical Science
Department of Psychology
Box 1853
Brown University
Providence, RI 02912

Cecelia McCarton, MD
Professor, Albert Einstein
Medical College
Rose F. Kennedy Center #820
1300 Morris Park Avenue
Bronx, NY 10456-1402

Matthew E. Melmed, JD
Executive Director, Zero to Three
National Center for Infants, Toddlers,
and Families
734 15th Street NW, Suite 1000
Washington, DC 20005

Bonnie Petrauskas
Pediatric Institute of
Johnson & Johnson
Grandview Road
Skillman, NJ 08558

Kyle D. Pruett, MD
Professor of Psychiatry
Yale University Child Study Center
230 South Frontage Road
New Haven, CT 06520

Arnold J. Sameroff, PhD
Professor of Psychology
Center for Human Growth &
Development
University of Michigan
300 N. Ingalls, 10th floor
Ann Arbor, MI 48109-0406

Holly Ruff, PhD
Professor of Pediatrics
Albert Einstein College of Medicine
Rose F. Kennedy Center
1300 Morris Park Avenue
Bronx, NY 10461

Steven P. Shelov, MD
Chairman, Dept. of Pediatrics
Maimonides Medical Center
Professor, Pediatrics
SUNY Health Sciences Center
Brooklyn, NY 11219

Daniel Stern, MD
Professor
University of Geneva
Bata 234 Center
Route De Drize 9
1227 Carouge Switzerland

Kathleen Tirpak, RN
Pediatric Institute of
Johnson & Johnson
Grandview Road
Skillman, NJ 08558

Edward Z. Tronick, PhD
Chief, Child Development Unit
The Children's Hospital
300 Longwood Avenue
Boston, MA 02115

Arlene S. Walker-Andrews, PhD
Professor, Rutgers University
Tillett Hall, 53 Avenue E
Piscataway, NJ 08854

John G. Warhol, PhD
Executive Director
The Warhol Institute
225 First Avenue
Atlantic Highlands, NJ 07716

Preface

Johnson & Johnson is pleased to re-introduce the highly regarded Pediatric Round Table series. Originally established in the 1970s, the goals of these conferences are to: foster the free exchange of the latest research in the field of infant development; to discuss the clinical implications of that research; and to make those findings available to all professionals working in the field of infant health. This new series of Pediatric Round Tables goes beyond its predecessors by including international experience in infant development and by utilizing electronic publication for global on-line access to the conference proceedings.

The faculty of this Pediatric Round Table: *New Perspectives in Early Emotional Development* represent the world's leaders in the field of infant development. Bringing years of experience from a variety of disciplines, the faculty shared their perspectives on the most effective ways to facilitate the healthy development of infants and families.

A common theme emerging from the Round Table focused on the role that everyone caring for infants plays in the "development of unique and healthy human beings," as well as the need for communication and cooperation among all individuals that influence young lives.

This publication is dedicated to James T. Dettre and Robert B. Rock, Jr. whose vision at Johnson & Johnson established these highly respected scientific round tables. Our goal is to continue to build and provide a library of current research and valuable information on childcare that features the world's leading scientists and health care specialists.

Julia A. Freedman
Director, Johnson & Johnson Pediatric Institute, Ltd.

Introduction

Research in child development has focused on a number of issues over the years. The early years paid strong attention to the major motor and fine motor milestones of young infants. Educating providers and parents about their young babies' capabilities, in terms of what they could do at various ages, from rolling over to sitting up to taking the first steps, was part of those early research outcomes. Certainly parents were better off knowing what their babies could do at different stages; just having the anticipation coupled with some knowledge allowed for a more satisfying relationship. The grist of "anticipatory guidance" offered by pediatricians over those early years of understanding child development were focused on those milestones and, I believe, offered some mutual ground of understanding and appreciation.

In the late 1930s and continuing thereafter, following the observations, research, and publications of Arnold Gessell and Beatrice Ilg, Margaret Mahler, Thomas Bowlby, Renee Spitz, and most definitively Chess, Thomas, Birch, and Escalona, child development began to broaden in its definition and scope. Beyond understanding what a baby could do, the energy and focus shifted to who a child was, what were they thinking, and what did the observed responses really mean. It was one thing to understand that a 1-month-old smiled responsively, it was yet another to appreciate the why and wherefore of that time of baby's life. It was an important recognition that many babies appeared to have a range of motor abilities, it was yet another to appreciate that babies had a range of behavioral differences as well, often recognizable from the first moments of life.

With the shift and broadening of much of the research, the inevitable dialogues regarding the importance of nature versus nurture ensued. What were the most important influences on a child's future direction and personality? Did the environment entirely determine the results of the growth process or was the wiring all predetermined before birth and there was little that could be done except for some fine tuning? Did the results of the research on sensory abilities reflect a predetermined state? Did the fact that some children from the same family seemed so different from the beginning and yet ended up with many of the same values and beliefs shared by all members of the family reflect the fact that child development was really the result of a mixture of nature and nurture? Finally, what determined the emotional responses of young infants and babies and could we know more about those responses by focusing the research on some of the newer technology and techniques of understanding?

The Johnson & Johnson Corporation has long been a proponent of achieving a higher level of understanding of child development and sharing that understanding with a broad range of other researchers, educators, and providers of care. Through a number of their efforts, they have brought real applications of this research understanding to the greater public as well. Their landmark series of child development symposia, published throughout the 1970s and 1980s, was critical to disseminating the information regarding the state-of-the-art knowledge at that time. Volumes on language, sensory needs and abilities, early infant stimulation techniques, and a number of others were intended to bring other child experts up to date with respect to newfound knowledge of the vast capabilities of the growing child.

This current volume represents a new stage in this educational process, and accompanies a number of new breakthroughs in our understanding of the potential influences on growing babies' development. Understanding the emotional development of babies and young children is the focus of these symposia. The organizers of these proceedings are of the deepest belief that a strong and well-constructed appreciation of the influences of the emotional development of growing infants and children can serve as the basis for more effective interactions, activities, and relationships over the course of the growing years of children. If the emotional development is understood, cared for, paid attention to, and nurtured, much of the work of the growth of the later years can be more productive and effective.

Simultaneously, our spectacular technology has permitted us to better understand the biology and neurochemistry of some of these stages of and influences upon emotional development. This symposium has brought those cutting-edge investigators together to share their latest findings in their area of expertise so that we may better understand how to most productively integrate their findings into usable interventions for all readership, researchers, educators, and practitioners alike. It is our intent to launch this new era in understanding the brain growth and capabilities of our young infants.

What are our goals for our children?

- To permit them to have confidence in the world around them

- To develop a sense of personal power

- To feel lovable and be able to love others

- To be able to recognize they are special and unique

- To value the importance of good communication with others

The tools, which are needed for many of these crucial steps in having the most effective interactions with our growing babies from the first days of life, are enclosed in this volume. It is hoped that appreciating them will permit wider, positive impact on our future generations; we are convinced it will!

Steven P. Shelov, MD

Section 1:
Critical Importance of
Emotional Development

Abstracts From Section 1. Critical Importance of Emotional Development

Biological Basis of Emotions: Brain Systems and Brain Development

Harry T. Chugani, MD

Functional neuroimaging techniques, such as positron emission tomography, have made it possible to noninvasively investigate brain metabolism during development. Studies have revealed a dynamic period of metabolic maturation and neuronal growth corresponding to the processes of synaptic proliferation and pruning of unused pathways. This physiologic plasticity is believed to be the biological basis for a "critical period" of learning and emotional development.

Temperament and Regulation of Emotion in the First Years of Life

Nathan A. Fox, PhD

Temperament is the tendency to express particular emotions with a certain intensity that is unique to each individual child. Although temperament seems to be biologically based, learning to regulate emotional expressions depends on caregiver input and socialization. Part of this process involves forming a trusting relationship with the infant so that he or she learns to rely on the parent to help "regulate" stressful or frustrating situations.

Early Emotional Development: New Modes of Thinking for Research and Intervention

Robert N. Emde, MD

Recent thinking about early emotional development in a context useful for pediatricians and other clinicians is reviewed in this chapter. Important functions of emotions are that they help define individuality, motivate approach or withdrawal from a situation, and communicate with caregivers. Emotional development in the first years of life may be seen as a series of predictable step-wise transitions when changes are pervasive and involve major re-orientation for children and families.

Biological Basis of Emotions: Brain Systems and Brain Development

Harry T. Chugani, MD

Introduction

Functional neuroimaging techniques have made it possible to noninvasively study energy metabolism in the developing human brain. This can be accomplished using positron emission tomography (PET) and the principles underlying the ^{14}C-2-deoxyglucose autoradiographic method developed by Sokoloff and colleagues.[1] With PET and the tracer 2-deoxy-2(^{18}F)fluoro-D-glucose (FDG), measurements of regional cerebral glucose utilization can be made during different stages of development and related to behavioral maturation, synaptogenesis, plasticity, and other neuromaturational phenomena.

Developmental Patterns of Cerebral Glucose Metabolism

The pattern of glucose metabolism in the newborn brain is fairly consistent (Fig 1) with the highest degree of activity in primary sensory and motor cortex, thalamus, brainstem, and cerebellar vermis.[2-4] The cingulate cortex, amygdala, hippocampus, and occasionally the basal ganglia may also show a relatively high glucose metabolism compared to most of the cerebral cortex in the newborn period.[5] The relatively low functional activity over most of the cerebral cortex during the neonatal period is in keeping with the relatively limited behavioral repertoire of newborns, characterized by the presence of intrinsic brainstem reflexes and limited visuomotor integration.[6,7] However, the relatively high metabolic activity of amygdala and cingulate cortex in newborn suggests an important role of these limbic structures in neonatal interactions and possibly emotional development.

Increases of glucose utilization are seen by 2 to 3 months in the parietal, temporal, and primary visual cortex, basal ganglia, and cerebellar hemispheres

Fig 1. Newborn pattern of cerebral glucose metabolism.

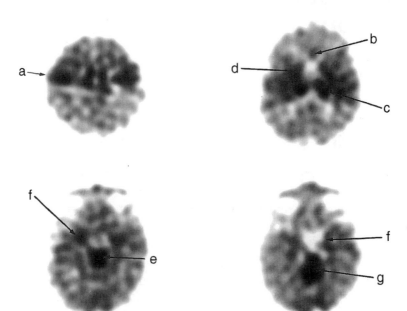

At this stage of development, glucose metabolism is most apparent in the sensorimotor cortex (a), cingulate cortex (b), thalamus (c), basal ganglia (d), brainstem (e), mesial temporal region (f), and cerebellar vermis (g). Metabolic activity is low in most of the frontal, parietal, temporal, and occipital cortex, as well as in the cerebellar cortex.

(Fig 2). These changes in glucose metabolism coincide with improved skills involving visuospatial and visuosensorimotor integration, the disappearance or reorganization of brainstem reflex neonatal behaviors, and evidence of increasing cortical contribution to the electroencephalogram.[6,8-10]

The frontal cortex is the last brain area to display an increase in glucose consumption. Starting between 6 and 8 months, lateral and inferior portions of frontal cortex become more functionally active (Fig 3) and eventually, between 8 and 12 months, the dorsal and medial frontal regions also show increased glucose utilization. These changes of frontal cortex metabolism come at a time when cognitively related behaviors, such as the phenomenon of stranger anxiety, and improved performance on the delayed response task

Fig 2. Pattern of cerebral glucose metabolism in a 3-month-old infant.

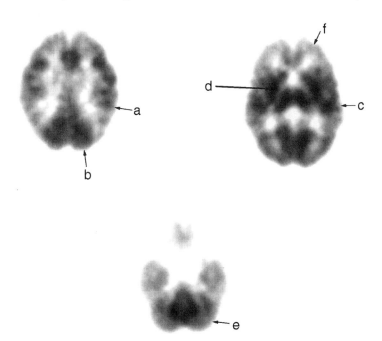

Glucose metabolism has increased in the parietal cortex (a), occipital cortex (b), temporal cortex (c), basal ganglia (d), and cerebellar hemispheres (e). Metabolic activity remains low in the frontal cortex (f).

begin to appear.[11-13] Increased glucose requirement in frontal cortex also coincides with the expansion of dendritic fields and the increased capillary density observed in frontal cortex during the same period of development.[14,15] By approximately 1 year of age, the infant's pattern of glucose utilization resembles qualitatively that of the adult.

From these observations, it appears that in the first year of life, the ontogeny of glucose metabolism follows a phylogenetic order, with functional maturation of older anatomical structures preceding that of newer areas.[2-4] In addition, the suggestion by Kennedy and colleagues that "at any given developmental age, structures having metabolic rates equal to or exceeding their mature levels are those that dominate the behavior at that age" appears to be

Fig 3. Pattern of cere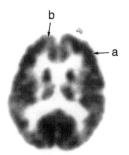   8-month-old infant.

Glucose metabolism has increased in the lateral portion of the frontal cortex (a) prior to the medial portion (b).

the case in human infant development because there is at least a general relationship between the maturational sequence of regional glucose metabolism and the behavioral maturation of the infant.[16]

Glucose Metabolic Rates

An important aspect of the PET technique is that it allows for the quantitative measurement of biochemical and physiological processes. Thus, even though the brain of a 1-year-old infant shows a similar distribution pattern of glucose utilization as that of an adult, the rate at which glucose is being used by various brain regions is different. In fact, a dynamic, protracted, and non-linear process of "metabolic maturation" is apparent at birth and lasts until early adulthood (16 to 18 years).

Birth to 4 Years

At birth, the regional or local cerebral metabolic rates of glucose utilization (LCMRglc) are about 30% lower than those seen in normal healthy young adults (Fig 4). Between birth and approximately 3 to 4 years, the cerebral cortex shows a dramatic increase in LCMRglc to reach levels that exceed adult rates by over twofold (Fig 4A,B). Such changes in LCMRglc are not observed in brainstem (Fig 4C), but a less dramatic increase is seen in the basal ganglia and thalamus (Fig 4D).

Fig 4. Absolute values of local cerebral metabolic rates for glucose (LCMRglc) for various brain regions vs age in normal infants, children, and young adults.

A. cerebral cortex (lobes);
B. selected cortical regions;
C. brainstem and cerebellum;
D. basal ganglia and thalamus.

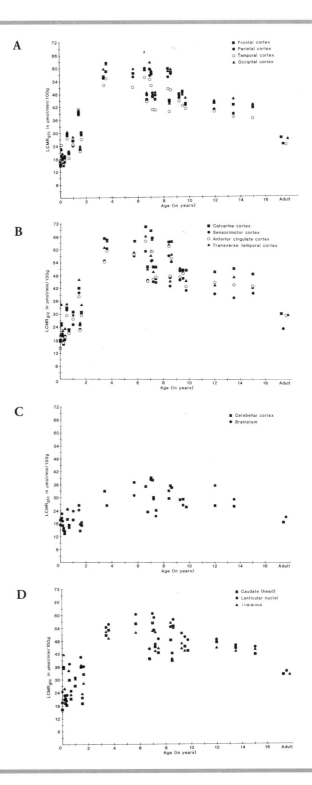

Middle Childhood

Between the ages of about 4 years and 9 to 10 years, the LCMRglc for cerebral cortex is essentially at a high plateau of over twofold the glucose utilization seen in adults[3,4] (Fig 4A,B). This observation confirms the earlier results of Kennedy and Sokoloff, who demonstrated that the average global cerebral blood flow (an indirect measure of energy demand in the brain) in nine normal children (aged 3 to 11 years) was approximately 1.8 times that of normal young adults.[17] Moreover, average global cerebral oxygen utilization was approximately 1.3 times higher in children than in adults.

Early and Late Adolescence

At about 9 to 10 years, LCMRglc for cerebral cortex begins to decline and gradually reaches adult values by 16 to 18 years[3,4] (Fig 4A,B). It should be noted that all regions in cerebral cortex studied show the *same timing* of developmental changes in LCMRglc. The time course is different only for basal ganglia and thalamus, whereas the brainstem does not show significant ontogenetic changes with glucose metabolism measurement.

Regressive Phenomena in Development

Since the initial description of the ontogeny of cerebral glucose metabolism in children, the relevance of these dynamic changes has been under active investigation.[3] For over half a century, it has been recognized that the brain of an immature rat consumes more oxygen and glucose than an adult rat brain.[18,19] For example, the utilization of both oxygen and glucose in excised rat cerebral cortex, striatum, cerebellum, and brainstem were shown to be higher during the period between the fourth and seventh postnatal weeks compared to adult values.[19] Studies performed in other species using either in vivo autoradiography or PET have confirmed the presence of a developmental period during which local cerebral energy demand, as measured by local cerebral blood flow (LCBF) and, more directly, LCMRglc, exceeds that of the adult.[20-22]

The ontogeny of cerebral glucose metabolism described in Fig 4 is not surprising considering the fact that regressive phenomena are not uncommonly seen during development of the nervous system.[23-25] Thus, there are periods during development when neurons, neuronal processes, synaptic contacts, neurotransmitters, and various receptors are in excess of those seen in the adult. The proliferation and overproduction of neurons in humans occur prenatally, whereas programmed cell death (apoptosis) begins prenatally and continues until about the second postnatal year.[26] Surviving neurons undergo a similar phenomenon postnatally characterized by overproduction of their arborization and synaptic contacts, followed by an elimination or 'pruning' phase.[27-29] Synaptic elimination in humans probably continues well into adolescence; for example, synaptic density in frontal cortex of children up to 11 years of age have been shown to exceed that in adults.[27]

Synaptic pruning is not a random phenomenon, but rather is based on activity-dependent stabilization. In other words, repeated neuronal activity involving certain circuits during a critical period will result in stabilization of those circuits rather than elimination during the pruning process.[30] The advantage of activity-dependent stabilization of neuronal pathways is that there will not be an unnecessary expenditure of genes to code precisely for the large number of connections in the brain. Rather, repeated early environmental exposure will serve to guide the molding of an optimum cortical cytoarchitecture for the individual's future needs. The molecular basis for the stabilization and retention of some pathways and vulnerability of others to be pruned or eliminated is an area of intense investigation. Recent studies have suggested that in the visual cortex of kittens, activity-dependent stabilization may involve activation of the N-methyl-D-aspartate (NMDA) subclass of glutamate receptors, associated perhaps with the expression of specific neuronal proteins.[31,32]

Neurobiological Correlates of Glucose Metabolism Ontogeny

Relationship to Synaptogenesis

Under normal circumstances, the major portion of glucose used by the brain is for the maintenance of resting membrane potentials.[33-35] Therefore, there should be a direct relationship between the degree of 'connectivity' and the energy demand of the brain in the resting state. This is, in fact, the case when one compares the ontogeny of LCMRglc in cerebral cortex (Fig 4A,B) with the developmental curve for synaptogenesis in humans.[27-29] Similar comparisons performed in the developing kitten and rhesus monkey have confirmed this notion.[21,22]

The ontogeny of LCMRglc in cerebral cortex may, therefore, provide an indirect measure of synaptogenesis in the brain. An analysis of the glucose metabolism curve (Fig 4A,B) suggests that the ascending portion of the curve seen between birth and 4 years represents the period of synaptic proliferation in cerebral cortex. The 'plateau' period of the curve seen during middle childhood represents the period of synaptic excess and exuberant connectivity associated with increased energy requirement by cortex compared to adults. This is also the critical period in development when the process of activity-dependent synaptic stabilization is at a maximum. With adolescence and losses from synaptic elimination, LCMRglc in cortex begins to gradually decline as shown by the gradual downslope of the metabolism curve because of diminishing energy requirement.[4,36]

Brain Plasticity

There have been many studies relating synaptogenesis to a critical period of developmental brain plasticity. Since the ontogeny of LCMRglc appears to be related to synaptogenesis, it may indirectly provide a marker for a critical period of developmental brain plasticity in humans and, therefore, analyses correlating synaptogenesis, LCMRglc, and brain plasticity may have important implications.

This relationship has been characterized in area 17 of the kitten visual system. In the kitten, synapses are sparse in this region at birth, and LCMRglc values are correspondingly low.[21,37,38] During the second and third weeks postnatally, there is a well-documented rapid increase of synaptic density which reaches a peak at about 70 days; this phase of synaptogenesis coincides with the period when LCMRglc values rise dramatically in area 17.[38,39] Moreover, the same period is characterized as a 'critical period' in the visual system of kittens. During this time, there is considerable plasticity manifested when the visual system is injured or experimentally manipulated.[40-44] This 'critical period' of development in kitten visual cortex extends from 3 weeks to about 3 months of life, during which LCMRglc values are high in this brain region. Subsequently, there is diminishing plasticity associated with regression of exuberant synapses and connections, and a corresponding decline of LCMRglc presumably due to diminished energy requirement.[45-47]

Interestingly, in the cat, the decline of LCMRglc in cerebral cortex is followed by a second, larger peak occurring at about 180 days. Only after 180 days did LCMRglc decrease to reach final adult values. The period at about 180 days appears not to coincide with any known major neuroanatomical changes in the cat brain, but rather is the time when cats undergo sexual maturation.[48] This timing of the gradual decline of LCMRglc in the cat at puberty is analogous to that in humans (Fig 4A,B). A similar relationship between synaptogenesis and LCMRglc has been shown in the developing rhesus monkey.[22,49]

Clinical Implications of Glucose Metabolism Ontogeny

The ontogeny of cerebral glucose metabolism appears to have profound implications in the study of human brain development, plasticity, and possibly child psychopathology. A central hypothesis in our laboratory is that at around 10 years, when LCMRglc in cerebral cortex begins to decline (Fig 4), developmental brain plasticity also begins to diminish in children. There is much support for this hypothesis in the clinical literature, only some of which will be reviewed below.

Children who have been deprived of exposure to language since birth, as for example those raised in the wilderness (so-called 'feral' children), can still acquire reasonably normal language skills but only if intense speech and language therapy is introduced prior to the age of 10 years.[50] Following damage to the language-dominant hemisphere, there is better recovery of language skills if the injury occurs prior to about 8 to 10 years than if the injury occurs later.[51,52] In fact, based on an extensive review of this subject, Lenneberg postulated that there must be a "critical period for language acquisition" ending at about the age of 10 years, after which there is a more limited (but not absent) potential to acquire language skills.[53]

Analyses in the human visual system have also suggested a similar timing of diminished plasticity in children. A number of studies have evaluated the upper age limit beyond which stimulus deprivation of one eye in young children, caused by monocular occlusion such as a cataract or certain kinds of strabismus, will induce an irreversible reduction of visual acuity known as amblyopia.[54] Two large clinical surveys have found that amblyopia can be prevented from occurring if the monocular occlusion is corrected prior to about 8 to 10 years of age, but not after.[55,56] In addition, the compromise in visual depth perception induced by unilateral enucleation (eg, for orbital tumors) can be minimized if enucleation is performed prior to about 8 years of age.[57]

The notion of an extended period during childhood when activity-dependent synaptic stabilization occurs has recently received considerable attention by those individuals and organizations dealing with early intervention to provide "environmental enrichment" and with the optimal design of educational curricula. Thus, it is now believed by many (including this author) that a biological "window of opportunity" when learning is efficient and easily retained is perhaps not fully exploited by our educational system.

Finally, there are investigators who believe that the onset of some forms of psychopathology may be related to various segments of the synaptogenesis curve. For example, Feinberg and colleagues have noted that the maturational curves for LCMRglc, synaptogenesis, and delta wave amplitude during sleep in children are similar, and can be best described with a gamma distribution model.[58] The proposal is made that since the early symptoms of schizophrenia occur at early adolescence when the maturational curves begin their downslope, errors in synaptic pruning localized to certain areas of the brain (eg, frontal cortex) may play an important role in the pathophysiology of this disorder.

References

1. Sokoloff L, Reivich M, Kennedy C, et al. The [14C] deoxyglucose method for the measurement of local cerebral glucose utilization: theory, procedure, and normal values in the conscious and anesthetized albino rat. *Journal of Neurochemistry.* 1977;28:897-916.

2. Chugani HT, Phelps ME. Maturational changes in cerebral function in infants determined by 18FDG positron emission tomography. *Science.* 1986;231:840-843.

3. Chugani HT, Phelps ME, Mazziotta JC. Positron emission tomography study of human brain functional development. *Annals of Neurology.* 1987;22:487-497.

4. Chugani HT. Development of regional brain glucose metabolism in relation to behavior and plasticity. In: Dawson G, Fischer KW, eds. *Human Behavior and the Developing Brain.* New York, NY: Guilford Publications, Inc; 1994:153-175.

5. Chugani HT. Neuroimaging of developmental non-linearity and developmental pathologies. In: Thatcher RW, Lyon GR, Rumsey J, Krasnegor N, eds. *Developmental Neuroimaging: Mapping the Development of Brain and Behavior.* San Diego, CA: Academic Press, Inc; 1996:187-195.

6. Andre-Thomas CY, Saint-Anne Dargassies S. *The Neurological Examination of the Infant.* London, England: Medical Advisory Committee of the National Spastics Society; 1960.

7. Von Hofsten C. Eye-hand coordination in the newborn. *Developmental Psychology.* 1982;18:450-461.

8. Bronson G. The postnatal growth of visual capacity. *Child Development.* 1974;45:873-890.

9. Parmelee AH, Sigman MD. Perinatal brain development and behavior. In: Haith M, Campos J, eds. *Biology and Infancy.* New York, NY: Wiley; 1983;11:95-155.

10. Kellaway P. An orderly approach to visual analysis: parameters of the normal EEG in adults and children. In: Klass DW, Daly DD, eds. *Current Practice of Clinical Electroencephalography.* New York, NY: Raven; 1979:69-147.

11. Kagan J. Do infants think? *Scientific American.* 1972;226:74-82.

12. Fuster JM. Behavioral electrophysiology of the prefrontal cortex. *Trends in Neuroscience.* 1984;7:408-414.

13. Goldman-Rakic PS. The frontal lobes: uncharted provinces of the brain. *Trends in Neuroscience.* 1984;7:425-429.

14. Schade JP, van Groenigen WB. Structural organization of the human cerebral cortex. *Acta Anatomica.* 1961;47:74-111.

15. Diemer K. Capillarisation and oxygen supply of the brain. In: Lubbers DW, Luft UC, Thews G, Witzleb E, eds. *Oxygen Transport in Blood and Tissue.* Stuttgart, Germany: Thieme Inc; 1968:118-123.

16. Kennedy C, Sakurada O, Shinohara M, Miyaoka M. Local cerebral glucose utilization in the newborn macaque monkey. *Annals of Neurology.* 1982;12:333-340.

17. Kennedy C, Sokoloff L. An adaptation of the nitrous oxide method to the study of the cerebral circulation in children; normal values for cerebral blood flow and cerebral metabolic rate in childhood. *Journal of Clinical Investigation.* 1957;36:1130-1137.

18. Himwich HE, Fazekas JF. Comparative studies of the metabolism of the brain in infant and adult dogs. *American Journal of Physiology.* 1941;132:454-459.

19. Tyler DB, van Harreveld A. The respiration of the developing brain. *American Journal of Physiology.* 1942;136:600-603.

20. Kennedy C, Grave GD, Jehle JW, Sokoloff L. Changes in blood flow in the component structures of the dog brain during postnatal maturation. *Journal of Neurochemistry.* 1972;19:2423-2433.

21. Chugani HT, Hovda DA, Villablanca JR, et al. Metabolic maturation of the brain: a study of local cerebral glucose utilization in the developing cat. *Journal of Cerebral Blood Flow and Metabolism.* 1991;11:35-47.

22. Jacobs B, Chugani HT, Allada V, et al. Developmental changes in brain metabolism in sedated rhesus macaques and vervet monkeys revealed by positron emission tomography. *Cerebral Cortex.* 1995;3:222-233.

23. Changeux JP, Danchin A. Selective stabilization of developing synapses as a mechanism for the specification of neuronal networks. *Nature.* 1976;264:705-712.

24. Jacobson M. *Developmental Neurobiology.* 2nd ed. New York, NY: Plenum; 1978:302-307.

25. Cowan WM, Fawcett JW, O'Leary DDM, Stanfield BB. Regressive events in neurogenesis. *Science.* 1984;225:1258-1265.

26. Rabinowicz T. The differentiated maturation of the human cerebral cortex. In: Falkner F, Tanner JM, eds. *Human Growth, Neurobiology and Nutrition.* 3. New York, NY: Plenum; 1979:97-123.

27. Huttenlocher PR. Synaptic density in human frontal cortex developmental changes and effects of aging. *Brain Research.* 1979;163:195-205.

28. Huttenlocher PR, de Corten C, Gary LJ, Vanderloos H. Synaptogenesis in human visual cortex: evidence for synapse elimination during normal development. *Neuroscience Letters.* 1982;33:247-252.

29. Huttenlocher PR, de Corten C. The development of striate cortex in man. *Human Neurobiology.* 1987;6:1-9.

30. Rauschecker JP, Marler P. What signals are responsible for synaptic changes in visual cortical plasticity? In: Rauschecker JP, Marler P, eds. *Imprinting and Cortical Plasticity.* New York, NY: Wiley; 1987:193-200.

31. Rauschecker JP, Hahn S. Ketamine-xylazine anaesthesia blocks consolidation of ocular dominance changes in kitten visual cortex. *Nature.* 1987;326:183-185.

32. Bear MF, Kleinschmidt A, Gu QA, Singer W. Disruption of experience-dependent synaptic modifications in striate cortex by infusion of an NMDA receptor antagonist. *Journal of Neuroscience.* 1990;10:909-925.

33. Mata M, Fink DJ, Gainer H, et al. Activity-dependent energy metabolism in rat posterior pituitary primarily reflects sodium pump activity. *Journal of Neurochemistry.* 1980;34:213-215.

34. Kadekaro M, Crane AM, Sokoloff L. Differential effects of electrical stimulation of sciatic nerve on metabolic activity in spinal cord and dorsal root ganglion in the rat. *Proceedings of the National Academy of Sciences USA.* 1985;82:6010-6013.

35. Nudo RJ, Masterton RB. Stimulation-induced 114CI2deoxyglucose labeling of synaptic activity in the central auditory system. *Journal of Comparative Neurology.* 1986;245:553-565.

36. Chugani HT, Phelps ME, Mazzlotta JC. Metabolic assessment of functional maturation and neuronal plasticity in the human brain. In: von Euler C, Forssberg C, Lagercrantz H, eds. *Neurobiology of Early Infant Behaviour.* Wenner-Gren International Symposium Series. New York, NY: Stockton Press; 1989;55:323-330.

37. Voeller L, Pappas GD, Purpura DP. Electron microscope study of development of cat superficial neocortex. *Experimental Neurology.* 1963;7:107-130.

38. Winfield DA. The postnatal development of synapses in the visual cortex of the cat and the effects of eyelid suture. *Brain Research.* 1981;206:166-171.

39. Winfield DA. The postnatal development of synapses in different laminae of the visual cortex in the normal kitten and in kittens with eyelid suture. *Developmental Brain Research.* 1983;9:155-169.

40. Morest DK. The growth of dendrites in the mammalian brain. *Zeitschrift fur Anatomie und Entwicklungsgeschichte.* 1969;128:290-317.

41. Hubel DH, Wiesel TN. The period of susceptibility to the physiological effects of unilateral eye closure in kittens. *Journal of Physiology.* 1970;206:419-436.

42. Spinelli DN, Hirsch HVB, Phelps RW, Metzler J. Visual experience as a determinant of the response characteristics of cortical receptive fields. *Experimental Brain Research.* 1972.

43. Pettigrew JD. The effect of visual experience on the development of stimulus specificity by kitten cortical neurones. *Journal of Physiology.* 1974;237:49-74.

44. Timney B. The effects of early and late monocular deprivation on binocular depth perception in cats. *Developmental Brain Research.* 1983;7:235-243.

45. Barlow HB. Visual experience and cortical development. *Nature.* 1975;258:199-203.

46. Hirsch HVB, Leventhal AG. Functional modification of the developing visual system. In: Jaconson M, ed. *Handbook of Sensory Physiology, Vol IX: Development of Sensory Systems.* Berlin-Heidelberg, Germany: Springer-Verlag; 1978:279-335.

47. Sherman SM, Spear PD. Organization of visual pathways in normal and visually deprived cats. *Physiological Review.* 1982;62:738-855.

48. Kling A. Behavioural and somatic development following lesions of the amygdala in the cat. *Journal of Psychiatric Research.* 1965;3:263-273.

49. Rakic P, Bourgeois JP, Eckenhoff MF, et al. Concurrent overproduction of synapses in diverse regions of the primate cerebral cortex. *Science.* 1986;232:232-235.

50. Curtiss S. Feral children. In: Wortis J, ed. *Mental Retardation and Developmental Disabilities.* XII. New York, NY: Brunner/Mazel; 1981;XII:129-161.

51. Basser LS. Hemiplegia of early onset and the faculty of speech with special reference to the effects of hemispherectomy. *Brain.* 1962;85:427-460.

52. Curtiss S. *Genie: A Psycholinguistic Study of a Modern-day "Wild Child."* New York, NY: Academic; 1977.

53. Lenneberg E. *Biological Foundations of Language.* New York, NY: Wiley; 1967:125-187.

54. Marg E. Prentice Memorial Lecture: Is the animal model for stimulus deprivation amblyopia in children valid or useful? *American Journal of Optometry and Physiological Optics.* 1982;59:451-464.

55. Awaya S. Stimulus vision deprivation amblyopia in humans. In: Reinecke RD, ed. *Strabismus.* New York, NY: Grune and Stratton; 1978:31-44.

56. Taylor V, Taylor D. Critical period for deprivation amblyopia in children. *Transactions of the Ophthalmological Societies of the United Kingdom.* 1979;99:432-439.

57. Schwartz TL, Linberg JV, Tillman W, Odom JV. Monocular depth and vernier acuities: a comparison of binocular and uniocular subjects. *Investigative Ophthalmology Visual Science.* 1987;28(Suppl):304.

58. Feinberg I, Thode HC, Chugani HT, March JD. Gamma distribution model describes maturational curves for delta wave amplitude, cortical metabolic rate and synaptic density. *Journal of Theoretical Biology.* 1990;142:149-161.

Temperament and Regulation of Emotion in the First Years of Life

Nathan A. Fox, PhD

Introduction

Perhaps one of the most important insights for new parents is that their new infant brings to the world his or her own set of individual characteristics which in no small way shape the world in which they all live. New parents are given a great deal of advice on how to feed their baby, how to get their baby to sleep through the night, and what to do with that baby when, in the mid-afternoon, he or she begins their "fussy period." Yet most of this advice is for the 'average' baby. And parents often do not have an average baby. Rather, their infant may exhibit a pattern of behaviors that sets him/her off from the average and may at times present challenges in parenting. These individual characteristics and patterns of behavior are what developmental psychologists call temperament. Temperament represents those characteristics that make an infant unique with regard to his or her daily responses to being fed, changed, bathed, played with, or put down for a nap. These characteristics have sometimes been ignored by developmentalists as well as advice givers. Yet temperament may represent an important construct around which the relationship between parent and child is formed, through which the pattern of daily interaction is constructed, and by which the infant's nascent personality emerges.

In modern developmental psychology, Thomas and Chess were the first to emphasize the importance of temperament in infant behavior and parenting.[1] These researchers recruited a sample of over 100 expectant families, and began a long-term study of infant and parent infant behavior. Thomas, Chess, and their colleagues visited families on a monthly basis, at which time they interviewed the parents, observed the infant alone and the mother and infant together. They took copious notes about the infant's behavior and the daily routine of the mother and infant. From these notes they generated lists of behaviors that infants exhibited. They then grouped these behaviors into nine dimensions or factors that they believed characterized the range of individual differences in the style in which infants responded to the range of normal events in their lives. For Thomas and Chess these factors represented the "how" of behavior. For example, in a daily activity like bathing, they observed differences in activity level, the degree to which infants adapted to the water, whether or not the baby "liked" the bath, and the intensity of their response to the activity.

The nine dimensions that Thomas and Chess produced are shown in Table 1. Each dimension ranges from high to low, and an individual infant could be placed anywhere on each of the nine dimensions. Obviously, the dimensions were not orthogonal to one another and infants who were placed high on certain dimensions could place high on others as well. From these clusterings Thomas and Chess created three classifications of infants: difficult, easy, and slow to warm up.[2]

Table 1.   Nine temperament dimensions of Thomas and Chess[1]

Activity level

Rhythmicity

Adaptability

Approach-withdrawal

Mood

Intensity

Attention span-persistence

Distractibility

Threshold of responsiveness

Since Thomas and Chess's original work there have been several conceptualizations of infant temperament, some of which have been offshoots of the Thomas & Chess model, while others have developed from different theoretical positions regarding the origins of temperament. Among the more recent temperament theories is one articulated by Rothbart and Derryberry.[3] Their model of temperament was initially based upon European temperament theorists such as Strelau who themselves were considered neo-Pavlovians regarding the etiology of individual differences.[4] Originally, Pavlov and his colleagues noted that there were differences among animals in their rate of conditioning. Pavlov attributed these differences to "strength of the nervous system" with animals having strong nervous systems taking longer to condition than animals with "weak" nervous systems. Pavlov's students, particularly those interested in human personality, expanded this notion in an attempt to understand individual differences in response to sensory stimulation. They reasoned that differences in response to a stimulus, as measured by the latency to respond, the threshold of response, the intensity of response, and the time needed to return to homeostasis were all a function of the strength of the individual nervous system. Individual differences in reactivity were the material which created temperament. Eastern European psychologists used models based on Pavlov to develop methods for assigning individuals to occupations.

Rothbart adapted this model to the study of individual characteristics of human infants. She reasoned that important differences in individual infant responses to the environment could be assessed via measurement of their reactivity. Reactivity in turn could be assessed by measurement of threshold to respond, latency to respond, and intensity of response. Rothbart proposed that reactivity could be assessed behaviorally and could be understood physiologically. That is, individual differences in reactivity were probably a function of differences in the manner in which autonomic, central, and hormonal systems respond.[5]

Rothbart felt that a second dimension to individuality was the degree to which infants could modulate reactivity. She proposed that infant temperament was comprised of differences in the degree to which infants reacted and regulated their reactivity. Whereas reactivity itself was the response to external stimuli, regulation was the manner in which the infant returned to homeostasis. Regulation could be best measured by the time it took the infant to soothe after the initial reaction. In subsequent writings she expanded on the dimension of regulation, and along with her colleagues have proposed that the regulation of behavioral reactivity comes to depend, more and more, on the development of specific cognitive systems that facilitate modulating behavioral reactivity. Rothbart has written extensively about the attentional system and its role in regulation of reactivity. She argues that this system is involved in modulating reactivity both physiologically and behaviorally. For example, the toddler's ability to be distracted when upset, or the degree to which the child can break set and move on, are important factors in his or her ability to regulate reactivity. This model has a distinct developmental component to it, in which the development of cognitive processes are seen as an integral part of the formation of infant temperamental style.[6] Although infants may be born with individual differences in reactivity, their regulatory capacities are far from complete at birth.

The notion that temperament could be conceptualized in terms of individual differences in reactivity has been further refined in the work of Goldsmith and Campos.[7] Both developmentalists come from a tradition in which they stress the importance of emotions in the psychological life of the child. For Campos and Goldsmith, emotions play an important functional role. They regulate internal psychological states and they regulate interpersonal and social interaction. In their attempt to integrate this functional view of emotions into a theory of temperament, Goldsmith and Campos utilized Rothbart's notion of reactivity. They argued that temperament may be defined as the manner in which infants express each of the discrete emotions. The expression of emotion may vary among individuals along the same dimensions as reactivity in Rothbart's model: threshold, latency to respond, intensity of response. For example, an infant may have a low threshold to express fear, a short latency of response, and a high intensity of response. This infant may be contrasted with one whose threshold to express fear is high, latency is long, and intensity is low when it is elicited. Thus, in Goldsmith and Campos's model, temperament may be described as individual differences in the tendency to express each of the different discrete emotions.

Our own work has utilized a definition of temperament that is a synthesis of the positions of Rothbart, Goldsmith, and Campos. It emphasizes the importance of individual differences in the expression of discrete emotions, but at the same time includes a broader definition of reactivity as well as an emphasis on regulation.[8] We view temperament as the set-point around which an infant reacts to unfamiliar or mildly stressful stimuli by expressing a predominant emotional response. The degree to which infants are aroused and the affect they express during that arousal best characterizes one infant from another. It also reflects the degree to which the infant is successful in modulating an emotional response. There are a number of critical points to this definition. First, it is proposed that there are differences among infants in the set-point or threshold by which they will respond to novelty or mild stress. Second, that reaction is characterized both in terms of the affect which is expressed and the degree of arousal (intensity of response). Finally, infants differ in the manner in which they "handle" that arousal; that is, the way in which they modulate that response. Differences in the predisposition to express specific emotions, to react with a certain intensity, and the disposition toward regulatory behaviors are thought to be governed by a neurophysiological system that includes limbic and frontal regions of cortex.[9]

A Broad View of Emotion Regulation

In a chapter written for the Society for Research in Child Development monograph *The Development of Emotion Regulation*, Pamela Cole and colleagues list seven dimensions they say are critical to understanding emotion regulation (as shown in Table 2).[10] The dimensions (from top to bottom) form an interesting developmental sequence. They indicate the issues that are critical during formative periods of infancy, preschool, and school years. For example, in the first years of life a critical aspect of development may be characterized in terms of the management of state-related processes. Cole et al address this by examining the role that emotional states have in regulating arousal. They list three dimensions: availability of a range of emotions; modulation of intensity of emotion; and fluid shifts in emotion. As it is necessary for the young infant to have a full range of states, to modulate these states, and to transition from one state to another, so too it is important that emotional behavior be governed by these same principles. An important characteristic of infant expressivity is their access to a full range of emotions. Infants who are predisposed to one particular type of emotion are very different from those who express a range of affects. Infants may also differ in the degree to which they are able to modulate a particular emotional state. One underlying cause of their inability to modulate affect intensity is the lack of fluid transition from one state to another. The end result may be an infant predisposed to negative affect, unable to modulate an intense reaction, and showing lack of fluid transitions to calmer states.

In the preschool years, the issues involving regulation of emotion are different. The child now finds himself in different contexts, interacting with peers and unfamiliar adults. There is a transition at this time from the toddler

---

Table 2. Seven dimensions of emotion regulation[10]

Access to a full range of emotions

Modulation of intensity and duration of emotion

Fluid smooth shifts in transition from one state to another

Conformance of cultural display rules

Integration of mixed emotions

Verbal regulation of emotional processes

Management of emotions about emotion

whose immediate needs are usually satisfied to the preschooler who must learn to wait his turn, who must realize that every toy in the store or every cereal on the shelf cannot be bought. The child learns that it is often inappropriate to laugh in certain contexts and that certain rules of conduct apply in specific situations. The development of rule-bound behavior and the increased ability for delay of gratification go hand-in-hand in the developmental processes in emotion regulation occurring in the preschool period. The child learns the display rules of his culture: when it is appropriate to laugh and when it is necessary to maintain a solemn expression. The child also learns to utilize verbal skills to modulate emotional responses. Here Cole's idea is similar to Rothbart's in placing emphasis upon the development of cognitive skills (in this case language) as an important element in the development of regulatory strategies. Finally, Cole et al emphasize an often-overlooked aspect of emotional development, the recognition of mixed emotions. At some point in early childhood the young child realizes that some situations are neither happy or sad, but may contain elements of both. The idea that one can feel more than one emotion simultaneously and that sometimes these emotions are conflicting is one recognized by adult emotion theorists as an important state, but seldom addressed in the developmental literature.

Emotion regulation does not take place in a vacuum, but most certainly develops within the framework of interaction and relationships. Parents provide more than just strategies for their infants and children to use in modulating emotional arousal. The very interaction between parent and child may in itself be a modulating force, as seen in the work of Myron Hofer.[11] Hofer has, through a series of experiments, detailed the nature of the interaction between a mother and infant rat pup during the first days of life. He found that aspects of this interaction regulate physiological as well as behavioral development. It is important to note that the aspects of this interaction that are modulatory do not necessarily involve the provision of food or heat to the pup but are behavioral in nature. As such, the *relationship itself* seems to have a modulatory effect upon the arousal system. The mother-infant relationship then may be viewed as a biobehavioral system, the outcome of which is the modulation of those physiological systems involved in emotional arousal.

A set of interactive factors may be viewed in parallel to Cole et al's seven dimensions and are important in understanding the effects of interaction on the development of emotion regulation as seen in Table 3. These factors form (from top to bottom) a developmental sequence parallel to that provided by

Table 3. *Emotion regulation at the level of interaction*

Maternal comforting and soothing of infant distress

Reciprocity and confirmation of affective states within the family

Provision of effective environments for the modulation of emotion

Use of peers as a source of affect modulation

Friendship and the development of intimacy as a context for regulation

Cole et al. For example, during early infancy, the mother provides soothing and comforting to her infant when the infant is distressed. This external source of emotion regulation is critical, particularly for the infant who does not have the internal resources to self-soothe.

During the first years, the infant presents parents with multiple instances of a variety of facial expressions during different contexts. Parental labeling of these expressions and subsequent validation of the infant's emotional states is also important for successful regulation. It is important that the infant understand that the feelings he/she has are not unusual and are shared within the context of the family. The matching and confirmation of infant internal states by the adult caregiver seems particularly important because it allows the infant to associate its feeling state with the shared state of another. One of the reasons that the "still face" paradigm is so successful is that it violates for the infant the shared affect state that he or she has established with the care-giver. Instead of returning a smile, the mother is asked to present a neutral, blank facial expression. Many infants will work to elicit a return smile in this instance.

A third dimension of caregiver interaction is the provision of effective envi-ronments for the modulation of emotion. Infants differ in the degree to which they can modulate their responses to external stimulation. As such, caregivers are often aware of the need to provide the infant with a quiet place that will enable self-regulation. Environments with a great deal of stimula-tion may be too chaotic or overwhelming for some infants and may not allow the child to develop the self-regulatory mechanisms necessary for appropriate emotion regulation. Parental input is critical here. For example, in the early months, parents may need a quiet room with dim lights to calm a fussy baby; later on it may be necessary to "remove" an infant from a situation which is too stimulating or exciting, and which does not allow the child sufficient latitude to modulate his or her reactivity.

As the child matures, age mates and peers become important agents of socialization. Children take cues from their peers as to what is amusing and how to react in certain situations. The peer group becomes an important source of affect modulation for the young child. To the extent that there is disorganization within the peer group, this may lead to inappropriate emotional behavior by individual children. Also, young children learn to "read" the affective cues of other children. They learn how to deal with the needs of other children within the group and how to modulate their own emotional responses when their immediate goals are not met. One prime example is with disputes over toys. Very early on, children learn (or do not learn) how to deal with conflict over object acquisition and how to modulate their own individual desires for toys.

A final dimension of importance in the development of emotion regulation and a source of important modulation is the formation of friendships within the peer group. Current research on the development of friendships in early childhood has stressed the importance of forming intimate relationships among older children. As children spend more time with peers they are increasingly exposed to the effects of other social agents on emotion, and have the opportunity to learn or practice regulatory strategies. Rejection by peers has a documented association with negative emotional states. Social rejection has been shown to induce negative affect in 7- to 8-year-old children. Moreover, even 5-year-old children appear to be aware that social rejection or verbal harassment will induce negative emotions, and that social nurturance, maternal help, or verbal support can remediate negative feelings. Sibling relationships as sources of emotion regulation become important in late childhood as well, and appear to have long-term consequences.[12,13]

For older children, adolescents, and adults, external sources of emotion regulation also include the responsiveness and support of peers (especially best friends), particularly during times of stress (for a review, see Rubin, Bukowski, & Parker).[14] Peer interactions create expectations about how potential social partners may behave. These expectations are emotionally laden and result in the individual's setting social goals, conjuring up means to meet those goals, and accessing alternate responses when the social partner fails to behave in a manner consistent with cognitive expectations.[15] In some cases, the child's expectations (which are drawn from previous interactions and the emotions resulting from them) lead to inappropriate social and emotional responses during peer interactions. Such inappropriate social situations lead inexorably to the individual's being isolated and rejected by the peer group. On the other hand, positive expectations of others, feeling secure in the company of others (peers), and the experience of positive social interactions may give the child confidence to explore the peer universe and develop social skills and competencies that result in peer acceptance and popularity.[14]

Issues in the Study of Emotion Regulation

Because emotion regulation in the developing lives of infants and young children is so important, we need to clarify exactly what we are studying and how we can go about completing research in this area. The following section outlines four issues that are critical in approaching the research of emotion regulation. These issues are applicable across development and can serve as a starting point for those interested in the study of emotion regulation.

What Is Being Regulated in Emotion Regulation?

This question is both conceptual and methodological, although the answers to both are clearly interrelated. Conceptually, we assume that individuals differ in the degree to which they react to environmental stimulation. Both the nervous system and behavioral responses contribute to these differences in reactivity. Indeed, the organization of behavioral responses is most probably similar to the organization of physiological responses to stimulation. A similarity for behavioral and nervous system responses may be that the system attempts to return to the resting state that existed prior to stimulation. Although it is true that the absolute energy level of resting states differ between individuals, it is still beneficial (behaviorally and physiologically) to remain in a resting state when not actively responding, in order to conserve energy. The principles of homeostasis most probably guide both behavioral and physiological regulation. Thus, one research imperative would be to measure emotion regulation across multiple systems, including physiological and behavioral responses. Such an approach must take into account the baseline pattern, the reactive response, and the attempt to return to "baseline." It is important that all three of these "conditions" be measured to provide the most complete picture of emotion reactivity and regulation.

What Is the Role of Context?

Emotions are a critical method of social communication between individuals. They provide information about an individual's internal state, but more importantly about an individual's reaction to a particular event. Thus, when an unfamiliar person walks into a room, most infants first look toward their mother to see how she responds to the person. This "checking" is known as social referencing and provides the infant with clues about the context in which the event (entrance of an unfamiliar adult) is taking place.

Often, an infant's response to a situation is guided by the context in which it occurs. For example, when they are almost 1 year old infants tend to respond with distress when their mother leaves them alone. This reaction, often known as separation protest, is much more likely to occur in an unfamiliar environment than at home. Here, context modifies the emotional response of the child. Context may also be a clue to the appropriateness of certain emotion expressions. As the infant gets older, context becomes even more important, because new rules and conventions about appropriate or inappropriate behavior depend upon context. For example, cultural norms are socialized by the family – in certain cultures it may be inappropriate for young children in public to laugh out loud. The child learns the display rules of the culture through parental socialization and with it the critical nature of context. Context is thus a critical variable that must be taken into account when formally analyzing differences in emotion regulation.

What Cognitive Skills Are Associated With Emotion Regulation?

The developing ability of the child to regulate emotion seems to indicate that processes are at work that mature over the first years of life that facilitate these developments. A number of workers have speculated about these processes. Among those mentioned are attention, and what may be loosely known as executive functions (such as the ability to switch set, to plan, to generate multiple option responses). Rothbart and colleagues have written about the role of attention in regulation of behavior.[6,16] They see attention as providing the child with "options" for response. Infants who are upset, for example, may be able to divert their attention away from stimuli which initiated the distress to other less aversive events.

For many young children, emotion dysregulation is not the result of excessive negative affect but the result of frustration in not obtaining a desired goal –

whether that goal is getting their favorite cereal or playing with their favorite toy. Many instances of emotion dysregulation and temper tantrums take place as a result of anger and frustration over blocked goals rather than distress. As the child gets older, he or she develops the ability to generate alternative strategies to achieve those goals. The ability to generate alternatives, to switch set, and plan successfully are important competencies involved in mature emotion regulation. Studies of these developing abilities are critical to understand mature emotion regulation.

Is "Good Regulation" Always the Dampening of Negative Affect?

Most often the process of emotion regulation is thought of as entailing the modulation of distress or negative affect in the young child. Of course, a large portion of emotion regulation involves the modulation of other emotions such as anger or joy. Anger in young children is often the result of frustration at being unable to achieve a goal. Infants as young as 6 months of age will display facial expressions reflecting anger when they cannot reach an attractive toy or have had a cookie taken away from them. Over the next few years, the young child must learn how to regulate that anger response. As most parents of toddlers know, this is not a trivial process and it is one which usually necessitates a good deal of parental guidance. The critical point here is that "good regulation" is the modulation of both positive or negative affect. Depending upon the situation and context, infants may display a range of different emotions with varying degrees of intensity. The task of bringing that system back into homeostasis or equilibrium may be difficult for emotions like anger, distress, or sadness. Differences in the degree of difficulty may be a function of the child's initial predisposition toward the expression of one type of emotion versus another.

Summary

The tendency to express particular emotions with a certain intensity is an important individual difference among infants and young children. This difference is known as the temperament of the child. The ability to modulate that expression is also an important competency for which there are important individual differences. Whereas temperament seems to be a biologically based difference, evident early in life, the ability to regulate emotions depends as much on caregiver input and socialization.

Children learn over the first years of life rules of appropriate social conduct. Included among these "rules" is the need to modulate emotions such as anger and distress when confronted with either frustrating or unfamiliar situations. One of the challenges of successful parenting is the task of providing children with strategies to utilize their own cognitive abilities in successful emotion regulation. This is a gradual process involving the formation of trusting relationships between caregivers and infants so that infants may realize that in the face of frustration or novelty, they can rely upon their parents to "regulate" the situation for them. Over time, the child develops these skills, transfers them to the peer group, and assumes an independent emotional life.

References

1. Thomas A, Chess S. *Temperament and Development.* New York, NY: Brunner/Mazel; 1983.

2. Thomas A, Chess S, Birch HG, et al. *Behavioral Individuality in Early Childhood.* New York, NY: New York University Press; 1963.

3. Rothbart MK, Derryberry D. Development of individual differences in temperament. In: Lamb M, Brown A, eds. *Advances in Developmental Psychology.* Hillsdale, NJ: Erlbaum; 1981;1:37-86.

4. Strelau J. *Temperament, Personality, Activity.* New York, NY: Academic Press; 1983.

5. Rothbart MK. Temperament and development. In: Kohnstamm G, Bates J, Rothbart MK, eds. *Temperament in Childhood.* Chichester, England: Wiley; 1989:187-248.

6. Rothbart MK, Posner MI. Temperament and the development of self-regulation. In: Hartlage LC, Telzrow CF, eds. *The Neuropsychology of Individual Differences: A Developmental Perspective.* New York, NY: Plenum Press; 1985:93-123.

7. Goldsmith HH, Campos JJ. Toward a theory of infant temperament. In: Emde RN, Harmon RJ, eds. *The Development of Attachment and Affiliative Systems.* New York, NY: Plenum Press; 1982;161-193.

8. Fox NA, Calkins SD. Pathways to aggression and social withdrawal: interactions among temperament, attachment, and regulation. In: Rubin KH, Asendorpf J, eds. *Social Withdrawal, Inhibition, and Shyness in Childhood.* Chicago, IL: University of Chicago Press; 1993.

9. Fox NA. Dynamic cerebral processes underlying emotion regulation. In: Fox NA, ed. The development of emotion regulation: biological and behavioral considerations. *Monographs of the Society for Research in Child Development.* 1994;59:2-3, Serial No. 240.

10. Cole PM, Michel MK, Teti LO. The development of emotion regulation and dysregulation: a clinical perspective. In: Fox NA, ed. The development of emotion regulation: biological and behavioral considerations. *Monographs of the Society for Research in Child Development.* 1994;59:73-102, Serial No. 240.

11. Hofer MA. Hidden regulators in attachment, separation and loss. In: Fox NA, ed. The development of emotion regulation: biological and behavioral considerations. *Monographs of the Society for Research in Child Development.* 1994;59:192-207, Serial No. 240.

12. Rubin KH, Asendorpf J, eds. *Social Withdrawal, Inhibition, and Shyness in Childhood.* Hillsdale, NJ: Erlbaum Associates; 1993.

13. Rubin KH, Chen X, Hymel S. The socio-emotional characteristics of extremely aggressive and extremely withdrawn children. *Merrill-Palmer Quarterly.* 1993.

14. Rubin K, Bukowski W, Parker J. Peer relationships. In: Damon W, ed. *Handbook of Child Psychology.* 5th ed. New York, NY: Wiley & Sons; 1998:3.

15. Rubin KH, LeMare LJ, Lollis S. Social withdrawal in childhood: developmental pathways to peer rejection. In: Asher SR, Coie JD, eds. *Peer Rejection in Childhood.* New York, NY: Cambridge University Press; 1990:217-249.

16. Rothbart MK, Bates JE. Temperament. In: Damon W, ed. *Handbook of Child Psychology.* 5th ed. New York, NY: Wiley & Sons; 1998.

Early Emotional Development: New Modes of Thinking for Research and Intervention

Robert N. Emde, MD

Introduction

This chapter of *New Perspectives in Early Emotional Development* reviews recent thinking about early emotional development in a context that can be useful for clinicians in pediatric settings. Beginning with some definitions and current views, the discussion leads to illustrations of adaptive functioning of early emotions in two areas: motivation and caregiving. Developmental transitions in emotion will then be reviewed, followed by some practical thoughts about assessing emotional availability.

Developmental Complexity and Emotions

Contemporary views of early emotions are framed by our appreciation of developmental complexity. Development involves changes within individuals over time, and the developing child is best understood in terms of increasingly organized complexity. Development, by definition, also involves dynamic exchanges within the environment. For the developing child, personal meaning is expanding, transforming, and reorganizing. Moreover, developing individuals are immersed in particular cultures and caregiving contexts. Meaning becomes organized to some extent in unique ways that carve out individual pathways for adaptation.[1-8] The clinician's job, therefore, is a tough one – to assess meaning in all of this complexity, for health as well as illness.

There are several reasons clinicians should be concerned with emotional development. The first is that emotions help define one's *individuality*. From the standpoint of an individual's experience, emotions define a sense of consistency; they set parameters for sensitivity and responsiveness, wherein a person comes to "feel right" (or otherwise) about his or her relation with the world.[9,10] From the standpoint of what others observe, emotional responses can be said to define temperament, which in turn can be regarded as an

individual's characteristic set of thresholds and latencies for such responses.[11,12] Clinicians can make use of the connections between emotions and
individuality. When a clinician gets in touch with a patient's emotional life,
that person is likely to feel understood – helping and healing then become
possible. Moreover, getting in touch with another person's emotional life can
help in working through a problem area, while appreciating its connection
with other areas (a clinical skill sometimes known as "systems sensitivity").[13,14]
Also, when clinicians help parents to appreciate their infant's temperament or
emotional individuality, caregiving attitudes may improve.[15]

A second reason is that emotions during early development have two central
adaptive functions that help define the meaning of experience. These are
motivation and *communication*. Emotions motivate an infant to either
approach or withdraw from a situation, to either maintain or terminate stimulation. Infant emotions are also linked to need states that may communicate
something that motivates caregiving by others. The linkage to need states
points to the other adaptive function of emotions – communication.
Emotions communicate intentions to people who not only observe emotions
but respond. Emotional signals are thus intrinsically connected with the
child's social functioning and social development. The communication of
pleasure, interest, surprise, or particular forms of distress all serve to guide
social exchanges and activities. Clinicians make use of these aspects of emotions as well. The clinician continually monitors emotional signals of the
child and parent in order to assess the degree of engagement or suffering.
Monitoring emotional expressions in infancy is especially important to understand the infant's intentions and state of well-being. It is not surprising that
clinicians sometimes refer to emotions as "the language of infancy," a language existing prior to the development of speech. After infancy, however,
emotional signals continue to provide a communicative background for social
discourse, as well as for clinical assessment.

In summary, assessing emotional development not only helps the clinician in
understanding individuality and meaning, but it may also enhance communications and have therapeutic benefits.

Thinking About Emotions: Three Helpful Views

Three current views take into account the adaptive functions of emotions
within a developmental systems framework. These views frame our current

thinking and bring considerable agreement to a field previously characterized by disagreement and diversity.

The first view is an *organizational/adaptive one.* Emotions were formerly regarded by many as reactive, intermittent, and disruptive events; now they are recognized as active, ongoing, and adaptive processes. They serve two kinds of adaptive functions: motivation within individuals and communication between individuals. In terms of motivation, there are two kinds of phenomena: short-acting emotions (which many following Paul Ekman[16] would consider "emotions proper") and longer-acting emotions (usually referred to as moods and temperaments). Emotional organization incorporates the principle of regulation, as is found in other psychobiological systems. In other words, there is a usual zone of regulatory adaptive functioning – and dysregulation is characterized by extremes, by either "not enough" or "too much" emotion.

A second view has to do with *complexity* – emotions are now seen as processes that have meaningful components and configurations. These components are often nonlinear and involve subsystems of appraisal, expectations, arousal, pleasure, pain, and autonomic and somatic feedback, as well as feedback from gestures, actions, and communications – all can occur in varying configurations. Adding to the complexity of this picture, different configurations of emotion may have components that are ordered in different ways in different contexts.[17-19]

The third view is *relational* and refers to the importance of context. Emotions used to be studied in an isolated, mechanical way. Now we appreciate that all processes of emotion involve significant person-environment relations. In other words, emotions are constructs that need to be understood in terms of the goals of the individual (with intentions and appraisals) in relation to the individual's environment.[18,20]

The preceding views of emotion may seem abstract, but they are useful for researchers and clinicians alike in light of ongoing discoveries in molecular genetics and developmental neurobiology.[21] In terms of the *organizational/ adaptive view,* it seems highly likely that types of emotion dysregulation will be clarified by discoveries of genetic and molecular aberrations. It is also possible that strength, competence, and mental health may be found to be fundamentally different from their "opposite" conditions of emotion dysregulation and disorder. If such is the case, it may make possible more effective interventions.

In terms of *complexity*, it seems certain we will understand more about the genetics of the components and configurations of emotion. In a related vein, we anticipate clarifications in terms of the *relational view* of emotions. The context specificity of components of emotional predisposition will be better understood with respect to particular situations. We have already learned that genetic expression can be profoundly influenced by environmental context.[5] We will undoubtedly learn much more about the particular contexts for emotional health, as well as for emotional illness.

Development

The three views about emotion are also useful in thinking about development – the changes that occur within individuals over time. In terms of the *organizational adaptive view,* changes sometimes involve a period of transition and reorganization; therefore early adaptational functions may be different from later ones. Thus, the first year-and-a-half of life is likely to be different in adaptive organization from the second and third years. In terms of *complexity*, developmental psychobiology involves increasingly organized complexity. Genetic and environmental influences with respect to components of emotional processes are likely to change with development. Similarly, new configurations of emotional processes are likely to emerge as well as new sets of genetic and environmental influences. As we learn more about the psychobiology of early development, we anticipate that complex organizations will illustrate features of continuity as well as change. In terms of the *relational view,* an increased complexity of person-environment relations includes the fact that transactions of experience will occur in particular circumstances, often within intimate and increasingly complex social relationships.

The MacArthur Longitudinal Twin Study provides an illustration of the changing aspects of genetic and environmental influences on emotion during the second and third years of life.[22] Our analyses of observed empathic responses in the child also illustrate the usefulness of the above views about emotion. Following the work of Zahn-Waxler et al, components of the toddler's empathy to the distress of another were coded from videotapes of some 200 twins.[23,24] Component emotional responses included such behaviors as cognitively oriented visual checking, emotional arousal, and prosocial activities such as helping, soothing, or sharing. Genetic influence at 14 and 20 months was indicated by substantially higher similarities in empathic responses of identical twins compared to fraternal twins. There was evidence of substantial environmental influence as well, but the patterns of genetic influence on component responses was different – indicating the usefulness of a components approach in thinking about developmental change.

Longitudinal results at 24 and 36 months of age in this study revealed continued genetic influence on empathic responses (cognitive, emotional, and behavioral arousal in response to the distress of another) but with a dramatic difference of testing conditions.[25] When an unfamiliar tester was the source of distress, a predominantly genetic influence on empathy was observed. But when the mother was the source of distress, predominant influences were of the shared environmental type (indicated by substantial similarities in both fraternal and identical twins). In other words, testing context made a big difference. Presumably, strong socialization influences shared by the twins in their day-to-day interactions with parents and others were a major influence in the context when mothers elicited the child's empathic response but not when responses were elicited by testers.

I would now like to return to some broader areas of adaptive functioning of early emotions that indicate their role in enhancing development. These areas include: 1) more general motivational tendencies; and 2) the caregiving relationship.

Emotions and More General Motivational Tendencies

The motivational and communicative functions of infant emotions are closely connected. As motives, emotions are inborn tendencies present in infancy that continue throughout life. Emotions are fostered by caregivers (who themselves are emotionally available) as they respond to the communicative signals of infant emotional states.[26] From the infant's point of view, there is a monitoring of experience according to what is pleasurable or unpleasurable. Such experiential states guide activity according to degrees of approach or withdrawal. From the mother's point of view, infant affective expressions guide caregiving. One needs only to think of the messages conveyed by an infant's cry ("Come change something") or by an interested, smiling expression ("Keep it up, I like it").

Then, during the middle of the infant's first year, a momentous development takes place. Emotional expressions of others take on a new meaning and are monitored in a new way. When confronted with a situation of uncertainty, the infant engages in social referencing, searching out emotional expressions of significant others in order to guide behavior accordingly. Thus, if mother smiles, the infant is encouraged to approach an odd-looking toy or a stranger, and if mother looks frightened or angry, the infant cancels an approach or retreats.[27,28] Social referencing adds a new level of shared meaning to the infant's affective monitoring.

Emotions also guide another motivational tendency. Research has documented that from the earliest days an infant has a tendency to explore the environment, seeking what is new in order to make it familiar – a process that Jean Piaget referred to as cognitive assimilation.[29] This tendency has also been studied as "mastery motivation" and "mastery pleasure."[30] More simply, we can refer to this as a directed tendency of the child to "get it right" about the environment. The emotions of interest, surprise, and pleasure often accompany such activities.

Emotions and the Caregiving Relationship

Another illustration of the adaptive functioning of infant emotions (for both motivation and communication) is seen in the caregiving relationship. Through repeated responses to infant emotional signals, caregivers respond appropriately with their own emotions and actions. Caregivers also help infants regulate their emotional states (for example, by making extended crying unnecessary or by promoting interested alert states). Over time the child learns such regulatory functions take over his or her own emotional regulation. Thus, emotion regulation experiences with caregivers become internalized by the developing child if there is consistency and the relationship is secure – as attachment researchers have emphasized. Indeed, the attachment researcher Alan Sroufe has elaborated attachment processes in aggregate as "the dyadic regulation of affect."[31]

This leads to another connected point. Development and its increasing complexity means that the infant's emotions are becoming more differentiated (in terms of their motivation and communication), at the same time as the context of the caregiving relationship is also undergoing development and revision. Infant emotional signals of joy, anger, fear, and surprise take on particular meanings that change to some extent as shared expectations change. Through repeated experiences with emotionally available caregivers, the child learns about emotional regulation and how emotions are communicated. During the second year, emotions are involved in negotiating responses to caregiver prohibitions; these exchanges involve interest, surprise, distress, anger, pleasure, and other emotions. Empathy, pride, and shame also typically develop during the child's second year as the onset of speech and better command of emotional communication give a richer expression of the child's emotional availability to the parent.[32] Overall, early emotional development offers repeated opportunities for emotional exchanges that not only involve conflict and its resolution but "attunement" as Daniel Stern has put it as the toddler develops new skills and emotional reactions.[33]

Developmental Transitions and "Milestones" in Early Emotional Development

Parents and clinicians often ask about "milestones." Can we say there are milestones – regular age-expectable sequences – in early emotional development? I used to be involved in "mapping expeditions" of the features of early emotional development.[34,35] But I have grown cautious about making such generalizations, in light of the three research-based views of emotion.

Table 1. Emotional development in the first 3 years

Emotions Developing in the First Year
> 0 - 6 Months
>> Distress / Crying
>> Happy or Joy / Smiling
>> Interest
>> Distaste ('Disgust')
> 6 - 12 Months
>> Anger
>> Fear
>> Sadness

Emotions Developing During the Second Year
> Pride
> Possessiveness
> Affection
> Generosity
> Anxiety

Emotions Developing During the Third Year
> Shame
> Envy
> Embarrassment

Components of emotions and their configurations change not only with development but also with contexts, in particular those involving experiences with caregivers. Most cautiously, therefore, I present the list in Table 1 that results from recent interview studies about prototypes of emotion mainly from middle-class Euro-American mothers in Denver.[36]

Based on my research and clinical observations over the past 30 years, it is generally safe to say that emotions of distress, happiness, interest, surprise, and distaste are present in the first 6 postnatal months. In the second 6 months anger, fear, and sadness appear. These results are admittedly from Denver mothers in a particular ecological niche but they are consistent with much of the literature.[31,37,38] Still, components of these emotions will vary in relation to their contexts – a consideration which becomes even more important during the child's second and third years. Components of emotions – such as appraisals, intentions, goals, and communicative styles – become increasingly varied in relation to their experiences with people. As might be expected, the mothers in our recent studies reported variations in these later-appearing emotions.

Thinking about developmental transitions rather than "milestones" provides a perspective that can be useful for clinicians. The idea of developmental transitions as periods of reorganization that can be opportunities for intervention (sometimes in the midst of stress and turmoil) is encompassed in T. Berry Brazelton's parenting book *Touchpoints* (Addison Wesley, 1992). René Spitz, in a pioneering theoretical monograph written in 1959, pointed out that infant development does not occur in a linear fashion but rather in a step-wise fashion. Spitz also pointed to times of psychobiological reorganization during these step changes that were indicated by new patterns of emotion. Today, we can schematically represent our knowledge of developmental transitions as in Fig 1. Ages during the transition are approximate, and individual variations in the timing of transitions become greater as the child gets older.[39,40]

As my colleague Joe Campos and I now think about such transitions, they are times in development when changes are pervasive, enduring, and involve major reorientations in person-environment relations. In other words, such transitions provide the setting for other changes in the child and family. Emotional communications are central to this process.

Seven such transitions can be designated from birth through 5 to 7 years – all having considerable clinical and research documentation.

Fig 1. Developmental transitions.

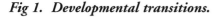

| 2-3 | 5-8 | 10-13 | 18-22 | 3-4 | 5-7 |
| months | months | months | months | years | years |

B

Developmental transitions occur in a stepwise sequence.

The first transition of birth has been well described by the Neonatal Behavioral Assessment Scale which also takes into account the adaptive functions of emotions. The emotional expressions of crying, interest/attentiveness, quiescence, and capacities for self-soothing are important aspects of the newborn's developing behavioral repertoire. These are used to assess states of need and motivation, as well as the clarity of communication of these states, for both clinician and caregiver. The rich variety of these emotional expressions serve also to indicate the newborn's uniqueness and individuality.[41,42]

In the six developmental transitions following the neonatal period, changes in emotional expression are prominent. They typically occur after other psychobiological changes have taken place. In particular they seem to provide communications that consolidate new roles of the child within the family.

The 2- to 3-month transition is typified by the onset and flowering of the social smile. It supplements an enhanced wakefulness and an enhanced capacity for eye-to-eye social contact, changes which in turn provide new opportunities for engagement and learning. Because of these features, we have often referred to this transition as "an awakening of sociability." Parents typically respond to these changes not only by increasing their own social interactions with the baby, but also by taking their baby outside of the home more and by increasing interactions with others. New parents have told us their baby at this time is less like a doll and more human.

The 5-month transition has been characterized as the onset of focused attachment and is often typified by the infant's distress or anxiety on the approach of a stranger and heightened distress upon separation from primary caregivers.

This is also a time when cognitive development is enhanced. Not only does the infant begin to remember goals when they are out of sight but the infant begins to have shared goals with caregivers.[29,33] Shared meaning in this sense is illustrated with peek-a-boo and similar games that begin during this transition period. The expectations and anticipatory sense of delight, as well as the infant's demonstrable knowledge of the routines in the peek-a-boo game, illustrate a shared sense of the past (knowledge of rules of the game) and of the future (expectations of what will come). Emotions become anticipatory in play, as well as in conditions of separation and distress.

In most infants at this time many of the relationship experiences with primary caregivers have become internalized in a person-specific way. Families now experience a further change in their infant's relation to them. Because of heightened distress, separation and substitute caregiving have different consequences than before.

The 10- to 13-month transition is marked by the onset of walking and its socio-emotional consequences. Clinicians, including Margaret Mahler and her colleagues, typified this time as one when the child often appears elated and begins to use emotions that communicate a sense of pride.[43] Young toddlers may also experience more distress at this time, because as they walk and are more autonomous, they experience consequences of caregiver prohibitions and other more distance-oriented emotional signals from adults. We found, in a longitudinal controlled study, that these emotional changes did not occur in all normal toddlers but rather tended to occur in those who began walking earlier.[44] Moreover, earlier walkers were also characterized by a particular emotional predisposition before, during, and after the transition – a predisposition for expressing distress upon physical restraint (such as in being dressed, put in a chair, or put to bed). This study also made us realize something about transitions we had not appreciated before: the importance of timing. Children who normally enter developmental transitions earlier may have different emotional experiences than those who enter transitions later in age.

The 18- to 22-month transition brings other momentous changes. This has sometimes been earmarked as the time of the "transition from infancy to early childhood" because the changes are major. Changes include the beginnings of self-reflective awareness, as well as the beginnings of multi-word speech.[45-47] Emotional changes include the acquisition of what has been referred to as early "moral emotions," such as "distress on the violation of standards" as Jerome Kagan has put it.[9] The toddler not only wants to "Get it right about the world," but sometimes becomes upset when an expectation about the way things *should be* is violated (for example, with a broken doll or a dirty toy). Empathy is another emotional change that becomes consolidated at this time. Toddlers respond to another's distress with personal expressions of concern and distress, accompanied by behaviors of caring, soothing, and helping – as Carolyn Zahn-Waxler, Marian Radke-Yarrow, and others have so amply demonstrated.[24,48] The onset of shame expressions may also occur at this time. Not surprisingly, the family again reorganizes the child's role during this transition. The child is held more responsible for intentions and for emotional regulation; socialization demands increase correspondingly.

The 3- to 4-year transition occurs when the preschooler becomes narratively competent. The ability to construct a narrative organization for emotion-laden experience is another momentous developmental acquisition – one wherein the child can represent past experience and future expectations in a coherent way, and can portray it in language and share it with another. Thus, the child can tell mother about what happened in daycare or with grand-mother when they were apart. The capacity for narratives, acquired during this transition, is also a giant step in being able to understand and regulate emotional life. Narratives, by their nature, are typically organized to deal with an emotionally unexpected situation or conflict. As such, they allow for "affective meaning-making" as Dennis Wolf and colleagues have put it.[49] Emotional tension moves to a high point in a narrative structure and then comes to some sort of resolution. Thus the understanding of family situa-tions, roles, and conflicts is often played out by the child using narratives. Narratives also allow for the playing out of alternative possibilities for future events, as Jerome Bruner has emphasized.[50] Assessing individual differences in preschoolers' emotion-laden play narratives now forms the basis for a research technique that gives us a window into the child's understanding of family relationships, as well as a variety of moral and emotional themes. Such narratives also link to the presence or absence of behavioral problems.[51-56]

Lastly, the 5- to 7-year developmental transition originally highlighted by Sheldon White is important and has recently been reviewed by Arnold Sameroff and Marshall Haith.[57,58] The transition is marked by enhanced cognitive, perceptual, and attentional capacities as well as capacities for social emotional regulation. All of these features reflect important neural-maturational developments and are associated with school readiness. The entry into school at this time initiates major changes in the child's role rela-tionships, not only with respect to the family but with peers and teachers.

Assessing Emotional Availability, Using Our Emotions, and Encouraging Adaptive Alternatives

Assessing emotional availability is an important feature of clinical practice. Emotional availability is a relational concept based on the knowledge that, in any caring relationship, a certain range of organized emotions is associated with continued involvement, intimacy, and developmental change. Being emotionally available is equivalent to communicating an openness toward an acceptance of another's feelings and expressed needs. Thus, it is not surprising that clinical and research experience both demonstrate that emotions can be a sensitive barometer of early developmental functioning in the child-parent system.[32,59-63]

If the child-parent relationship is healthy, sustained pleasure and mutual interest should be evident, as well as a well-modulated range of emotional expressions, both negative and positive. The clinician will see evidence of this in the child, the parents, and in their interactions. If the relationship is not functioning well, one sees little pleasure and the range of emotional expressions is restricted; replacing expressions of interest there may be evidence of avoidance, "turning off," or apathy. Maladaptive patterns such as fearfulness and vigilance or sustained anger and hostility may also be apparent, and in extreme circumstances there may be sadness and depression.

Clinical experience has taught us that assessment of emotional availability is in one sense straightforward and in another sense not. In one sense clinicians have long found emotions to be central. Expressed discomfort is a basis for consultation, and therapeutic progress is monitored through observation and empathy; moreover, patients' emotional expressions reveal how they feel. In another sense, there is an aspect of this kind of assessment that is not straightforward. A difficulty emerges from the relational nature of emotional availability – in order to assess emotional availability, the clinician must use his or her feelings and be emotionally available. This is not often easy with children. For example, their expressions of sadness and depression are painful to acknowledge when they are experienced by adults as resonant responses. Discomforts of this sort probably contributed to the fact that childhood depression went unacknowledged for so long, and that painful observations of child abuse went unappreciated for decades.[64,65] Because of the empathic difficulties in seeing the implications of pain in infants and toddlers, we have often referred to this aspect of emotional availability as "Coming to grips with the painfully obvious."

Conclusion

In concluding, I would like to direct our attention to another new area of thinking that has been previously neglected. This involves the child's early imagination and the development of future-oriented processes.[66-68] Imagination is an adaptive psychological function of emotional significance, and it deserves more attention. It is through exercising imagination that the child, parent, and clinician can envision new combinations and better possibilities.[32,69] As adults, we often acknowledge that imagination in play, movies, and art adds enrichment to our lives by showing us alternative worlds. We often forget that with children, viewing alternative possibilities is also vital for social exchange and for other aspects of everyday functioning. The child needs to see another's view for effective communication, and to see alternative possibilities when a goal is blocked or a conflict is encountered.

At 3 to 4 years of age children develop narrative capacities that allow them to organize meaningful alternative personal worlds of emotional significance and to express them to others.[49,50] Alternative imaginary worlds allow the child to try out varying expectations in a future-oriented way. As Inge Bretherton has put it, the narratively competent young child can organize emotionally meaningful experiences according to an "as if" imaginative mode that can lead to a "what if" cognitive mode.[68] Alternative possibilities can be created, envisioned, and in a sense "tried out" in advance.

Recent observations have underscored a surprising developmental feature in terms of the child's early imagination. Children as young as 2 are able to transform reality while playing without being confused and they can experience pleasure with their caregivers when doing so. This is quite different from a traditional psychoanalytic view that the young child normally has difficulty distinguishing fantasy and imagination from reality. It is also surprising as to the extent to which imaginative capacities can be seen to develop in important ways at the very dawn of language (for example, soon after the onset of multi-word speech).

The following vignette from a 24-month-old is presented as an example of early imagination (Fig 2).[69] This child was videotaped and recorded in one of our studies and was seated between his parents, who were eating dinner at home. The child begins making motions and sounds with his bread. We refer to the vignette as "A Horse Made From Bread."

Fig 2. A horse made from bread.

Mike:	(looks at bread, clicks tongue)
Mother:	Boy, Mike, you're eating a really nice dinner.
Mike:	(plays with bread, "gallops" across table)
	Look a horsie. Look horsie, Mama.
	(holds bread towards Mother)
Mother:	Does that look like a horsie?
Mike:	Yeah. My bread horsie.
Mother:	Is that your bread horsie? (chuckling)
Mike:	(Bread horsie breaks apart)
	Fall off.
Mother:	Uh-oh.
Mike:	Put him together.
Mother:	Well, I don't know. Once you take bread apart I don't know that you can put it back together again.
Mike:	(Undistinguishable utterance)
Mother:	Kinda like Humpty Dumpty.

The above example is among many we have recorded in our studies that illustrate early imaginative transformations at 2 years of age. Our research group would emphasize that research on early imaginative capacities and their variations is at an early phase. It seems likely, though, that such variations are considerable and that many children, particularly under conditions of environmental deprivation and stress, show less of such abilities. Certainly, children who are stressed may at times confuse elements of the imaginary with what is real, especially when they feel not in control, frightened, sleepy, or ill. The implications of early variations in this ability are as yet unclear. What does seem clear is that these are areas of major emotional significance for many children and their families. It also seems clear that as interventionists, we will soon be presented with increasing opportunities for learning about variations in future-oriented processes and emotion-laden imaginative processes in young children, as well as the implications of these processes for fostering adaptive alternatives in development. This will occur as we learn more about the particulars of *biological variation* from advancing knowledge of molecular genetics and cognitive neurosciences and as we learn more about the particulars of *cultural variation* from advancing knowledge of our increasingly diverse and interconnected society.

References

1. von Bertalanffy L. *General System Theory Foundations, Development, Applications.* New York, NY: Braziller; 1968.
2. Boulding K. General systems theory: the skeleton of science. *Management Science.*1956;2:197-208.
3. Platt JR. *The Step to Man.* New York, NY: Wiley; 1966.
4. Werner H. *Comparative Psychology of Mental Development.* New York, NY: International Universities Press; 1957.
5. Gottlieb G. *Individual Development & Evolution.* New York, NY: Oxford University Press; 1992.
6. Hinde RA. Developmental psychology in the context of older behavioral sciences. *Developmental Psychology.* 1992;28(6):1018-1029.
7. Sameroff AJ. Developmental systems: contexts and evolution. In: Hetherington E (ed); Mussen PH (series ed). *Handbook of Child Psychology, Vol 1. Socialization, Personality, and Social Development.* New York, NY: Wiley; 1983:237-294.
8. Thelen E, Ulrich BD. Hidden skills. *Monographs of the Society for Research in Child Development.* Serial No. 223. 1991;56(1).
9. Emde RN, Biringen Z, Clyman RB, Oppenheim D. The moral self of infancy: affective core and procedural knowledge. *Developmental Review.* 1991;11:251-270.
10. Emde RN. Mobilizing fundamental modes of development – an essay on empathic availability and therapeutic action. *Journal of the American Psychoanalytic Association.* 1990;38(4):881-913.
11. Goldsmith H, Campos J. Toward a theory of infant temperament. In: Emde RN, Harmon RJ, eds. *The Development of Attachment and Affiliative Systems.* New York, NY: Plenum; 1982:161-193.
12. Goldsmith HH, Campos JJ. Fundamental issues in the study of early temperament: the Denver twin temperament study. In: Lamb M, Brown A, eds. *Advances in Developmental Technology.* Hillsdale, NJ: Erlbaum; 1986:232-283.
13. Fleming J, Benedek T. *Psychoanalytic Supervision.* New York, NY: Grune & Stratton; 1966.
14. Lennard HL, Bernstein A. *The Anatomy of Psychotherapy.* New York, NY: Columbia University Press; 1960.
15. Field TM. Effects of early separation, interactive deficits and experimental manipulation on infant-mother face-to-face interaction. *Child Development.* 1977;48:763-771.
16. Ekman P. Moods, emotions, and traits. In: Ekman P, Davidson RJ, eds. *The Nature of Emotion.* Oxford, England: Oxford University Press; 1994:56-67.
17. Scherer KR. On the nature and function of emotion: a component process approach. In: Scherer KR, Ekman P, eds. *Approaches to Emotion.* Hillsdale, NJ: Lawrence Erlbaum; 1984:293-318.
18. Lazarus RW. *Emotion & Adaptation.* New York, NY: Oxford University Press; 1991.
19. Ellman JL, Bates EA, Johnson MH, et al. *Rethinking Innateness: A Connectionist Perspective on Development.* London, England: The MIT Press; 1996.
20. Campos JJ, Campos RG, Barrett KC. Emergent themes in the study of emotional development and emotion regulation. *Developmental Psychology.* 1989;25(3):394-402.
21. Emde RN, Robinson J, Corley R. Proceedings of the National Institute of Mental Health Conference on Developmental Plasticity. June 1996.
22. Plomin R, Emde RN, Braungart JM, et al. Genetic change and continuity from 14 to 20 months: The MacArthur Longitudinal Twin Study. *Child Development.* 1993;64(5):1354-1376.
23. Zahn-Waxler C, Radke-Yarrow M, King RA. Child rearing and children's prosocial initiations toward victims of distress. *Child Development.* 1979;50:319-330.

24. Zahn-Waxler C, Radke-Yarrow M, Wagner E, Chapman M. Development of concern for others. *Developmental Psychology.* 1992;28:126-136.

25. Emde RN. Data on file.

26. Emde RN. Mobilizing fundamental modes of development – an essay on empathic availability and therapeutic action. *Journal of the American Psychoanalytic Association.* 1990;38(4):881-913.

27. Sorce JF, Emde RN, Campos J, Klinnert MD. Maternal emotional signaling: its effect on the visual cliff behavior of 1-year-olds. *Developmental Psychology.* 1985;21(1):195-200.

28. Emde RN. Social referencing research: uncertainty, self, and the search for meaning. In: Feinman S, ed. *Social Referencing and the Social Construction of Reality in Infancy.* New York, NY: Plenum Press; 1992:79-94.

29. Piaget J. *The Origins of Intelligence in Children.* 2nd ed. New York, NY: International Universities Press; 1952.

30. MacTurk RH, Morgan GA, eds. *Advances in Applied Developmental Psychology: Vol 12. Mastery Motivation: Origins, Conceptualizations, and Applications.* Norwood, NJ: Ablex Publishing Corporation; 1995.

31. Sroufe LA. *Emotional Development; The Organization of Emotional Life in the Early Years.* New York, NY: Cambridge University Press; 1995.

32. Emde RN, Robinson JL. Guiding principles for a theory of early intervention: a developmental-psychoanalytic perspective. In: Shonkoff J, Meisels S, eds. *Handbook of Early Childhood Intervention.* In press.

33. Stern D. *The Interpersonal World of the Infant.* New York, NY: Basic Books; 1985.

34. Emde RN, Izard C, Huebner R, et al. Adult judgments of infant emotions: replication studies within and across laboratories. *Infant Behavior and Development.* 1985;8(1):79-88.

35. Fuenzalida C, Emde RN, Pannabecker BJ, Stenberg C. Validation of the differential emotions scale in 613 mothers. *Motivation and Emotion.* 1981;5(1):37-45.

36. Nikkari D, Emde RN, Campos JJ, Kubicek LF. The emotion prototypes questionnaire: a new instrument for the toddler. Data on file.

37. Izard CE, Huebner R, Risser D, et al. The young infant's ability to produce discrete emotional expressions. *Developmental Psychology.* 1980;16(2):132-140.

38. Campos JJ, Barrett KC, Lamb ME, et al. Socioemotional development. In: Haith M, Campos JJ, eds. *Handbook of Child Psychology: Vol I.* New York, NY: Wiley; 1983:783-915.

39. Spitz RA. *A Genetic Field Theory of Ego Formation.* New York, NY: International Universities Press; 1959.

40. Emde RN, Gaensbauer TJ, Harmon RJ. Emotional expression in infancy: a biobehavioral study. *Psychological Issues, A Monograph Series, Inc.* Vol 10, No. 37. New York, NY: International Universities Press; 1976.

41. Brazelton TB. *Infants and Mothers: Differences in Development.* New York, NY: Delacorte Press; 1969.

42. Sameroff AJ. Summary and conclusions: the future of newborn assessment. In: Sameroff AJ, ed. *Organization and Stability of Newborn Behavior.* Monographs of SRCD. Serial No. 177. 1978;43(5-6):102-117.

43. Mahler MS, Pine F, Bergman A. *The Psychological Birth of the Human Infant: Symbiosis and Individuation.* New York, NY: Basic Books; 1975.

44. Biringen Z, Emde RN, Campos JJ, Appelbaum MI. Affective reorganization in the infant, the mother, and the dyad: the role of upright locomotion and its timing. *Child Development.* 1995;66(2):499-514.

45. Lewis M, Brooks-Gunn J. Toward a theory of social cognition: the development of self. In: Uzgiris I, ed. *New Directions in Child Development: Social Interaction and Communication During Infancy.* San Francisco, CA: Jossey-Bass; 1979:23-33.

46. Kagan J. *The Second Year: The Emergence of Self-Awareness.* Cambridge, CT: Harvard University Press; 1981.

47. Fenson L, Dale PS, Resnick JS, et al. Variability in early communicative development. With commentary by M. Tomasello and C. B. Mervis and by J. Stiles. *Monographs of the Society for Research in Child Development.* Serial No. 242. 1994;59(5).

48. Radke-Yarrow M, Zahn-Waxler C, Chapman M. Children's prosocial dispositions and behavior. In: Herrington EM (ed); Mussen PH (series ed). *Handbook of Child Psychology.* New York, NY: Wiley; 1983.

49. Wolf DP, Rygh J, Altshuler J. Agency and experience: actions and states in play narratives. In: Bretherton I, ed. *Symbolic Play. The Development of Social Understanding.* Orlando, FL: Academic Press, Inc (Harcourt Brace Jovanovich, Publishers); 1984:195-217.

50. Bruner JS. *Actual Minds, Possible Worlds.* Cambridge, MA: Harvard University Press; 1986.

51. Bretherton I, Ridgeway D, Cassidy J. Assessing internal working models of the attachment relationship; an attachment story completion task for 3-year-olds. In: Greenberg MT, Cicchetti D, Cummings EM, eds. *Attachment in the Preschool Years; Theory, Research, and Intervention.* Chicago, IL: The University of Chicago Press; 1990.

52. Buchsbaum HK, Emde RN. Play narratives in thirty-six-month-old children: early moral development and family relationships. *The Psychoanalytic Study of the Child.* 1990;40:129-155.

53. Warren SL, Oppenheim D, Emde RN. Can emotions and themes in children's play predict behavior problems? *Journal of the American Academy of Child and Adolescent Psychiatry.* 1996;34(10):1331-1337.

54. Oppenheim D, Nir A, Warren S, Emde RN. Emotion regulation in mother-child narrative co-construction: associations with children's narratives and adaptation. *Developmental Psychology.* 1997;33(2):284-294.

55. Oppenheim D, Emde RN, Warren S. Children's narrative representations of mothers: their development and associations with child and mother adaptation. *Child Development.* 1997;68(1):127-138.

56. Toth SL, Cicchetti D, Macfie J, Emde RN. Representations of self and other in the narrative of neglected, physically abused, and sexually abused preschoolers. *Development and Psychopathology.* 1997;9:781-796.

57. White SH. Evidence for a hierarchical arrangement of learning processes. In: Lipsitt LP, Spiker CC, eds. *Advances in Child Development and Behavior.* New York, NY: Academic Press; 1965.

58. Sameroff AJ, Haith MM, eds. *The Five to Seven Year Shift.* Chicago, IL: University of Chicago Press; 1996.

59. Emde RN. Emotional availability: a reciprocal reward system for infants and parents with implications for prevention of psychosocial disorders. In: Taylor PM, ed. *Parent-Infant Relationships.* Orlando, FL: Grune & Stratton; 1980:87-115.

60. Sorce JF, Emde RN. Mother's presence is not enough: the effect of emotional availability on infant exploration. *Developmental Psychology.* 1981;17(6):737-745.

61. Emde RN, Gaensbauer TJ, Harmon RJ. Using our emotions: some principles for appraising emotional development and intervention. In: Lewis M, Taft L, eds. *Developmental Disabilities in Preschool Children.* New York, NY: SP Medical & Scientific Books; 1981:409-424.

62. Emde RN, Easterbrooks MA. Assessing emotional availability in early development. In: Frankenburg WK, Emde RN, Sullivan JW, eds. *Early Identification of Children at Risk: An International Perspective.* New York, NY: Plenum; 1985:79-101.

63. Biringen Z, Robinson J. Emotional availability in mother child interactions: a reconceptualization for research. *American Journal of Orthopsychiatry.* 1991;6:258-271.

64. Emde RN, Harmon RJ, Good WV. Depressive feelings in children: a transactional model for research. In: Rutter M, Izard CE, Read PB, eds. *Depression in Young People: Developmental and Clinical Perspectives.* New York, NY: Guilford Press; 1986.

65. Radbill SX. Children in a world of violence: a history of child abuse. In: Kempe CH, Helfer RE, eds. *The Battered Child.* 3rd ed. Chicago, IL: University of Chicago Press; 1980:3-20.

66. Harris P, Kavanaugh R. Young children's understanding of pretense. *Monographs of the Society for Research in Child Development.* Serial No. 231. 1993;58(1).

67. Haith MM, Benson JB, Roberts RJ Jr, Pennington BF, eds. *The Development of Future-Oriented Processes.* Chicago, IL: The University of Chicago Press; 1994.

68. Bretherton I. Representing the social world in symbolic play: reality and fantasy. In: Bretherton I, ed. *Symbolic Play: The Representation of Social Understanding.* New York, NY: Academic Press; 1983.

69. Emde RN, Kubicek L, Oppenheim D. Imaginative reality observed during early language development. *International Journal of Psycho-Analysis.* 1997;78(1):115-133.

Section 2:
Research Perspectives

Abstracts From Section 2. Research Perspectives

Mother and Infant: Early Emotional Ties

Marshall Klaus, MD

Recent behavioral and physiologic observations of infants and mothers have shown them ready to begin interacting in the first minutes of life. Included among these findings are the newborn infant's ability to crawl towards the breast to initiate suckling, and maternal-infant thermoregulation. The attachment felt between mother and infant may be biochemically modulated through oxytocin; encouraging attachment through early contact, suckling, and rooming-in has been shown to reduce abandonment.

Mothers' Sensitivity to Infant Signals

Lewis A. Leavitt, MD

The cry, among all of an infant's signals, is particularly influential in the developing pattern of mother-infant interaction – if a mother successfully terminates crying, she may gain confidence; if unsuccessful, she may begin to focus on her perceived inefficacy. Pediatricians and nurses who work with mothers of young infants need to carefully evaluate what mothers "think" about their successes and failures in dealing with daily childcare. Helping mothers "reframe" their perceptions of their infants may be a simple but powerful intervention to optimize interactions with their infants.

Mothers' Emotional Needs

Daniel Stern, MD

In most families, mothers contribute substantially to the new baby's emotional environment and development. Because such mother-infant interaction is crucial, a mother's emotional context is very relevant to infant development. This chapter of *New Perspectives in Early Emotional Development* addresses the relationships that a mother requires in order to regulate her maternal or parental capacities that enable the baby to develop appropriately.

Attachment: Role of the Father

Kyle D. Pruett, MD

Fathers make definite contributions to infant development and are now spending more time with their children than in many past decades. This chapter reviews the most compelling research on the developmental importance of fathers, including father-infant attachment and interaction, and differences between maternal and paternal interaction styles. Results of a long-term study of primary caregiving fathers are also presented.

Learning and Emotion in Babies

Lewis P. Lipsitt, PhD

The systematic study of the sensory and learning processes of babies is a rather recent science; indeed, infants far surpass what we "knew" about their capacity for learning a few decades ago. Emotion and learning are closely intertwined, as behaviors that elicit positive emotional responses are repeated and learned. Understanding these processes can optimize care of newborns by both professionals and parents.

Emotions and Social Development: Infants' Recognition of Emotions in Others

Arlene S. Walker-Andrews, PhD

Infants generally begin to recognize emotional expressions after 6 months of age; some reports have even observed recognition in neonates. Emotional recognition is important for social referencing, in which infants "read" their parents' expressions to understand events. Three methods for studying how infants come to recognize emotion are described in this chapter: peek-a-boo, matching faces and voices, and multimodal presentation.

Language Development and Emotional Expression

Lois Bloom, PhD

The relation of language and emotion in development is most often thought about in terms of how language describes emotional experiences with words that name different feelings. However, children typically do not begin to use these words until language development is well underway, at about 2 years of age. Given the relatively small number of words for naming feelings and emotions, and the redundancy between emotion words and the expressions they name, understanding how emotion and language are related in early development requires looking beyond just acquisition of specific emotion words.

Mother and Infant: Early Emotional Ties

Marshall Klaus, MD

Introduction

In the past 10 years, several provocative behavioral and physiologic observations in both infants and mothers have altered our perception of their readiness to begin interacting in the first minutes of life. In addition, two simple interventions for mothers and their infants in the perinatal period have led to new insights into their relationship around the time of birth.

This report will describe and integrate these new findings and observations and discuss how they will alter current caregiving practices in the perinatal period and their implications for further research.

The Breast Crawl

The most visually striking of these observations is the ability of a newborn, if left quietly on the mother's abdomen after birth, to crawl up to her breast, find the nipple, and start to suckle.[1] If the infant is dried thoroughly and placed on her abdomen and not taken from the mother for the next 60 minutes, the baby begins a five-part sequence. For the first 30 minutes the newborn rests and looks at his mother intermittently. Between 30 and 40 minutes, lip smacking and mouthing of the fingers begin, followed by an outpouring of saliva onto the infant's chin. Then the baby begins to inch forward using his legs, which push strongly into the mother's lower abdomen. When he reaches the tip of the sternum he bounces his head into her chest. While moving up, he often turns his head from side to side. As he comes close to the nipple, he opens his mouth widely, and after several tries makes a perfect placement on the areola of the nipple.

The odor of the nipple appears to guide the journey. If the right breast is washed with soap and water, the infant will crawl to the left breast, and vice versa.[2] If both breasts are washed, the infant will move to the nipple that is painted with the amniotic fluid of the mother. This trip was made by 15 of

16 babies from a group of mothers who did not receive pain medication and whose infants were not taken away, bathed, and given vitamin K or eye ointment (Fig 1).[3] For newborns not making the crawl on their own, when placed between the breasts, there is also usually a delay of 30 to 40 minutes before he moves towards the nipple. The infant reaches the target just as effectively, but with a different pattern of behavior. Instead of beginning to suckle, many infants just lick the nipple and their hands. These observations should be taken into consideration in institutions where standard maternity policy is to attempt to place infants on the breast immediately after birth.

Fig 1. A baby boy less than 1 hour old crawls up his mother's body and latches onto her breast by himself, clockwise from left. (Photo courtesy of Marshall Klaus and Linnart Righard)

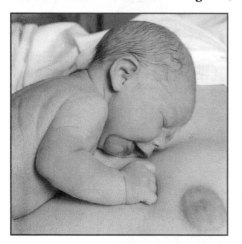
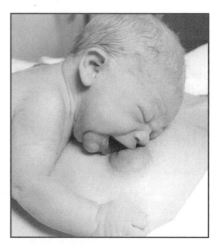
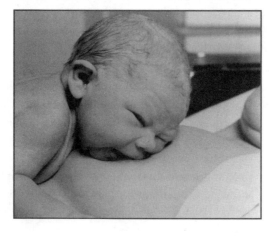

Thermoregulation

A perfect complement to the infant's ability to crawl to the breast is the mother's capacity to keep him warm on the journey. A mother can maintain her infant's body temperature as successfully as elaborate, high-tech heating devices when her nude, dry infant is placed skin-to-skin on her chest.[4] In addition, this skin-to-skin contact has a calming and reassuring effect on the baby. For the first 90 minutes following birth, infants held skin-to-skin on their mothers' chests hardly cried at all compared with infants who were placed in bassinets after being dried and wrapped in blankets[5] (Fig 2).

Fig 2. Separation distress call of the human neonate in the absence of maternal contact. Crying time in seconds for infants skin-to-skin on their mothers' chests for full 90 min ■; infants in cots for 45 min, and then skin-to-skin on their mothers' chests for 45 min ■; infants in cots for 90 min ▨.

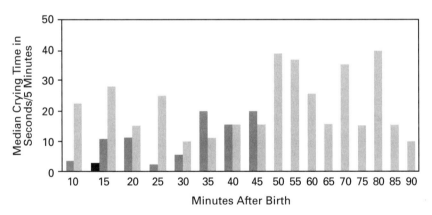

Adapted from Christensson K, et al. *Acta Paediatrica.* 1995;84:468-473.

The Baby-Friendly Initiative

In bringing a common context to these new observations, it is necessary to note that many studies have revealed that a mother will breast-feed more successfully and for longer periods of time when she is permitted to have early contact, an opportunity for suckling in the first hour, and rooming-in with her infant. In 1990, to increase breast-feeding throughout the world, UNICEF incorporated these interventions into a 10-point program titled

"The Baby-Friendly Initiative." Other elements of The Initiative included: a breast-feeding plan for the hospital; the absence of bottles or pacifiers; and closure of the newborn nursery. With UNICEF's encouragement, more than 50% of births in some countries now occur in "Baby-Friendly" maternity hospitals.

This large-scale change in care has been accompanied by an unexpected positive observation in several countries. In places where a disturbing number of babies had been abandoned by their mothers in the maternity hospital, the introduction of early contact with suckling and continuous rooming-in has significantly reduced the frequency of this sad outcome. For example, a hospital in Thailand reported a drop in abandonment from 33/10,000 to 1/10,000 after becoming "Baby Friendly."[6] In one maternity hospital in St Petersburg, Russia, abandonment was initially 5.5-6/1,000 during the years 1990-1992; the rate dropped to 3/1,000 within the next 3 years after adopting "The Baby-Friendly Initiative." Similar observations have been made in the Philippines and Costa Rica.

In my observations in 11 hospitals in the Philippines, mothers were feeding their babies every 45 to 75 minutes throughout their waking hours. This was possible because in a "Baby-Friendly" hospital, the newborn infant is frequently left in the mother's bed during the entire maternity stay. Is this reduced abandonment the result of early or increased mother-infant contact, the increased sucking stimulation, or all three?

Several reports address this issue. First, O'Connor et al carried out a randomized trial of 277 mothers in a hospital with a high incidence of parenting disorders.[7] On the first 2 days of life, one group saw their infants for 20 minutes every 4 hours (the usual and customary amount of time); the experimental group had their infants with them a similar amount of time *plus* an additional 6 hours daily. Ten children in the control group and two in the experimental group experienced abuse, failure to thrive, abandonment, or neglect in the next 17 months of life. A similar study in North Carolina of 202 mothers and infants during the first year of life found 10 cases of failure to thrive, neglect, or abuse in the control group, compared to 7 in the group that had extended contact.[8] When the results of these two studies are combined in a meta-analysis, the statistical probability (*P*) that additional mother-infant contact in the first days of life reduces later abuse and neglect is greater than .054.

The Role of Oxytocin

Suckling in the first hours of life may also contribute to reduced abandonment. Swedish researchers noted that if an infant's lips touched her mother's
nipple in the first hour of life, the mother kept her baby 100 minutes longer
every day than mothers who did not experience suckling until later.[9]

It should be noted that when the infant suckles from the breast, there is an
outpouring of 19 different gastrointestinal hormones in both the mother and
infant, including insulin, cholesystokinin, and gastrin. Five of these hormones stimulate the growth of the baby's and mother's intestinal villi. As a
result, with each feeding, there is an increased intestinal surface area for
nutrient absorption. The hormonal release is stimulated by the touch of
the mother's nipple by her infant's lips. This increases oxytocin in both the
mother's and infant's brains, which stimulates the vagus nerve, which then
causes the increase in the output of gastrointestinal hormones. Before the
development of modern agriculture and grain storage 10,000 years ago, these
responses in the infant and mother were essential for survival when famine
was common.[10]

Only small amounts of oxytocin reach the brain via the bloodstream, the
blood-brain barrier being essentially impermeable to the hormone. Within
the brain, oxytocin receptors are supplied by endogenous production. The
increase of brain oxytocin in the mother results in slight sleepiness, euphoria,
a higher pain threshold, and increased love for the infant. High plasma oxytocin concentrations are also associated with sleepiness, suggesting that during
breast-feeding higher blood levels are associated with increased brain levels.

Plasma oxytocin was found to be elevated following birth among women
who held their infants skin-to-skin; notably the oxytocin peaked following
expulsion of the placenta.[11] After one or two suckling periods, the blood
oxytocin became elevated with each breast-feeding. These increased levels
may enhance the bonding of the mother to her infant as well as contract
the uterine muscle to prevent bleeding. Do these findings help explain the
observation made by nurses in France in the 19th century, when many poor
women were giving up their infants? They noted that mothers who breast-fed
for at least 8 days rarely gave up their babies.

Labor Support

A meta-analysis of 11 randomized trials reported that continuous support during labor by an experienced woman (known as a *doula*) significantly reduced the length of labor, the need for pain medications, operative vaginal delivery, and, in many cases, the number of cesarean sections.[12] In one of the 11 studies, impressive behavioral differences were observed 6 weeks postpartum wherein a significantly greater proportion of women in the doula group were breast-feeding than in the control group (51% vs 29%).[13] These mothers took an average of 2.9 days to develop relationships with their infants compared with 9.8 days in the control group. At 6 weeks, they were significantly less anxious, had scores on a depression test significantly lower than those of the control group, and had higher levels of self-esteem. The supported mothers often rated their babies as *better* than standard babies, more beautiful, clever, and strong; in contrast the control group mothers rated their infants as being *almost* as beautiful, clever, and strong as standard infants. This suggests that the care a mother receives in labor may in part determine the way she cares for her infant.

Recommendations for the Future

Most needed in the future are further studies to confirm that continuous social support in labor also improves the psychological health of the mother and has parenting benefits such as reducing the incidence of child abuse. Further studies are also needed to explore the effect of "Baby Friendly" initiatives in altering later maternal behavior.

Applications to Practice

These findings suggest that care provided in the perinatal period must be reviewed thoroughly. All parents of healthy infants should be offered early contact and the opportunity to get to know their infants before bathing, vitamin K, and eye ointment are instituted. In addition, breast-feeding and rooming-in should be encouraged for all mothers during the short (48-hour) hospital stay. Furthermore, because continuous labor support is associated with improved obstetrical outcomes and parental involvement, it is time that no mother labors alone without continuous support by a skilled woman.

References

1. Widström AM, Ransjo-Arvidson B, Christensson AS, et al. Gastric suction in healthy newborn infants: effects on circulation and developing feeding behavior. *Acta Paediatrica Scandinavia*. 1987;76:566-572.

2. Varendi RH, Porter J, Winberg J. Does the newborn find the nipple by smell? *Lancet*. 1994;344:989-990.

3. Righard L, Blade MO. Effect of delivery routines on success of first breastfeed. *Lancet*. 1994;336:1105-1107.

4. Christensson K, Seles C, Moreno L, et al. Temperature, metabolic adaptation and crying in healthy newborns cared for skin-to-skin, or in cot. *Acta Paediatrica Scandinavia*. 1992;8:488-503.

5. Christensson K, Cabrera T, Christensson E, et al. Separation distress call in the human neonate in the absence of maternal body contact. *Acta Paediatrica*. 1995;84:468-473.

6. Buranasin B. The effects of rooming-in on the success of breast-feeding and the decline in abandonment of children. *Asia-Pacific Journal of Public Health*. 1991;5:217-220.

7. O'Conner S, Vietze K, Sherrod KB. Reduced incidence of parenting inadequacy following rooming-in. *Pediatrics*. 1980;66:176-182.

8. Siegel E, Baumann ES, Schaefer MM. Hospital and home support during infancy: impact on maternal attachment, child abuse and neglect and health care utilization. *Pediatrics*. 1980;66:183-190.

9. Widström AM, Wahlburg W, Matthiesen AS. Short-term effects of early suckling and touch of the nipple on maternal behavior. *Early Human Development*. 1990;21:153-163.

10. Uvnäs-Moberg K. The gastrointestinal tract in growth and reproduction. *Scientific American*. 1989;78-83.

11. Nissen E, Lilja G, Widström AM, Uvnäs-Moberg K. Elevation of oxytocin levels early postpartum in women. *Acta Obstetrica Gynecologica Scandinavia*. 1992;74:530-533.

12. Hodnett, E. Support from caregivers during childbirth. In: Neilson JP, Crowther CA, Hodnett ED, et al, eds. Pregnancy and childbirth modules of the Cochrane database of systematic reviews (database on disk and CD-ROM, The Cochrane Collaboration; Issue 2. Oxford: updated software, 1997).

13. Wolman WL. *Social Support During Childbirth: Psychological and Physiological Outcomes*. Johannesburg, South Africa: University of Witwatersrand; 1991. Thesis.

Mothers' Sensitivity to Infant Signals

Lewis A. Leavitt, MD

Introduction

The infant cry, among all the signals that infants emit, is particularly influential in the developing pattern of mother-infant interaction. The infant cry as a signal of distress presents one of the first challenges faced by parents. If successful at terminating crying, a mother may gain confidence in her own effectiveness; if unsuccessful, the mother may begin to focus on her own perceived inefficacy. Mothers' perceptions of an infant, as well as their style of coping with the infant, are in part based on experiences and expectations developed prior to the infant's birth.[1] During the early weeks and months of mother-infant interaction, mothers perceive their own infant's signals filtered by expectations of and models of infant behavior constructed from past experience.[1-6]

My laboratory has been engaged in the development of experimental techniques to evaluate mothers' responsiveness to infant signals and how this responsiveness is related to mothers' cognitive sets and experiences. In this paper I will review some of our findings that demonstrate the importance of mothers' experiences and perceptions in determining their responsiveness to their infants. Our findings suggest that pediatricians and nurses who work with mothers of young infants need to evaluate carefully what mothers "think" about their babies, and their successes and failures in dealing with daily childcare. Helping mothers "reframe" their perceptions of their infants may be a simple but powerful intervention to optimize interactions with their infants.

Parental Perceptions and Expectations

The first study I would like to discuss involved mothers and fathers watching a videotaped presentation of an infant in both a smiling and crying state.[7] The same infant was described in a paragraph as either a typical (normal), difficult, or premature baby. The same cry, when labeled as coming from a difficult or premature infant, was more aversive to fathers and mothers than when it was labeled as a cry of a typical infant. This result demonstrates the importance of parental perceptions and expectations in determining processing of infant signals. It emphasizes the importance of framing or labeling the experience of interacting with an infant on responses for that infant.

In another study of mothers watching videotapes of crying and smiling infants, we asked mothers to rate their own infants' temperaments.[1] Those mothers who rated their infants as "easy" in temperament were more physiologically responsive to a change in infant signal (measured by heart rate) than mothers who rated their infants as difficult. This finding demonstrates a mother's perception of her infant is associated with physiological response to infant signals. The next step, of course, was to examine what this implied.

In a longitudinal study,[1] we measured mothers' heart rate responses to videotaped infants in the laboratory when the infants were 4 months old. We then observed the same mothers feeding their infants when the infants were 9 months old, and then at 15 months assessed the infants on a cognitive measure. We found that mothers who were more physiologically responsive to infant signals were more behaviorally sensitive to their infants during feeding. Moreover, these infants paired with more behaviorally sensitive mothers had more mature scores on a cognitive task (object concept on the Uzgiris and Hunter Scale). With this study we found a link between our laboratory assessment of mothers' responsiveness and an actual behavioral assessment of mother-infant interaction. We also have a link between physiologic response, behavioral response, and infant development.

The Role of Experience

Another aspect of mothers' experiences with an infant's cry is the role of her experience in childcare success in shaping infant interaction. When mothers interact with their infants, they develop experiences of success as well as failure in managing the demands of childcare. Effectively soothing a crying child can provide the mother with the model of herself as a competent and successful caregiver. Unfortunately, occasions may arise which lead a mother to perceive herself as ineffective. Learned helplessness theory[8,9] provides a model for understanding this process. In a large number of studies it has been shown that experience with events that are perceived as "uncontrollable" leads one to expect that this state of uncontrollability will continue.

In a set of experiments,[3,4] we modeled in the laboratory the experience of being unsuccessful in controlling an infant cry. Mothers listened to a sequence of infant cries and were asked to perform an intervention (moving a handle or pushing a button) to terminate the cry. Mothers were placed in three groups. Group I mothers were "helpless"; no effort by them could stop the cries. Group II could readily stop the cries, and Group III was a yoked control group who simply heard the same amount of crying as Group I.

We then gave each group a subsequent task in which all the subjects could stop the cries. We found that Group I, the group exposed to uncontrollable failure, was debilitated in the second task. That is to say, they performed less well than both control groups in stopping the cries in the second task.

We then performed an intervention. We told mothers after the uncontrollable task that performance in the second task was unrelated to the performance on the first. This intervention reversed the debilitation of the experience of failure.

In another experiment, we labeled the same cries used in all the experimental sessions as coming from a difficult baby. We found that this labeling of the cry debilitated performance across the board on a solvable task of stopping the infant cries.

These experiments in the laboratory give us a model for understanding the role of experience and mental representation of the infant as a scaffolding which shapes mother-infant interaction. The experiments also suggest interventions a clinician may use in helping reframe the picture of representation a mother has of her infant.

Forming a Realistic Sense of Efficacy

We have proposed that mothers develop a sense of their efficacy in accomplishing childcare tasks based on her experience with success and failure. We have examined this experimentally by using a laboratory task which assesses mothers' estimates of how effectively they accomplish the task of terminating an infant cry.[10] In the laboratory, mothers are presented with a series of cries and asked to either press or not press a button to terminate the cries. Following the task, they are asked to rate their success. In fact, the task was designed so that neither button response was more effective than the other, so a mother's estimate of control (or success) is an estimate of her "illusion" of control.

One week later they were tested on the same learned helplessness task described earlier. We also measured mothers' heart rate responses to the cries. Our results showed that mothers with a high illusion of control were more susceptible to helplessness in the learned helplessness task; ie, experience with uncontrol had a debilitating effect on later performance. Moreover, mothers with a high illusion of control showed less of an "attentive" heart rate response to an impending cry. This experiment suggests that a high illusion of control may be a maladaptive response to the performance demands of childcare. It suggests that helping mothers form a "realistic" picture of what contingencies are like in interacting with infants may be beneficial.

Sensory Sensitivity

Carrying our investigation of mothers' responsiveness to infant cries a step further, we have examined sensitivity at a sensory level in the laboratory.[6] We asked whether a mother's cognitive set (how she rates her child, easy or difficult) and coping strategy (illusion of control) affects the actual processing of an infant signal. We used the methodology of Signal Detection Theory[11,12] to examine to what degree variation in maternal response to an infant cry is due to differences in signal processing (ie, sensitivity at the sensory level) or due to differences in the response (or decision-making system). In other words, does illusory control affect how sensitive mothers are to the actual acoustic signal of the cry or does it affect their bias to respond or not respond to a cry? The methodology of the experiment requires mothers to listen to cries constructed with systematic small variants from a standard cry and determine whether the cries were the same or different. We found that mothers who exhibited high illusory control were least sensitive in detecting differences between cries, and that labeling the same cry as coming from a "difficult" versus an "easy" baby changed sensitivity.

This study, in conjunction with our other studies, demonstrates that the cognitive set of a mother – developed through her experience with her infant, her expectations of her infant, and her developing sense of her own efficacy in childcare – is associated with physiologic and behavioral response to infant signals. Moreover, this cognitive set and the coping style developed in conjunction affect the processing of the physical signals emitted by the infant.

Our experiments suggest that clinical interventions of reframing or reinterpreting infant behaviors may play an important role for mothers of typically developing infants and especially for mothers of atypically developing infants.

The signals of atypically developing infants (for example, premature infants and infants with Down's syndrome) may be filtered and interpreted in a fashion which hinders optimal mother-infant interaction.[7,13] Our laboratory methods provide us with an approach to determine the important components determining mother-infant interaction. They can be used in evaluating components of proposed clinical interventions.

Conclusions

There are, of course, many variables which affect mother-infant interaction. Our experiments have shown that mothers' perceptions of their infants, their expectations, and their assessments of their own effectiveness are associated with important variations in physiological and behavioral responses to infant signals. These variations, in turn, are associated with infant development. Clinicians must attend to these aspects of the developing mother-infant relationship to help foster optimal child development.

References

1. Donovan WL, Leavitt LA. Early cognitive development and its relation to maternal physiologic and behavioral responsiveness. *Child Development.* 1978;49:1251-1254.

2. Donovan WL, Leavitt LA. Maternal self-efficacy and infant attachment: integrating physiology, perceptions, and behavior. *Child Development.* 1989;60:460-472.

3. Donovan WL, Leavitt LA. Physiologic assessment of mother-infant attachment. *American Academy of Child Psychiatry.* 1985;24:65-70.

4. Donovan WL, Leavitt LA. Simulating conditions of learned helplessness: the effects of interventions and attributions. *Child Development.* 1985;56:594-603.

5. Donovan WL, Leavitt LA. Physiology and behavior: parents' response to the infant cry. In: Lester B, Boukydis CFZ, eds. *Infant Crying: Theoretical and Research Perspectives.* New York, NY: Plenum; 1985.

6. Donovan WL, Leavitt LA, Walsh RO. Cognitive set and coping strategy affect mothers' sensitivity to infant cries: a signal detection approach. *Child Development.* 1997;68:760-772.

7. Frodi A, Lamb ME, Leavitt LA, Donovan WL. Fathers' and mothers' responses to infant smiles and cries. *Infant Behavior and Development.* 1978;1:187-198.

8. Abramson LY, Seligman MEP, Teasdale JD. Learned helplessness in humans: critique and reformulation. *Journal of Abnormal Psychology.* 1978;87:49-74.

9. Seligman MEP. *Helplessness: On Depression, Development and Death.* San Francisco, CA: Freeman; 1975.

10. Donovan WL, Leavitt LA, Walsh RO. Maternal self-efficacy: illusory control and its effect on susceptibility to learned helplessness. *Child Development.* 1990;61:1637-1647.

11. Green DM, Swets JA. *Signal Detection Theory and Psychophysics.* New York, NY: Wiley; 1966.

12. Macmillan NA, Creelman CD. *Detection Theory: A User's Guide.* Cambridge, MA: Cambridge University Press; 1991.

13. Stevenson MD, Leavitt LA, Silverberg SB. Mother-infant interaction: Down syndrome case studies. In: Harel S, Anastosiow NJ, eds. *The At-risk Infant: Psycho-socio-medical Aspects.* Baltimore, MD: Paul H. Brookes; 1985:379-388.

Mothers' Emotional Needs

Daniel Stern, MD

Introduction

In most families mothers contribute substantially to the new baby's emotional environment and development. Because such mother-infant interaction is crucial, a mother's emotional context is very relevant to infant development. This chapter of *New Perspectives in Early Emotional Development* will address the relationships that a mother requires in order to regulate her maternal or parental capacities that enable the baby to develop appropriately.

Positive Holding Environment

An often-told story about a new mother in her first days of being a parent goes like this. She was asked, "What was the most psychologically supportive interaction you had during the hospital stay after the baby was born?" She replied, "Well, my answer's a little funny. The person who really mattered the most to me was the cleaning lady. She came in every morning at 7:15 and she would stop by my bed, really look at me and the baby and we'd talk. She was a grandmother. She was about 55 and she'd say, 'Oh, how are you doing this morning? How's the baby? Oh, the baby looks good. Well, how did it go last night?' Every day I looked forward to her visit."

To this new mother, this visit by a kindly grandmother was the most psychologically supportive thing that happened for her. Of course, the visits by the doctors and nurses and her husband were essential, but if you asked her what was the high point – in terms of establishing her new role in life – it was this grandmother.

This special kind of relationship is hard to define, and difficult to name, so I use Donald Winnicott's old term of the "positive holding environment." It has to do with psychologically framing, holding, and contextualizing the mother in such a way that she feels validated, encouraged, supported. You don't have to teach her. You don't have to advise her. You do have to give her a benign regard. You have to create some kind of psychological holding condition so that she feels free to explore her own basic repertoire of maternal behavior and to try them out with a certain amount of confidence. It is like a psychological doula following birth, to complement Dr Klaus's doula during labor.

This observation is important for two major reasons. First, it points to a real need on the part of women that isn't being met. Second, although this may be perfectly obvious, there is a theoretical and research gap, and not enough work has been done on it.

Approaches to Parent and Infant Psychotherapy

I've spent a lot of time in the last few years looking at different forms of parent/infant psychotherapy. It turns out that there is actually a great deal of convergence in what different schools of thought and training actually do (shown in Fig 1, which diagrams the interactions between the behaviors and representations of mothers, fathers, babies, and therapists).

Fig 1. Interaction between mother, father, baby, and therapist.

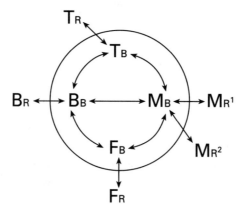

B_B is the baby's behavior; T_B is the therapist's behavior; M_B is the mother's behavior; F_B is the father's behavior. B_R is the baby's representation; T_R is the therapist's representations; $M_R{}^1$ is the mother's representations before therapy, $M_R{}^2$ is her representations during the therapeutic alliance; F_R is the father's representations.

The mother has representations in mental sets or preconceptions about what's going on, as does the baby, the father, and the therapist. A different set of maternal representations (M_R^2) exist when she is in the therapeutic relationship. This means that the mother's representations or conceptions of who she is and who her baby is may be different when she is in a therapeutic relationship than when she is alone.

Let's look at five different approaches.

- The psychoanalytically oriented people address themselves to the mother's representations, what was problematic with her before and which of her conflicts are now getting played out with the baby.

- For people who work in a more behavioral fashion, the port of entry into the system is through the interaction and largely the mother's behavior.

- Others are interested in what they would call the representations that are permitted by virtue of the mother being in the corrective attachment experience with her own mother.

- A developmental pediatric approach focuses on what the baby can do and showing that to the parents.

- Family systems theory approaches the mother, father, baby together.

All of these techniques are approximately equal in effectiveness. One of the reasons that they all work is that they spend an enormous amount of time and effort creating a positive therapeutic alliance. Positive is a very important part. The specificity of the approach is relatively unimportant compared to creating this positive context.

The Motherhood Constellation

The question to me became "What is it about this positive therapeutic holding environment that works?" Or stated another way, "What are mothers really concerned with? What are the things that constitute the necessary experiences or difficult areas in becoming a mother? What provides the context that permits her to become an adequate mother?"

Here's the picture that emerged. When a mother becomes pregnant and has a baby, she starts to form a new psychic or mental organization that I call the motherhood constellation. Whatever her main organizing principles were before, they get moved off center stage and the motherhood constellation becomes preeminent. The constellation remains prominent for a variable time period depending on the woman, the culture, and the home/work situation. Then very slowly, months or years after the baby's birth, the motherhood constellation progressively moves into the background, but it never goes away. It can be immediately re-activated if there's something wrong with the child and she has to become a mother again. For example, if a child who is 7 months or 7 years becomes sick. It then comes right into the center again. It doesn't disappear. It simply is relatively deactivated.

Protect the Newborn

What's in this constellation and why is it important? The first thing that almost all mothers will tell you is that their major concern is the task of keeping the baby alive and protected. When they get home from the hospital it is the most organizing and preoccupying central theme of their lives. There is nothing that comes close to it. All mothers have a set of fears which, at least in our society, are totally characteristic. They're afraid the baby may stop breathing so they go to the baby's crib several times the first couple of nights to make sure. If you try to stop her, the anxiety level becomes unbearably high. Similarly, she's afraid that when she's bathing the baby, he may slip through her soapy fingers and bang his head on the tub. When she changes the baby she fears he will fall off the changing table. These are all totally normal fears yet we don't have a good theory for thinking about how to approach them.

I think that they're not only normal and necessary, but they're the price that a mother pays from both biology and culture that place a high value on babies. This creates a powerful theme to protect her baby that often leaves a mother exhausted and overworked. One of the reasons that she needs to be contextualized is most mothers do not know what to do with the fear and fatigue that's created by this survival theme during the newborn period. It's very hard to deal with alone. It requires a good holding environment in order to be well tolerated and well dealt with.

Love and Attachment

The second theme in this constellation is what I call love and attachment. Here the mother asks, "Am I a competent human being? Can I love somebody? Will they love me? Will I be able to recognize that they love me? Will I be able to love my baby in a special way so that he will become my baby and not just any baby?" These are very tough questions because the whole process of being with a baby in those early interactions requires a lot of unusual things. For the most part, the process of being with a newborn is nonlinear, spontaneous, and dynamic. This requires that the mother feel quite competent in her spontaneity, her generosity, her ability to do all of these things – this is very hard for her to do if she isn't appropriately psychologically "held."

Because of this process, mothers spend a vast amount of time watching other mothers – to see what the other mother knows that she doesn't know, or what she can learn from her. The big question here is something like, "Am I a natural mother? And if not, what can I do to become one?" For professionals, this means that mothers know better than you do what they don't do well. Mothers know deeply and fully the things that they do poorly or are incapable of doing. On the other hand, what they don't generally know is what they do well and how they can use those skills. This is one of the reasons that they require a positive holding environment. Criticizing the mom is counterproductive.

Creating the Maternal Matrix

The third theme is that a mother creates around herself something I call a maternal matrix. This is some kind of network of one or more experienced mothers or experienced parents. Someone who has been a successful parent is the necessary person to create the holding environment.

This whole process starts to form in pregnancy when women start to have thoughts and fantasies and recollections about their own mothers. There's a turning point in the woman's mind when she becomes much less interested in men and much more interested in women. She becomes much more interested in her mother, not as a woman, or a worker, or as a wife to her father, but as a mother. The relationship that a mother has with her own mother is something of extreme importance in creating the new mother's psychological context.

Another piece of evidence comes from a study that we conducted in Boston along with Ed and Kathryn Weinberg. In a phone interview with new mothers we asked: "Who stayed at home with you after you came home from the hospital? Who phones you?" And so on. The data was very clear that the person who does it the most was the new mother's mother. Relatively speaking, next in line were other experienced women on the mother's side of the family – sisters or aunts with children. After that were experienced mothers on the father's side, then the woman's female friends who already had babies. Males friends tended to talk about the baby for 5 minutes then move on to what's going on at the office.

Now, when you add up all the contacts, what effectively happens is most women create for themselves a matrix of experienced women with whom they have contact anywhere between 6 and 12 times a day for several months. So this business of a matrix is not something that's theoretical. It's something that most women actually create during this period of time.

The last reason I think a maternal holding context is important is that a woman is concerned with her past experience with a mothering figure. For example, we know the present context in which a memory is elicited is important because it determines the choice of memory fragments and how they are put together. The baby in its entirety – seeing, feeling, and hearing the baby – is a very powerful memory inducer that elicits neural circuits, some of which have not been used for a very long period of time, some of them going back to her infancy, or to her childhood. So that the presence of her baby elicits the past experience that the woman has had with other maternal figures in her own life. The fantasy that most women have, at least in our culture, is that they would like to be surrounded by a benign grandmother. This is the nature of the desired relationship that they would most like to have for this positive holding environment.

Conclusions

A major practical implication of helping mothers have the emotional environment they need is that intervention techniques alone will never work. You need to establish a good relationship in which the technique is positioned. And not just anyone can do this – you need someone who has been selected for the process. If we're going to be training people to create the emotional environment so interventions can take hold, these people have to be highly selected. Unfortunately we spend most of our time training people, not selecting them. There's no question that people who do this well have a highly specific set of characteristics, but there is no good, fast way to select them. We can teach the intervention techniques but as far as establishing the positive holding environment is concerned, we need to select. This may be contrary to some of our current practices, but I think it's absolutely necessary to move to a new paradigm.

Attachment:
Role of the Father

Kyle D. Pruett, MD

Introduction

At the close of our millennium, we find fathers and babies having more to do with each other than in many previous decades. The dramatic movement into the work force of women of child-bearing years, the softening of sexual stereotypes subsequent to the achievements of the women's movement, and expressed longing among men for deeper meaning in their lives have conspired to bring men into close contact with their babies, whether they want it to not. Joseph Pleck's[1] review of the last 20 years of father involvement research concludes that fathers' proportional engagement (caregiving and play) with their children, though still less than half of that with mothers, is up by a third over the last generation. Fathers' overall availability and accessibility to the child, however, has increased by one half. Documented time spent with younger children ranges from 2.8 to 4.9 hours per day, with a heavy dose on the weekends, not the 12 minutes a day cited in the media. Federal surveys of child care arrangements of employed moms indicate that fathers are as common a source of child care as are child care centers and family day care homes. So, if they are around more, exactly what are they doing and how is it affecting their babies' development?

Twenty years ago, we said we wish we knew. Now, we can say we wish we knew more, because we have learned much in the interim, but still not enough. Fathering continues to be thinly represented in child development literature as a whole, from developmental psychology through pediatrics and nursing to psychopathology. Phares and Compas[2] reviewed research in all major journals dealing with clinical child development published between 1984 and 1992, and found that nearly half of all reported studies involved mothers only. Roughly one quarter of the remaining studies did include father-related material, but did not bother to differentiate its effects. The remaining quarter did measure father-child effects and consistently found them. So, when researchers bother to look for father effects, they *always* find them. They concluded that over-reliance on mother variables has fostered not only an incomplete database with regard to child development, but also a heavily gender-biased one; "Relations cannot be found among variables not investigated."

It is interesting to speculate why this circumstance exists. Fathers have been harder to access in the past, given the way data have been collected. The influence of the researcher's gender seems unlikely, as men and women are both well represented among authorship. Discussions among the Yale Father Study Group in the 1980s suggested that it is exciting and developmentally appropriate, but potentially conflictual for the infant, to "...have to look away from the mother in order to see the father...." But a separation is a separation, and perturbations cause distress. Researchers themselves may have similarly felt less sanguine about turning away from mothers to find fathers, even in the laboratory.

Research does remind us that infants develop in messy, complex social systems and that fathers make unique contributions to that system. How fathers respond to the system, their influence upon it, the way they attach to their babies, how those ways differ from mothers, and what difference it all makes to early infant development are the focus of this paper, reviewing the most compelling literature addressing the first 2 years of life. Original research from my own 10-year longitudinal study of infants raised by primary caregiving fathers in intact families will then be summarized. Finally, implications for clinical practice and suggestions for further research will be discussed.

Paternal Responsivity to Infants

Attachment theory is embedded in the concept that when infants signal their needs, and adults respond appropriately, secure infant-parent attachments ensue; but does this hold for men as well as women? Frodi and Lamb[3] found no sex differences in psychophysiologic responsiveness to videotapes of quiescent, smiling, or crying infants. These findings were extended to investigate 8- and 14-year-old males and females in a similar research design, and Frodi et al[4] concluded there were "no biologically-based sex differences in responsiveness to infants."

Fathers of infants were found to be equally anxious as mothers about leaving their infants in someone else's care.[5] The men's skills at identifying their babies are also equivalent to women's. Israeli fathers who were blindfolded and olfactory blocked were still able to recognize their infants by touching their hands, as were their mothers.[6] Newborn nursery observations by Parke and Sawin[7] documented that fathers responded to infant cues regarding satiation, burping, soothing, etc as effectively as mothers. Fathers spontaneously adjust their speech patterns when interacting with infants, speaking more slowly, in shorter phrases, using multiple repetitions of a musical nature.[8]

Fathers' and mothers' perceptions of their infant's temperament are correlated, but not highly. This suggests that moms may be more sensitive to different infant tendencies and characteristics, have different internal experiences of their infants, and/or that their personalities affect their perceptions.[9] In my own research of primary caregiving fathers,[10,11] I found that fathers were often more sensitive to their children's distress than moms, suggesting this may in fact be a total-time-with-proximal-caregiver variable, and less dependent on gender. Paternal responsivity has also been shown to vary depending on the amount of infant care responsibility fathers assume.[12]

Individual characteristics in paternal engagement that do exist were shown by Belsky et al[13] to remain stable over time, especially at 3 and 9 months, although paternal sensitivity is certainly affected by other variables. Satisfaction with marital partners is especially important for paternal engagement.[14] Cox et al[15] also reported that fathers in warm and confiding marriages have more optimistic attitudes toward their 3-month-olds than did men in less satisfying or successful marriages. Dickie and Matheson[16] further elucidated the importance (and unidirectionality) of spousal support by reporting that fathers' interactions with infants were more heavily influenced by the quality of the marital interaction than were mothers' interactions. The same is also true of the influence of marital satisfaction on the father's involvement with medically compromised infants.[17] In summary, most fathers exhibit sensitivity to their infants, especially if supported by his partner (but not exclusively so). That attachment forms readily, especially in relation to amount of father-infant interaction over time.

Father-Infant Attachments

How might we know if an infant had formed an attachment to its father? Studies begun by Kotelchuck in the 1970s assumed that such an attachment would reveal itself in separation protest.[18] Twelve-month-old infants (and subsequently 15-, 18-, and 21-month-old infants) protested whether left alone by mother or father; showed positive relief upon reunion; and lost the drive to explore in the interim. When separated from only one parent, half preferred mother, 30% preferred father, and 20% showed no clear preference. Spelke et al[19] elaborated these findings for highly involved fathers, finding that their infants protested less overall, and showed delayed separation protest in general. Still there is no determinative data for 6- to 9-month-old father-infant pairs, when the most vigorous maternal attachment behavior is in evidence.[20] Cohen and Campos[21] did show that, although 10-month-olds showed preferences for their mothers as "secure bases" after brief separations, fathers were clearly preferred over strangers, giving credence to the fact that infants did attach to fathers hierarchically and differentially.

In an important study of attachment classification of mothers, fathers, and their infants, Steele, Steele and Fonagy[22] analyzed father and mother differences in the Strange Situation Procedure. They found that the mother's Adult Attachment Interview scores influenced (but did not predict) the father-infant experience. This suggests that fathers and infants form unique "states of mind concerning attachment in ways that influence each other." Further evidence regarding this unique state of mind can be found in Ferketich and Mercer's[23] investigations of paternal attachment in experienced and inexperienced fathers. She found no difference between experienced and inexperienced fathers with regard to the intensity of their attachment, indicating that the love relationship formed with subsequent infants is as unique as the first.

Lamb's landmark longitudinal study[24] of mother-infant and father-infant attachment was begun in 1974 to try to categorize the unique components of father-infant attachment. Home observations of 7-, 8-, 12-, and 13-month-old infants revealed no preference for either parent on attachment behavior measures. This changed in the second year of life, when boys showed preferences for their fathers, while girls showed no consistent preference for either parent. Lamb[24] concluded that earlier claims of a hierarchy among attachment figures, with the more proximal caregiver becoming preferred, was not upheld by home observational data. Furthermore, Lamb observed that when infants in the study were stressed, attachment behavior increased and they organized their behavior around whichever parent was more proximal. Interestingly, when both parents were present, 12- and 18-month-olds turned to mom, while at 8 and 21 months there was again no preference. So that if there is any hierarchical period, it is relatively short-lived, and may not endure.

Abelin's[25] work on the father as a "significant other" for older autonomy-seeking toddlers (as they feel the need to be more separate from the mother) may explain why the hierarchical period may be short-lived. He suggests that around 18 months, toddlers develop the capacity to observe the father's appreciation of the mother as distinct from their own appreciation of her.

Lamb further speculated that the father's interest in play may enhance their importance and that when such a characteristic is missing (such as in the Swedish father studies with Hwang and Frodi),[25] infants develop clearer preferences for their primary caregiver. Overall the infant-father connection is enhanced by paternal involvement, although mothers are still the preferred attachment figure in most families where she provides the bulk of intimate care. Nevertheless, early and powerful attachments between infants and fathers have been seen in myriad studies.

Father-Infant Interaction Profile

There is huge variation in the amount of father-infant interaction in any given culture.[26] Munroe[27] observed mother-child and father-child contact in Belize, Kenya, Nepal, and American Samoa, and found vast differences in father presence and absence, infant care time, competence, and maternal support for father involvement. Clearly, father-infant interaction is affected by many external factors. Fathers in dual-career Anglo-European families were more involved,[28] as were encouraged and prepared fathers. Lind[29] found that Swedish fathers, when taught child care techniques and encouraged consistently over time (short term does not work), remained involved long after infancy. Preterm babies are known to draw fathers into deeper levels of involvement than comparably healthy babies.[30]

But the most robust finding is that the *quality*, not the quantity of the social interaction between father and infant facilitates the infant's connections to people and other sources of stimulation.[31,32] Yet practice helps make perfect – quality connections are probably also practiced connections.

Mother and Father Differences in Infant Interaction

Durable and different maternal and paternal styles are consistently found in father-infant and mother-infant pairs. Clarke-Stewart[33] found in observations of 6-month-old infants that fathers tended to engage in more physically stimulating and unpredictable play than mothers. Not surprisingly, such interaction elicited more positive responses from infants, and later from toddlers,

meaning that children seek out this type of behavior from fathers and reinforce it. Fathers tend to report greater satisfaction in more active pursuits
with their young children, so it is mutually gratifying. They seem to have a
penchant for making even the mundane routines more intensely physical
endeavors, pushing the stroller, taking a bath, etc.

In verbal and nonverbal communication with infants, fathers use shorter,
staccato-like bursts of language and physical stimulation, while mothers were
more modulated and predictable.[30] Infants respond more positively to being
held by fathers between 7 and 13 months, probably because mothers pick
them up for caretaking, while fathers pick them up to play, or in response to
the infant's request.[34] Father care tends to be more disruptive and unpredictable than mother care, and fathers can be more intrusive than mothers.[35]

Lamb concludes that fathers and mothers do not simply play differently –
play itself is an important component of father-infant relationships,[24] as
shown in African-American Euro-American cohorts.[36] The origins of these
differences elude explanation, although social role plays a major part. Field[37]
and Pruett[10] found that primary caretaking fathers resembled traditional
mothers more than secondary caretaking fathers, although playfulness and
"noncontaining interactions" remained stable regardless of level of interaction.

An enduring debate began 24 years ago when Maccoby and Jacklin[38] suggested that mothers and fathers treat their sons and daughters differently from
one another. Although they found differences, they felt that differential
socialization of sons and daughters was probably not caused by sex differences. The latest contribution to the debate is a meta-analysis by Lytton and
Romney[39] of 172 studies. They concluded the only consistent influence was
a very small (0.3 to 0.5 of one standard deviation) engagement in play with
sex-typed toys or games. Furthermore, any trends favoring parental sex difference in interaction style diminished with age. The authors concluded: "The
present meta-analysis has demonstrated a virtual absence of sex-distinctive
parental pressures."

Regarding all the documented mother-father differences in interaction with
infants, I feel that the majority of the development-enhancing intimate transactions that grow healthy, loving infants will eventually turn out to be gender
neutral. These will most likely be proven to be experientially enhanced, and
not fundamentally skewed by the intriguing differences between fathering and
mothering styles. Mothers and fathers share much of the competent nurturing domain, and that is what matters to children.

Developmental Importance of Fathers

A meta-analysis[40] of 11 studies observing fathers in the Strange Situation Procedure reported that infants tended to have similar types of attachment to both mother and father. The impact of variations in paternal behavior and attachment was investigated by Cox and Bithoney.[41] Fathers who were affectionate, had positive attitudes, and spent more time with their 3-month-olds would more likely have securely attached infants at 12 months. But the quality of care matters, not just the quantity. Easterbrooks and Goldberg[42] found children's adaptations were enhanced by the amount, sensitivity, and quality of their father's involvement, with quality being a more potent predictor than the extent of involvement.

The innate physical differences between mother and father can be quite stimulating to the infant when experienced in apposition to each other. Dad's typically larger size, deeper voice, coarser skin, smell, physical attributes, and habits all combine to offer a distinctly different buffet of potential attachment behaviors. This very differentness may aid the infant in earlier and better recognition of mother or father. Such recognition may create an early paradigm for appreciating unique features that distinguish identifying attributes of important objects. This may well predispose the infant to heightened awareness of different social styles and thereby enhance social competence.

Longitudinal Follow-up of Infants of Primary Nurturing Fathers at 10 Years

The First Year

To determine the effects of intimate paternal care on the development of young children, and to differentiate potential idiosyncratic properties of paternal care from primary caregiver effects, I began a small longitudinal pilot study of children raised primarily by fathers in intact families.[43] The study assessed the developmental profiles of 17 infants aged 2 to 22 months, the psychological characteristics of the fathers and mothers, the fathers' nurturing patterns, and the marital relationship patterns.

The 17 families recruited had a broad range of income and education. Eight of the fathers were unemployed, but the rest were graduate students, blue-collar workers, sales representatives, artists, computer programmers, real estate brokers, lawyers, writers, or small businessmen. Incomes ranged from nothing to $125,000 annually. The mothers were nurses, secretaries, teachers, taxi drivers, welfare recipients, blue-collar hourly workers, or sales representatives. Their incomes, if employed, ranged from $8,000 to $75,000 a year. Of the 17 children, 8 were male and 9 were female, and 16 of the 17 were first born. Parents ranged in age from 19 to 36 years, mean ages for fathers and mothers were 24 and 25, respectively. Few of the fathers had previous child-care experience, although most had siblings. The father was the primary caregiver, usually also the house manager, cook, and cleaner. Although arrangements differed from house to house, he was expected to carry the bulk of emotional responsibility for his offspring. The mothers were, however, very active in the care of the infants when they were home, usually in the evenings and on weekends. Sixteen of the 17 women continued to breast-feed for at least 3 months, although on average they returned to work after 6 weeks.

The infants were evaluated in the presence of their mothers and fathers using the Yale Developmental Schedules,[44] a composite of standardized instruments evaluating motor, language, adaptive problem-solving, and personal-social competence by chronologic age. Extensive home visits were conducted, and personal and developmental histories taken for the children and their parents.

In general, the children's performance was active and robust. They were competent and occasionally scored above expected norms. The youngest groups of infants (age 2 to 12 months) performed several of the adaptive, problem-solving tasks at the level of babies 2 to 4 months their senior. Personal social skills were also ahead of schedule. The older babies (age 12 to 22 months) performed as well. An interesting qualitative stylistic characteristic emerged frequently. These infants seemed to be attracted to, and comfortable with, stimulation from the external environment, and not restricted to feeling comfortable only within the intimacies of the parent-infant realm. These babies also seemed to expect that their diligence and curiosity would be appreciated and tolerated. They expected that play would be rich, interesting, exciting, and reciprocated by the adults that entered their lives.

> Twenty-two-month-old Helen knocked over her tower of 10 small red cubes, which she had so carefully and proudly constructed a moment before, with a round-house sweep of her small fist. She sat forward quickly on the edge of her high chair, and with a broad smile, fixed her eyes on the examiner with the excited anticipation that he would reciprocate appropriately and preserve the game she has just started, asking quizzically as though mid-conversation, "...So, yeah?" It was as though there was little in the world that could not yield to her eventually.

We also observed that these men had achieved the reciprocal nurturing attachment so critical to healthy infant development. The depth and rapidity of the attachment often amazed the fathers themselves. They did not, however, consider themselves to be "mothering." Although initially when they were confused or uncertain, many thought about their spouses or mothers, within weeks they usually abandoned the mental portrait of themselves as stand-ins for a woman. Interestingly, they kept their sense of growing confidence to themselves, as though it was very unusual or it might not last. They switched routinely, although at differing rates, to thinking of themselves as parents in their own right. They read their babies well, and their caregiving responses were observed to conform well to their babies' most complex needs. As to the slightly precocious performance of the infants and toddlers, it seemed this was a benefit of having two deeply involved parents, as well as a competent primary caregiver.

Follow-up at 2 and 4 Years

All the families were re-evaluated at 2 years and 4 years.[45] Second children had been born into seven of the families. Fathers continued to serve as the primary parent in eight families, including four that now had second children. This was particularly surprising because families initially thought that the father would the primary caregiver for only a year. Mothers had meanwhile become the primary parent in three families, all of whom had second children. Fathers had returned to work or school in six families with second children, and had ceased to serve as the primary parent. There had been one parental separation in which the father had retained custody.

Still there were no signs of psychological vulnerability among the children. The quality of their relationships, the level and range of emotional maturation, or the ability to handle everyday stress did not differentiate these children from their more traditionally reared peers. Standardized testing using the Yale Developmental Schedules showed some slowing of the precocious functioning in the adaptive and personal social domains. Comfortable dependencies, zest for life, assertiveness, drive for mastery, and the usual childhood worries showed up on the semi-structured diagnostic play sessions with both boys and girls.

A certain emotional flexibility appeared as these children described their interactions with friends and playmates. There were rudimentary signs they might be developing resilience and flexibility in certain areas of their personality, particularly in the ease with which they moved back and forth between feminine and masculine behavioral roles – not identities, but roles.

If anything was unique about their internal images of themselves or their parents, it was the sense of their father as a nurturing force. Empirical evidence would continue to mount throughout the remainder of the study that having a father as a primary nurturing figure stimulates more curiosity and interest in fathers as procreators than is found in most traditionally raised children. The children in this study saw their fathers (and mothers) as makers of human beings.

Follow-up at 6 and 8 Years

Six- and 8-year follow-up found secure gender identities in place and good school performance. The children now clearly demonstrated a strong interest in nurturing behavior in their interactions with peer groups and extended families.[11]

Fifteen families were still available for study after 8 years. The children, now 8 to 10 years old, seven female and eight male, were interviewed in extensive diagnostic family interviews, as developmental competence was no longer a question.[46] Eleven fathers were still in major caretaking roles. Three more siblings had been born, and a second divorce was pending. Interestingly, both marriages that failed had decided earliest to have father in the primary nurturing role. Both seemed enamored of the plan intellectually from the beginning, and gave it a "good go." Both mothers felt that the child care decision had played some role in the marital distress.

The 8-year data could be summarized almost wholly by the concept of generativity. Each of the 15 children had an ongoing commitment to growing, raising, or feeding something: plants (both house and garden) were watered and potted and propagated. Pets were nurtured, fed, walked, trained, even bred. In general, they all husbanded and shepherded a panoply of living things. Caretaking was valued as an activity in and of itself. Competence, spiced with competitiveness with other propagators, was obvious in their caretaking skills and their pride in exhibiting their "progeny." This is a particularly robust version of the developmental line of caretaking in boys as put forward by John Munder Ross.[47]

All the children had chores – the younger, the more menial – but none was just "make work." A work ethic was expressed and espoused by the children. They also knew a great deal about their parents' work, what they did, where they did it, and with whom they did it. In Katelin's words:

> "He makes pots and plates and stuff out of clay, and then puts them in a box of brick stuff. He's really good at it. He starts a fire in there and then he looks in. It gets really hot, like a volcano, and if you went in there you'd get cooked. When the pots come out, they're gorgeous – so he charges a lot of money for them."

The products of the children's work, especially the creative work, was everpresent in their homes. Susan's father, a textbook salesman, had carefully framed and hung her best pictures throughout the house. Katelin's artwork hung in the kitchen. Allen, as a 5-year-old, had been interested in birds with "big beakers who liked to bite noses." He was now a devoted bird watcher and member of the Connecticut Audubon Society. He had earned money for his own spotting scope, and his pencil and watercolor bird renderings were everywhere in the home. Helen's favorite shell and beach glass collections were scattered throughout the house.

Although our focus is on children, it is worth commenting on the fathers' increased comfort level with parenting. In general, fathers and mothers felt less competitive with each other about parental discretion and power.

> Helen's father: "I have staying home down to a science. I am motivated to be home."

> Helen's mother: "His ideas about the kids and home are better than mine. I really like work and I'm good at it."

Also, fathers continued to turn their own childhood wishes for a more involved father into actually *being* a more involved father.

> Allen's father: "The more experience I have loving Allen, and being involved in his growing up, the more my old hurts about my father and his distance from me seem to heal. Funny, I thought it would be the other way around. You know, make it worse, not better. It's better the way it is between Allen and me."

Follow-up at 10 Years

After 10 years, 14 families remained available for study. The children ranged from 10 to 12 years of age, with six boys and eight girls. Siblings ranged from none to three. Nine of the families still had fathers sharing in, or serving as, the major caretaker in the family: cooking, transporting, helping with homework, disciplining, etc. The other five families had mothers at home either half or full time, with the father still serving full time in out-of-home work. There had been a second divorce, and the family chose not to continue participating in the study.

We conducted a 1½-hour semi-structured interview with the child alone with one interviewer. Although open-ended enough to follow child's narrative, interview data was collected about school performance and attitudes, health, moods, recurrent or important dreams, friendships, interests in art and sports, family relationships, gender issues of role and stereotype, and life goals or plans.

To address the contextual issues, the interviewer and an observer also conducted a 1½- to 2-hour semi-structured family interview after the individual assessment. The family interview was conducted with the child and family, typically at the family home.

Helen. Helen now described herself as a "soccer junkie," and was in her uniform and pads for her interview. Her father had been her coach up to this year, "…because we both thought we needed a break from each other. He thought he knew everything about soccer, and I did too, until I went to soccer camp last summer and learned more than he could teach me. I miss having my dad at practice, but I'm playing great!" As for her friendships, she beamed as she reeled off a list of six best friends, three of them boys. She organized a mixed indoor soccer league in the off-season, and made up rules "to be fair to everyone." This was obviously a source of great joy for her.

How was Helen feeling about both of her parents these days? She felt close to both and felt they knew her well, describing them as being "different, not better, not worse." She experienced her dad as easier to "hang out with" than her equally loving and loved mother. "My mom is neat, but she kinda nags. My dad is cool."

We wondered if self-awareness might benefit from being so in touch with both parents that a child sees himself reflected in two differing styles of caring and teaching. Helen described the value of both parental styles:

> "Dad tolerates my confusing life better than Mom. When I changed my mind thousands of times about who was coming to my birthday, he just let me be nuts for a while and said, 'Let me know when you're done being crazy about this.' Mom would have gone crazy with me, and that's not the best way to handle my being nuts."

In the family interview with her 8-year-old sister and parents, Helen and her father teased each other vigorously and mercilessly about who knew more about soccer, the Red Sox, the "Spice Girls," etc. Her mother and sister rolled their eyes, giving them a gentle "knock-it-off" sign, with little effect. Still, though Helen and her father communicated well and enjoyably, her nonverbal connection was more with her mother, leaning her back against her mother's chest as she wove their fingers together. Her father, when asked about any changes in the way the family was getting along these days, replied with mild but audible distress, "Helen doesn't tell me as much about her life as she used to." To which Helen replied, "Oh, Dad, stop complaining, I'm supposed to have a private life *sometime*." The mother gave her a warm hug from behind, as though to reward her daughter's declaration of growing autonomy, while giving a reassuring glance to her husband across the room.

Though well defended, it was still clear that Helen's 38-year-old father, who now worked 30 hours out of the home in a job that was "just OK," was feeling a new remoteness, benign though it may be, in his relationship with his older daughter. His wife had recently been promoted, and was involving Helen in some office work, lending lunch, travel, and social time to the mother-daughter life. While Helen and her father remained affectionate and close, she was now confiding more in her mother (while also arguing more), and volunteered that she preferred to have her mom do the driving to the movies and the mall, because "Dad embarrasses me in public sometimes because we are so close and he thinks he knows me so well."

Later in the interview, we asked Helen to explain "embarrassed." To her it meant, "He likes to joke about stuff in public, like he wants my friends to know that we are close. But it feels kind of awkward, having him do that around my buddies, especially my girlfriends. He is my Dad, but he is a guy – he can't help it!" It was as though Helen had discovered a father in whom gender had achieved a new salience for their relationship.

Allen. Allen, now 11, compared how his mom and dad gave him instruction: "Mom teaches like a teacher: 'Remember this – remember that.' Dad plays with me a lot and tries to sneak in the learning." His father corroborated this description: "While playing with him, I try to teach him to compete hard but fair (I don't let him cheat), how to deal with frustration and losing (we don't play for a while if he starts to whine and complain), how to reinforce new skills and how to handle power and aggression." (Allen: "He doesn't use all his strength all the time, but I do!")

The oldest of three, Allen is especially proud of his responsibilities with regard to his little sister. He taught her to "ride a bike, and use the potty" and is starting to teach her to read. He winks to the interviewer as he says "read," indicating he knows full well she merely memorizes what comes next in his dramatic readings of *Curious George.*

His role as a caretaking older brother was valued by his siblings, who kept "telling him secrets" during the interview. When pressed to reveal their content by his mother, Allen said, "They are just us kids talking, Mom, nothing to worry about." When asked about any recent changes in the way the family was getting along, the mother responded, "Allen seems to be giving me a pretty hard time these days, right, Buddy?" Allen fell silent for a moment, looking more thoughtful than wounded. "I think that's right, Mom. You are bugging me about my homework, my room, how long I'm in the shower, or on the phone – you are all over me." The father broke in with a slight edge in his voice, leaning forward aggressively in his chair to cut off the "angle of fire" between his wife and son: "It's not quite that bad, but there is more arguing than there used to be, with both of us. You don't listen the way you used to, especially to your mother." The younger sister, age 7, both excited and made anxious by this interchange, spontaneously yelled "Fight! Fight!" and humorously brought the "confrontation" to a close when Allen swept her up in his arms and lovingly called her a "troublemaker." She squealed in delight and queried, "Me? No! You're the troublemaker!"

In this family, the continuity of communication and closeness was transforming around Allen, and his parents were both reacting strongly. The mother felt that Allen was arguing with her more, but that they still managed to feel loving toward one another. Allen's father appreciated Allen's beginning search for autonomy and felt less threatened by it. In the meeting he closed his reflections on the interview by saying, "I could never imagine talking with my parents about myself and my feelings the way Allen did here today, I would have been too worried they'd be hurt or they wouldn't get it. I'm proud of him for saying what he feels, and of us for getting it."

In his individual interview, Allen described a recurrent dream that started when he began the 6th grade:

> He is riding his brand new trick bike back and forth along a country road with his Mom and Dad at opposite ends of the road. He remembers that the road signs say "One way, this way" but he ignores them and just keeps riding faster and faster back and forth until it starts to rain. He comments that it's a "weird dream" because he'd "never bike alone – his friends are always with him." He adds later that he "remembers feeling a little scared riding one way, but not the other."

Sorting out his loyalties, even at this age, is hard work, even for the unconscious.

General Findings

While we have focused only on two families in this review, we analyzed all the interview and family interview data for the study population and found that the children are still developing well in the relevant domains and their families continue to handle their maturational needs reasonably well, despite the changes brought about by imminent adolescence. Again, no statistically significant data could emerge from such a small pilot study, and a control group is not possible, so we are informed by only the most robust consensual findings in this population, while being challenged to understand those things which surprise us. But there did emerge several interesting trends in both the children as individuals, and in the families' nurturing dyads.

The most robust finding 10 years into the study was that the father's gender became more important to his parental identity. Early in his caregiving career, his nurturing behavior, motivation, and overall parental characteristics had outweighed the contribution of his gender. But now, his masculine gender emerged as a central attribute in his ongoing relationship with his child on the threshold of adolescence. The parallel ascendancy of gender in the life of his pubescent child is undoubtedly catalytic, rendering a new focus on this previously peripheral attribute in their identities.

Harmonically, the mother's femininity also assumes new salience, but with a slightly different meaning for the preteen. Her femininity had always been an important attribute because it was part of what defined her "differentness" from the father. This enhanced her power as the "important other" in the child's struggle for differentiation from the father, especially in the child's pre-school life. Now, in the developmental era when the child is no longer mere-ly rehearsing psychological and sexual autonomy, but differentiating "for real," her femininity clarifies and affirms her son's heterosexual interests, and simultaneously reassures and challenges her daughter. It's as if she can say, "Trust me, I showed you before that it is OK to look beyond your father's love, and to look for me, and with me, for a wider world."

The most vigorous clinically apparent finding at this level of investigation was that the eight girls and six boys felt that their friendships and relationships with peers of both genders were very satisfying, and that gender was less important than the overall quality of friendship. Gender polarization seemed a marginal rather than central issue. This was striking in its equanimity, because of the usual anxiety and conflict that typically suffuses previously comfortable and companionable peer relations in this era. More typically, gender differences become far more salient, as sexual and physiological repro-ductive differentiation asserts itself in the arrival of puberty. Teasing, jokes, and sadistic humor all arrive to bind the conflict and anxiety that accompany this relational change.

But for the children in this study, the companionable humor and communi-cation of latency survives still. The kids themselves are aware that they have a surprising number of friends across gender lines (especially compared to their peers) that still come comfortably to birthday parties, go to movies, commu-nity events, and occasional religious festivities as real friends, and not, as Katelin said, "potential honeys."

This trans-stereotypic clustering of friendships is rather counter-intuitive for the young adolescent population. We theorize that having your father as a primary nurturing figure during early developmental maturation, while your mother stayed very close (most mothers continued to breast-feed after return-ing to work), creates a bedrock trust and comfort with present and future male *and* female objects. Herein the gendered aspects of those relationships may be less salient than the overall quality of the relationship. How long this relative ease will endure, and what role it plays in late adolescence when sexual differentiation is more complete and the search for intimacy in the sexual context is more libidinized, is a matter for further study.

Research and Practice Applications

Now that we have come to know that paternal presence is a positive and powerful force in the lives of young children, let's review what we know about how it happens. Pleck[1] reviewed the sociodemographic predictors of father involvement:

Fathers

1) Are more involved with sons than daughters, especially when older, less so when young

2) Are less involved with older than younger kids, though father involvement declines less proportionally to mothers' decline in involvement

3) Are more connected to first-born sons than later-born children, to the prematurely born, and to those with difficult temperaments (both trends noted in mothers as well)

4) Are more involved the more children they parent

5) Involvement with children has not been consistently found to be related to socioeconomic characteristics, race, or ethnicity.

These data draw the profile of the way fathers "naturally" involve themselves with their children without intervention. Unfortunately, there is a paucity of reliable data evaluating the effectiveness of programmatic or practice-based enhancement of father involvement. Still, reviews and descriptions of particularly effective fathering programs and consensus strategies for promoting responsible fathering have been compiled by Doherty et al.[48] Drawing from these reports and my own research and clinical experience, the following recommendations and strategies are presented which apply our research knowledge to best practices:

1) Critical developmental touchpoints should be used to encourage father involvement. Pregnancy and childbirth (of course), but also illnesses, entrance into child care and school, marital separation, or job loss are all opportunities for health and/or service personnel to reach out to the father and support increasing involvement. Entry into adolescence and divorce are two especially vulnerable periods where decreasing father connection can significantly increase a child's risk for trouble. Even family courts have begun to recognize this risk, and parenting classes for divorcing mothers and fathers are increasingly available (although unfortunately of uneven quality). These are all wide-open windows of opportunity that should not be missed by pediatricians, nurses, early childhood educators, early care providers, or policy makers.

2) Encourage fathers to establish legal paternity. In the event of marital separation, a father has a better chance of staying active in his child's life if he commits his own personal and emotional resources to fatherhood. He has to stay active in the child's and mother's life, benefitting his child's development over the long haul (most true for nonresidential fathers).

3) As fathering is fused with providing, for most men, employment remains a critical element in involvement. This is especially salient for nonresidential fathers who tend to withdraw from their children when out of work. The reverse can also be true, implicating child involvement as a catalyst to returning to employment (this is an important, unresearched question to date).

4) Child care staff at all levels need reminding and training to promote responsible fathering. High expectations of father involvement need to be held by everyone, not just children. Otherwise the windows close and opportunities vanish. As we have seen in the research and prevention literature, "parent" means mother 75% of the time. Professionals need reminding of the significance of the paternal presence or they, by habit alone, leave them out of appointments, procedures, intake questionnaires, parent conferences, hospital visits, workshops, etc. Specific training and reminding for both male and female workers to encourage father-child involvement is economically and developmentally frugal.

5) Mothers need ongoing encouragement to support their partners' involvement with their children. Because of the societal expectation that mothers will be the central figures in their children's lives, it may not be easy, or even obvious, that encouraging her spouse to care for their baby will serve the child's needs. Some women give lip service to paternal involvement, but then feel anxious or critical about the lack of skill men initially show in caretaking. In fact, men need the same opportunity to learn on the job the way women do. Consequently, we need to support mothers through the anxious beginnings as Dad practices, in order to promote the long-term benefits of competent father care to her, her child, and her marriage.

6) Fathers need to be encouraged to work with fathers. Since men are less typically group affiliative than women, they tend not to gather, physically or emotionally, around such a critical issue in their lives as fathering. Yet experienced fathers are a tremendous resource for both residential and nonresidential fathers. Although this remains a researchable question, the support that fathers can offer to one another at difficult times, and the modeling of robust and competent fatherhood, are routinely mentioned by fathers who have been "rehabilitated" or sustained through experiences that threatened their being responsible fathers. Mother-only groups are very useful to at-risk moms, and the corollary holds for fathers too. Father to Father, a community-based, easily replicable program with broad applicability, and initiated by Vice President Al Gore, uses experienced fathers as its chief resource, and is highly regarded.

Confident though such recommendations may seem, we are still far from a comprehensive father-inclusion paradigm. Many special circumstances of fathering remain insufficiently understood or even identified. The variety of the fathering experience is as varied as the mothering experience. And as our society increasingly complicates itself, the inclusion of fathers with different experiences becomes even more critical. Ethnic differences are finally getting their just due; gay fathering, however, particularly of young children, remains uninvestigated systematically. Fathers are only just beginning to be included in critically important research on family violence, a particularly egregious oversight.

In the end, fathering, like mothering, exists simultaneously for the baby and the family. It is influenced first by past experience, spousal expectations, economics, personal and marital values and behaviors, and last by our very own professional and institutional practices. The former requires our understanding, the latter our commitment and action.

References

1. Pleck J. *Paternal Involvement, Levels, Sources, and Consequences.* New York, NY: John Wiley & Sons; 1997.
2. Phare V, Compas BE. The role of fathers in child and adolescent psychopathology: make room for daddy. *Psychological Bulletin.* 1992;111:387-412.
3. Frodi AM, Lamb ME. Sex differences in responsiveness to infants: a developmental study of psychophysiological and behavioral responses. *Child Development.* 1978;49:1182-1188.

4. Frodi AM, Murray AD, Lamb ME, Steinberg J. Biological and social determinants of responsiveness to infants in 10- to 15-year-old girls. *Sex Roles.* 1984;10:639-649.

5. Deater-Deckard K, Scarr S, McCartney K, Eisenberg M. Paternal separation anxiety: relationships with parenting stress, child-rearing attitudes, and maternal anxieties. *Psychological Science.* 1994;5: 341-346.

6. Kaitz M, Lapidot P, Bronner R, Eidelman AL. Parturient women can recognize their infants by touch. *Developmental Psychology.* 1992;28:35-39.

7. Parke RD, Sawin DB. The family in early infancy: social interactional and attitudinal analyses. Paper presented at the meeting of the Society for Research in Child Development; March 1997; New Orleans, LA.

8. Blount GB, Padgug EJ. Mother and father speech: distribution of parental speech features in English and Spanish. *Papers and Reports on Child Language Development.* 1976;12:47-59.

9. Lamb ME, Frodi AM, Hwang CP, Frodi M. Interobserver and test retest reliability of Rothbart's Infant Behavior Questionnaire. *Scandinavian Journal of Psychology.* 1983;24:153-156.

10. Pruett K. *The Nurturing Father.* New York, NY: Warner Books; 1987.

11. Pruett K. Consequences of primary paternal care: fathers and babies in the first six years. In: Greenspan S, Pollock G, eds. *The Course of Life, Vol 3, Middle and Late Childhood.* New York, NY: International Universities Press; 1991:73-94.

12. Donate-Bartfield D, Passman RH. Attentiveness of mothers and fathers to their baby's cries. *Infant Behavior and Development.* 1985;8:385-393.

13. Belsky J, Gilstrap B, Rovine M. The Pennsylvania Infant and Family Development Project: I. Stability and change in mother-infant and father-infant interaction in a family setting at one, three, and nine months. *Child Development.* 1984;55:692-705.

14. Belsky J. Experimenting with the family in the newborn period. *Child Development.* 1985;56: 407-414.

15. Cox MJ, Owen MT, Lewis JM, Henderson UK. Marriage, adult adjustment, and early parenting. *Child Development.* 1989;60:1015-1024.

16. Dickie J, Matheson P. Mother-father-infant: who needs support? Paper presented at the meeting of the American Psychological Association Convention; August 1984; Toronto, Canada.

17. Darke PR, Goldberg S. Father-infant interaction and parent stress with healthy and medically compromised infants. *Infant Behavior and Development.* 1994;17:3-14.

18. Kotelchuck M. The infant's relationship to the father: experimental evidence. In: Lamb ME, ed. *The Role of the Father in Child Development.* New York, NY: Wiley; 1976:329-344.

19. Spelke E, Zelazo P, Kagan J, Kotelchuk M. Father interaction and separation protest. *Developmental Psychology.* 1973;9:83-90.

20. Bowlby J. *Attachment and Loss: Vol 1. Attachment.* New York, NY: Basic Books; 1969.

21. Cohen LJ, Campos JJ. Father, mother, and stranger as elicitors of attachment behaviors in infancy. *Developmental Psychology.* 1974;10:146-154.

22. Steele H, Steele M, Fonagy P. Associations among attachment classifications of mothers, fathers, and their infants. *Child Development.* 1996;67:541-555.

23. Ferketich S, Mercer RT. Paternal-infant attachment of experienced and inexperienced fathers during infancy. *Nursing Research.* 1995;44:31-37.

24. Lamb ME. The development of mother-infant and father-infant attachments in the second year of life. *Developmental Psychology.* 1977;13:637-648.

25. Abelin EL. Triangulation, the role of the father and the origins of core gender identity during the rapprochement subphase. In: Lax R, Bach S, Burland A, eds. *Rapprochement.* New York, NY: Aronson; 1980:151-169.

26. Engel PL, Breaux C. *Is There a Father Instinct? Fathers' Responsibility for Children.* Boulder, CO: Westview; 1994.

27. Munroe. Data on file.

28. Gottfried AE, Gottfried AW, Bathurst K. Maternal employment, family environment, and children's development: infancy through the school years. In: Gottfried AE, Gottfried AW, eds. *Maternal Employment and Children's Development: Longitudinal Research.* New York, NY: Plenum; 1988:11-58.

29. Lind R. Observations after delivery of communications between mother-infant-father. Paper presented at the meeting of the International Congress of Pediatrics; October 1974; Buenos Aires, Argentina.

30. Yogman MJ, Dixon S, Tronick E, et al. The goals and structure of face-to-face interaction between infants and their fathers. Paper presented at the meeting of the Society for Research in Child Development; March 1977; New Orleans, LA.

31. Schaffer HR, Emerson PE. The development of social attachments in infancy. *Monographs of the Society for Research in Child Development.* 1964;29:94. Special issue.

32. Lamb ME. The changing roles of fathers. In: Lamb ME, ed. *The Father's Role: Applied Perspectives.* New York, NY: Wiley; 1986:3-27.

33. Clarke-Stewart KA. And daddy makes three: the father's impact on mother and young child. *Child Development.* 1978;49:466-478.

34. Belsky J. Mother-father-infant interaction: a naturalistic observational study. *Developmental Psychology.* 1979;15:601-607.

35. Frascarolo-Moutinot F. *Daily Paternal Involvement and Parent-Child Relationships* [in French]. Unpublished doctoral dissertation, University of Geneva. 1994.

36. Hossain Z, Roopnarine JL. African-American father's involvement with infants: relationships to their functional style, support, education, and income. *Infant Behavior and Development.* 1994;17:175-184.

37. Field T. Interaction behaviors of primary versus secondary caretaker fathers. *Developmental Psychology.* 1978;14:183-184.

38. Maccoby E, Jacklin C. *The Psychology of Sex Roles.* Stanford, CA: Stanford University Press; 1974.

39. Lytton H, Romney DM. Parents' differential socialization of boys and girls: a meta- analysis. *Psychological Bulletin.* 1991;109:267-296.

40. Fox NA, Kimmerly NL, Schafter WD. Attachment to mother/attachment to father: a meta-analysis. *Child Development.* 1991;62:210-225.

41. Cox JE, Bithoney WG. Fathers of children born to adolescent mothers. Predictors of contact with their children at 2 years. *Archives of Pediatric and Adolescent Medicine.* 1995;9:962-966.

42. Easterbrooks MA, Goldberg WA. Toddler development in the family: impact of father involvement and parenting characteristics. *Child Development.* 1984;53:740-752.

43. Pruett K. Infants of primary nurturing fathers. *The Psychoanalytic Study of the Child.* 1983;38: 257-277.

44. Provence S, Naylor A. *Working With Disadvantaged Parents and Their Children.* New Haven, CT: Yale University Press; 1983.

45. Pruett K. Oedipal configurations in father-raised children. *The Psychoanalytic Study of the Child.* 1985;40:435-456.

46. Pruett K, Litzenberger B. Latency development in children of primary nurturing fathers: eight-year follow-up. *The Psychoanalytic Study of the Child.* 1992;47:85-101.

47. Ross JM. Fathering. *International Journal of Psycho-Analysis.* 1979;60:317-327.

48. Doherty WJ, Kouneski EF, Erickson MF. *Responsible Fathering: An Overview and Conceptual Framework.* Washington, DC: Report prepared for the Administration for Children and Families and the Office of the Assistant Secretary for Planning and Evaluation of the United States Department of Health and Human Services; October 1996.

Learning and Emotion in Babies

Lewis P. Lipsitt, PhD

Much like the law of gravity, the laws of learning are always in effect.
– Scott Spreat and Susan Rogers Spreat, *Learning Principles*

Statements of fact are always either true or false, but our knowledge about them always remains to an extent uncertain or incomplete.
– Charles C. Spiker, 1955, Course teaching notes, Univ. of Iowa[1]

Introduction

The study of perceptual and learning processes in humans is of rather recent origin relative to many other scientific endeavors, such as the study of gravity, electricity, and fluid mechanics. Interest in the learning and sensory processes of *babies* is even more modern. Thus our knowledge base about the behavioral and psychophysiological capacities of infants, including motivational processes and emotional characteristics, is still quite inadequate relative to the scientific sophistication and practical wisdom that we would like to have.

Only in the last few years, for example, has the definitive advice of pediatricians been given that babies in the first few months of life are best put in their cribs to sleep on their backs rather than in the prone position – in order to reduce the risk of sudden infant death. Even so, the debate about this particular child-rearing practice continues, because many pediatricians believe there is a significant risk, in the supine position, that the infant may regurgitate its food.

By the same token, child developmentalists, behavior scientists, and the medical community continue to debate, and individuals among them argue heatedly about, such matters as (1) how soon a mother can return to employment after the birth of her baby and still feel secure that the child is not thus put at developmental or emotional risk; (2) whether circumcision is a traumatic experience for a baby; (3) how early a baby can detect its own mother's voice, and the effect of reading, or simply talking, to a baby from the earliest days and weeks of life; (4) how early infants can remember, and how long those memories last, and (5) whether there is such a phenomenon as 'recovered memory,' whereby an experience of a young child may be forgotten by the child for many years, only later to become a vividly recaptured recollection.

New Perspectives and Old Misapprehensions

Significant strides have been made by increasing numbers of basic and clinical researchers of babies over the past half century. The "blooming, buzzing confusion" of infancy, as William James characterized the earliest days and weeks of human life, is gone forever. Indeed it never existed for the normal, full-term robust baby, and certainly no longer exists in the minds of parents and pediatricians familiar with the fulsome accounts now available of the behavioral and cognitive competencies of infants. Human babies are very orderly in their ways; they actually behave according to laws (even like the rest of us) which can be explored, discovered, confirmed, reconfirmed, and celebrated

The accessibility of the infant for the systematic observation of developmental regularities, in humans generally and in individuals as well, was recognized in the early writings of Freud, Piaget, and other theorists. They believed, based upon empirical study, that early experience is an important determinant of later behavior, along with genetic disposition, and that, as an anonymous New Englander put it, "while people are mostly the same, what little differences there are seem powerful important."

Today, the sensory and learning capacities of the young infant, even the newborn, far exceed those with which the baby had been credited historically. At least with respect to certain kinds of learning, it is not absurd to suggest that the very young child may never again in its life be as fast at learning as during the newborn period and the succeeding few months.

It is important to look at what we do know through careful clinical observation and laboratory investigation, and to note that we have indeed come a long way. In view of our interest at this time in new perspectives, it is not a bad idea to reflect on William James and the extant wisdom of his day, as we have done, and to take a quick look at other "ancients" and their perspectives.

Ghosts in Our History

Time and tradition dictate that we frequently assimilate overly simplified or completely erroneous information from our intellectual forebears. John B. Watson, the noted "father of behaviorism" in America, is often misrepresented by students, especially those who have just (correctly) learned that Watson is an icon in the field of child development and behavioral psychology, as having said that "all behavior is learned."

Watson, however, was in fact a well-trained physiologist, and a believer in the importance of heredity, just as Pavlov was. He was a major proponent of the supposition that *all* behavior is founded in emotion, and that the earliest manifestations of behavior in the human infant are essentially of an emotional nature. In a now-classic treatise, he described an array of nonconditioned, congenital, or hereditarily given responses: *fear, rage,* and *love.* He elaborated with the following statement:

> *"An emotion is an hereditary 'pattern-reaction' involving profound changes of the bodily mechanism as a whole, but particularly of the visceral and glandular systems."* [2]

This celebration of the importance of heredity shows that Watson obviously had great respect for genetic underpinnings of behavior, even as he advocated, foolishly as we now suppose, that fathers should greet their children with handshakes rather than hugs. Had Watson's scientific career not been interrupted suddenly by an emotional and behavioral (amorous) relationship, we might have found Watson today as much a significant contributor to the literature of and our knowledge about emotional development as to that on the developing learning processes of children.

Misconceptions through the ages continue. Just as Watson continues to be appreciated for some odd reasons, so does Freud become surrounded with inappropriate classic misapprehensions. Freud did not claim, despite suppositions to the contrary, that there is an unconscious element in every aspect of behavior or mental functioning.

Although elaboration of the "behaviorism" inherent in Freudian theory will carry us too far from our mission here, it should be noted that the widely held presumption that Freud's interest in mentalisms, particularly unconscious processes, precluded interest in overt behavior (or in the science of experimental psychology) is false. An excellent treatise on this aspect of Freudianism by Gustav Bergmann,[3] although much ignored, is nonetheless available. What is quite true is that Freud concerned himself very little with direct observations of infants, or even older children. He wrote about infancy and childhood on the basis of patients' retrospective reports. However, many of his successors, notably Daniel Stern (this volume), are well known for their intense involvement in direct observation of the infant, and for their systematic substantiation of inferences drawn from those observations. This contemporary innovation lends credibility to aspects of Freudian theory about infantile behavior that it might otherwise not have had. In particular, Freud was very clear that from the earliest days of life, babies have strong proclivities for special cathected objects and events, particularly mother and the stimuli and styles of attachment behavior that she provided. By the same token, infants may object strenuously and unmistakably to noxious events in their environment. The psychological defense behaviors which humans manifest at later ages, and which become persistent patterns of behavior for which Freud is noted as the master cataloguer, are grounded in infantile experience.

The Problem With Emotions and Behavior

Communications about the nature of learning, behavior, emotional expression, and motivation are often hampered by denials that emotional reactions, as mental phenomena, have anything to do with overt behavior. After all, the argument goes, a person can be angry without it showing. And, by the same token, a relatively unperturbed person can look quite angry in his or her behavior.

The concepts of *emotion* and *behavior* have become so compartmentalized that experts in the study of emotional development hardly give even a tip of the hat to Watson's characterization of the earliest psychological characteristics of the human infant as *fear, rage,* and *love.* What could be more emotional than fear, rage, and love? Yet the notion is perpetuated that Watson had little or nothing to do with emotional development, only conditioning – and then only classical conditioning. In fact, Watson used an *operant* conditioning style of training, which involves quite a different set of procedures from those of classical Pavlovian conditioning.

As for operant conditioning procedures, parents have been doing this kind of training for eons. For example, the child engages in some behavior like that which is desired, perhaps pulling himself almost to a standing position. In anticipation that this is a prelude to walking, parents express their glee to the child with each successive approximation to a standing position. Later, the pleasure of the parents is expressed on the occasion of the first step, then the second, and progressively with each advance in the child's behavior. Much shaping of the child's behavior occurs through the presentation of contingent stimulation like this. That the expressed pleasure of the parents is meaningful to the child, and coaxes him on, is apparent from the way in which the child continually refers back with smiles and other measures of satisfaction to the parents. He will soon see that he can't clap for his own performance and pull himself up at the same time. This is not the start of, but is one of many examples of, self-regulatory behavior of the young child.

The young child sorts out, in part due to differential reinforcement administered by the caring persons in her environment, those aspects of the skill that can be, each by itself, satisfactorily performed and followed by pleasure. This reinforcing or rewarding aspect of behavioral development has not been sufficiently acknowledged, historically, largely because of the enormous influence of biological determinists, both on the science of human development and on parents' understandings of what child development is about. Gesell,[4] for example, insisted that development is essentially genetically programmed, that successive stages will be arrived at in due time, and that neither facilitative nor interfering stimulation will affect the rate of the child's hereditarily determined mental growth. The profound effects of environmental and experiential influences, in interaction with maturational and congenital factors, have been incontrovertibly documented, and must now be heeded.

Denigration of the importance of experience on children's development and behavior has led to some flagrant devaluations of the influence of the environment on children's welfare, and on social programs and policies that might otherwise benefit youngsters growing up in America. The national attitude toward maternal leave, child care, enhancements of school budgets, and the implementation of after-school programs has been generally negative, relative to other advanced nations such as the Scandinavian countries, France, and others, to say nothing of the special disregard our society seems to have for the devastating influences, perhaps one of the best-documented facts in the study of child development, that poverty has on the well-being of children.

The Legacy of Developmental Dichotomies

The historic dichotomization of the many different influences on human growth and development has had a pernicious effect on the way in which we regard life-span influences. The human organism does not, as it makes its way through development, compartmentalize the genetic and environmental influences on its behavior.

Neither do other psychological dichotomies work in the way that our language often suggests. Dichotomous "manners of speaking," whether relating to learning and emotion, sensation and perception, or conscious and unconscious ideation, are heuristic fictions created for the benefit of simplified discourse. Developmental psychology is, perhaps more than many other scientific fields, victimized by the entrapments of words.

I come to the point, then, that in our zeal to study conditioning processes of infants, and in our eagerness to understand the origins and changing patterns of emotion in development, we have acted as if there are separate and clearly distinctive processes underlying them. This is, however, patently false. Those who study emotions and emotional development simply cannot avoid the conditioned aspects of emotional reactivity, nor the mechanisms and processes which by now have been so carefully documented in the laboratory. I will provide an example shortly of a "condition of infancy" which is best explicated by drawing upon the conjoint effects of both neuromotor capacities of the infant and the experience of the baby to create a neuropsychogenic pattern of behavior. The constellation of behaviors involved in the scenario, in which the baby's response to brief respiratory occlusions is of vital importance, could not appear without contributions from neuromuscular and central nervous system maturation, on the one hand, and experience, on the other.

The Nature of Infancy

Recent years' advances in the study of infant behavior and development have led to the well-supported conclusion that normal full-term humans are capable of perceiving stimulation in all sensory modalities, and are able to engage in classical conditioning, operant learning, and the learning of discriminations, even in the first month of life.[5,6]

Although most studies conducted in infant laboratories are of "positive" or "approach" responses, such as sucking, rooting, smiling, and tugging at mobiles, a few studies (eg, Watson and Rayner[7]) and naturalistic evidence indicate clearly that avoidance, aversive, and escape behaviors are also conditionable.

Learned approach and learned avoidance responses are almost invariably mediated by positive and negative hedonic qualities, such as intense pleasure or pain, moderate satisfaction or annoyance, or other "feeling" characteristics. It is practically impossible to speak separately of emotion and learning. Michael Lewis[8] has addressed the phenomenon of anger, for example, in connection with the emergence of emotions. At about 2 months of age, he says, infants will become angry if a "learned instrumental act is removed" from the possibility of occurrence. His observation lends itself to our supposition that learning and emotion, in this case "anger," are often conflated in a complex psychological event.

Lewis[8] also talks of "surprise" in 6-month-old infants. Under conditions in which "children were taught an instrumental arm-pulling response, the children showed surprise at the point when they discovered that the arm-pull could turn on a [photographic] slide." The synergistic occurrence of a habit, then, and the manifestation of emotional surprise in one behavioral event or sequence of events furthers the present thesis that learning and emotion go hand in hand from the earliest months of life. Lewis adds: "Surprise can reflect either a violation or a confirmation of expectancy." Expectancies are, of course, typically based upon prior experience, learned models of the way the world is, the way things operate, and the usual consequences of one's own behavior. Infants even in the first month of life, while not yet superb information processors, utilize historical information proactively for behavioral and emotional self-regulation.

Pleasure and the Precocity of Babies

Rather contrary to the usual appreciation of the very young infant, babies by 2 months of age manifest proactive patterns of behavior based on prior experience. Even 6-week-old children have been shown to engage in repetitive behaviors which are instrumental in effecting previously experienced changes in the environment.[6]

Such self-regulation seems to be based on a primary level of executive function, in the form of deliberate *approach* and *avoidance* behavior. This is mediated by the pleasantness (hedonic quality) of the response consequences that ensue. Like other humans, babies are responsive from the earliest moments of life to the pleasures and annoyances afforded by the environment, particularly as consequences of their own behavior.

That babies derive pleasure and experience annoyance from their own behavior is the bedrock of learning and emotion in the first year of life. Even babies, like older individuals, can distinguish between a more pleasurable stimulus and a lesser, and the hedonic properties of an experience are determinants, along with other stimulus features, of whether the behavior will be repeated in the future.

Human infants are capable of *preferring.* There are some visual stimuli to which they will turn their heads more frequently, and concentrate their gaze on. Relatedly, newborns change their sucking and other mouthing behavior depending on how sweet the fluid is for which they are sucking.[9-10] They suck more times per minute for sweeter fluids, even as they slow down their sucking within bursts of sucking, probably to savor the sweeter fluid. By 1 week of age, infants have been shown to prefer their own mother's odor to the odor of another infant's mother. Examples of this sort of differential responding, or preferential behavior, can be found for infants in every sensory modality.

As it happens, such preferential responding, evident in the first days of life and found in increasingly complicated styles as the child matures and assimilates more experience, is the sine qua non of learning. Learning depends upon the assimilation of sensory experience, and the capability of preference, ie, to like some experiences more than others. The child is capable of learning because, as with his elders, Thorndike's Law of Effect[11] is in place: those behaviors which are followed by a "satisfying state of affairs" will tend to be repeated when the occasion arises again, while those behaviors which are followed by annoyance or pain will occur less frequently, and may result in long-term exclusion from the behavioral repertoire.

The expression "satisfying state of affairs" is, of course, a phrase connoting emotional reactivity. Thorndike is not irrelevant to contemporary analyses of behavioral and emotional interactions between mothers and their infants. When "flat affect," "resistance to contact with others," and "gaze aversion" are noted in nonnurtured institutionalized orphans, the terms have a special meaning. They connote suppression or extinction of normal or usual behavioral patterns of babies who have not had the misfortune of being subjected to such abject conditions as have prevailed in Eastern European orphanages in recent times.

Pleasure and annoyance as psychological dispositions are aspects of emotional reactivity. They are revealed in part through indices of autonomic nervous system responsivity, such as the heart-rate response, or crying. Such emotional reactivity may be accompanied by neuromotor components, as in sucking on a sweet-delivering nipple, or pulling the hand away from a hurtful stimulus. The quality of the infant's response, including its approach and avoidance characteristics, signal the pleasure or annoyance inherent in the experience.

An especially striking index of emotional annoyance in the baby is crying behavior, which occurs under conditions of tissue damage or deprivation. Crying is a conditionable behavior. Whereas it might occur under distressing physical stimulation, such as a loud noise, a bump on the head, or a bad taste, it may subsequently occur on the basis of learned anticipation. For example, parents have often noted that their toddler sitting near a refrigerator door that slams may at first jump in response to the sound of the door; but after several such occasions, the child will jump before the door slams, simply at the sight of the door closing.

A similar situation exists with respect to pleasant taste sensations. After a great deal of experience, as occurs in real life, the pleasures associated with taste and the ritualistic feeding regimen may lead to craving. Craving is an appetitional pattern of behavior involving strong approach responses, both neuromotor and emotional, which, when thwarted, may lead to enormous psychological excitement, regret, and anger. Craving is both emotional and conditionable.

The Perturbable Infant

Even the well-nurtured, wanted baby of parents who have fallen in love with him or her, under the best of circumstances will be perturbed on occasion by environmental events. Some such experiences can quickly become major family crises as, for example, when a 3-year-old child has a temper tantrum during his older sister's piano recital. Such occasions are behavioral and emotional, and are often the consequence of some learning process that is not easy to follow as to its origins, and are even more difficult to address as to their "curability."

There are some conditions of early infancy that have that same kind of stress-evoking durability, and for which, as with the condition called colic, we tend to find ourselves devoid of antidotes! Perhaps we do not often enough look to the specific behaviors involved, or have the necessary confidence in an environmental and behavioral analysis, to look at the instigating circumstances that promoted the behavior in the first place and the reinforcing events that perpetuate it.

Fortunately, we have a test instance taught to us by a wise pediatrician who adopted a behavioral approach to the understanding of, and eventual treatment of, breast-feeding problems. Mavis Gunther reported her initial observations in a *Lancet* article,[12] then expanded on her theory in a volume on the *Determinants of Infant Behavior*.[13]

Aversive behavior sometimes occurs in the human newborn when biological threat exists.[14] In its milder forms, such behavior is manifested in withdrawal responses of the baby to intense stimulation, such as bright lights, painful touch, unpleasant odorants, loud noises, and so on. The amount of active response to such threats is proportional to the intensity of the aversive stimulation. When the annoying stimulation persists, the baby often becomes agitated and cries.

Gunther described such a situation in newborns and explained the anger that can be evoked in babies under rather specific conditions. A particularly striking pattern of behavior may be seen in newborns when they experience the threat of respiratory occlusion. This can happen when they press their faces fleetingly against a mattress, or when their respiratory passages are blocked with mucous or regurgitated fluids.

Stimulation that supports or threatens such "smothering" tends, Gunther said, to elicit a response sequence consisting of five components. She described this behavior as a "fixed action pattern," using an ethological term of biologists studying stereotypic species-specific response sequences. The five-stage response sequence, she said, is often found in the natural course of breast-feeding of the infant. The baby will have the nipple in its mouth, with a tight pressure seal around it, preventing any respiration through the mouth.

The nostrils are the only source of oxygen. The baby objects to, and defends itself against, further respiratory occlusion with an adaptive sequence of responses, going to the next increasingly vigorous behavioral defense on the "list" if the earlier coping tactic does not free the respiratory passages for breathing:

(1) side-to-side head waving,

(2) head withdrawal, with backward jerks and grimacing,

(3) facial vasodilation,

(4) arm jabbing, and

(5) crying.

In fact, Gunther reported that she observed "one-trial learning" in which, following an episode of the sort just described, babies would, when put to the same breast again, turn their heads in the opposite direction.

This continuum of responses is, from all appearances, a build-up of angry behavior. It abates when the threatening or noxious stimulation is removed or reduced. From Gunther's poignant descriptions of the phenomenon, one realizes that once the infant is successful through its progressively aggressive pursuit of air, there occurs an enormous sigh of relief that can only be described as rewarding.

Especially striking are Gunther's observations of breast-feeding babies in the arms of their mothers, particularly new mothers who had had little experience with babies. Some mothers, either because they have not observed other women breast-feeding a baby, or due to some awkwardness of build or posture, would inadvertently smother their babies for brief times. These episodes of respiratory occlusion at the breast elicited the fixed action pattern of behavior, to the point that some infants went through the entire sequence of defensive behaviors culminating in the relief associated with crying and thrusting the nipple from their mouths. Mothers who avoided this "crisis" were those who deftly utilized their fingers to hold the breast away from the infant's nostrils.

The fixed action pattern (FAP) of the baby has the effect of freeing the respiratory passages, by displacing the offending object or by impelling the mother to adjust her feeding position. The freeing from occlusion is a reinforcement condition that may increase the probability of the FAP's occurrence again under this and similar conditions in the future. From what we know of the shaping of behavior through reinforcement, it is not unthinkable that the angry response may occur subsequently in a shorter period of time, or even anticipatorily to less intense stimulating conditions.

To carry the learning prospects still further, it is possible that the behavior previously executed directly to stimulus instigators might be adopted as a coping pattern in other situations where arousal has reached "panic" proportions. We may be describing here the origins of "aggressive behavior" mediated by anger which had been initially generated from circumstances different from those in which the behavior was first learned.

That such defensive behaviors are necessary for survival, and that the learned consequences of experiences like these may be of considerable importance in understanding the ontogeny of aggression and other learned patterns of behavior, may go without saying.[15] Perhaps a modicum of such experience is necessary for babies to learn life-long coping skills or useful defensive patterns of behavior. An excess of such experience might, on the other hand, conduce to a pattern of reactivity characterized by anger and aggression. Of special interest is the possibility that the *inability* of a baby to defend itself against episodes of respiratory occlusion may forecast a hazardous first year of life, particularly during that window of time, 2 to 5 months of age, when behavior gradually shifts from a reflexive basis to become increasingly under the control of learned responses.

When the Torch Is Passed

The behavior of human infants, like that of other mammals, is mediated by subcortical brain structures in the earliest days of life. Over the course of the next 2 or 3 months, there is a gradual shift of executive function to cortical structures. Mediation by these eventually acquired responses is based largely on experience, especially those which facilitate learning. The early reflexes appear in many instances to be preludes of and preparations for the to-be-acquired responses. For example, normal, full-term babies born under conditions of minimal perinatal stress have strong, obligatory grasp reflexes; they engage in stepping reflexes; and they exhibit stereotypic swimming reflexes when placed in water.

McGraw[16] has shown that these and other reflexes are transformed over the first weeks of life from obligatory behaviors to slower, more deliberative, "voluntary" patterns of behavior. Based upon the neurophysiological evidence available to McGraw at the time of her writing, she concluded that the neuromuscular maturation of the infant, and particularly the rapid maturation of cortical structures in the first few months after birth, enabled the transition of the infant's behavioral repertoire from largely reflexive functioning to a repertoire of largely learned functioning.

This transition from reflexive to learned function may operate in the following way. A reflexive response is usually elicited by a stimulus condition that is fairly obvious. The grasp reflex is stimulated by pressure on the palms of the baby. The stepping reflex is stimulated by pressure against the soles of both feet. The rooting reflex is produced by a touch to the face by the side of the mouth. The respiratory occlusion reflex occurs in response to dimininished availability of air or the threat of such occlusion produced by an object blocking the nose and mouth. In the normal course of events, these reflexes are exercised, in some infants more strongly than in others. The "practice" of reflexes which have a rewarding effect, such as relief from smothering, will tend to provide "learning trials," such that in later stages of development, when the intense reflex has waned, a learned anticipation of reward for engaging in that pattern of behavior will be manifested. This learned consequence of reflex functioning is probably at the root of much self-regulatory behavior of the infant and young child, and may well be responsible for most babies "knowing what to do" when threatened with respiratory occlusion after the primary control of behavior has shifted from subcortically mediated reflexive functioning to what McGraw called "voluntary" or learned functioning mediated by cortical structures. It is quite possible that the crib death will eventually be understood partly in terms of failure of that transition to occur effectively. Epidemiological statistics indicate that some 90% to 95% of all crib deaths occur in that critical 2-to-5-month age period when the baby makes the transition from the early mode of behavior to the later. Prior to 2 months of age, the baby is essentially free of critical occlusion because of the presence of a safety reflex; after 4 to 5 months of age, the learned "voluntary" aspects of behavior provide the safety net.

Summary and Reflections

Most human babies come into the world with all sensory systems functioning, and they are capable of learning. Their perceptual processes and learning capabilities have been rather well studied by now, although much remains to be discovered, particularly about the wondrous ways in which nature and nurture, heredity and the environment, congenital dispositions and experience work synchronously and symbiotically to shape the developmental destinies of individuals.

Child development experts are not entirely satisfied with their expertise in predicting life-span destinies from early behavioral characteristics, social indices, family attributes, or schooling, but the study of specific processes and mechanisms of early development and behavior has yielded some helpful hints as to what may be possible to know in the future. At the very least, they are confident that early life experiences are of inestimable importance, in that severe deprivation of sensory and learning opportunities, as well as the chance to become attached to a loving, trusted other person usually results in developmental retardation, intellectual incompetency, and insufficient capacity for engaging in close, caring relationships with others.

Fortunately, most children, even those reared under handicapping conditions, are resilient in at least some areas of psychological functioning, especially fortuitous insults that are not long-lasting. Later experience, it seems, can help deleteriously affected children to overcome the assaults of abuse, poverty, emotional deprivation, and early cognitive deficits. Just how these compensatory mechanisms can be best implemented, and for whom, is a matter of social policy as well as scientific exploration and documentation.

Some adverse developmental destinies that are reached early and with either tragic finality or life-span consequences require much more scientific attention by child development researchers than they have been afforded thus far. Among these are the so-called sudden infant death syndrome, and the failure-to-thrive phenomenon. Some advances have been made in understanding crib death as in part due to the environmental conditions of the sleeping infant and the *experience* of respiratory occlusion. Similarly, failure to thrive in young children has yielded to alterations in the *environment* in which the child lives.

Behavioral problems of infancy must be researched by experts in behavior analysis, and should be addressed therapeutically and preventatively by applied developmental scientists, among others.

References

1. Spiker CS. Lecture notes, *Research Methods in Child Psychology*. Iowa City, IA: University of Iowa; 1955.

2. Watson JB. *Psychology From the Standpoint of a Behaviorist*. 2nd ed. Philadelphia, PA: Lippincott; 1924.

3. Bergmann G. Psychoanalysis and experimental psychology. In: Marx MH, ed. *Psychological Theory*. New York, NY: Macmillan; 1951.

4. Gesell A. Maturation and the patterning of behavior. In: Murchison C, ed. *A Handbook of Child Psychology*. Worcester, MA: Clark University Press; 1933.

5. Lipsitt LP. Learning in the first year of life. In: Lipsitt LP, Spiker CC, eds. *Advances in Child Development and Behavior. Vol 1*. New York, NY: Academic Press; 1963.

6. Rovee-Collier C, Lipsitt LP. Learning, adaptation, and memory in the newborn. In: Stratton P, ed. *Psychobiology of the Human Newborn*. New York, NY: John Wiley & Sons; 1982.

7. Watson JB, Rayner R. Conditioned emotional reactions. *Journal of Experimental Psychology*. 1920;3: 1-14.

8. Lewis M. The emergence of human emotions. In: Lewis M, Haviland JM, eds. *Handbook of Emotions*. New York, NY: Guilford Press; 1993.

9. Lipsitt LP. Developmental psychobiology comes of age. In: Lipsitt LP, ed. *Developmental Psychobiology: The Significance of Infancy*. Hillsdale, NJ: Lawrence Erlbaum Associates; 1976:109-127.

10. Lipsitt LP. Toward understanding the hedonic nature of infancy. In: Lipsitt LP, Cantor JH, eds. *Experimental Child Psychologist: Essays and Experiments in Honor of Charles C. Spiker*. Hillsdale, NJ: Lawrence Erlbaum Associates; 1986:97-109.

11. Thorndike EL. *Animal Intelligence*. New York, NY: Macmillan; 1911.

12. Gunther M. Instinct and the learning couple. *Lancet*. 1955;1:575.

13. Gunther M. Infant behavior at the breast. In: Foss B, ed. *Determinants of Infant Behavior*. London, England: Methuen; 1961:37-44.

14. Lipsitt LP. Critical conditions of infancy. *American Psychologist*. 1979;34:973-980.

15. Lipsitt LP. Infant anger: toward an understanding of the ontogenesis of human aggression. Unpublished paper presented at the Department of Psychiatry, The Center for the Health Sciences, University of California at Los Angeles, March 4, 1971.

16. McGraw M. Maturation and behavior. In: Carmichael L, ed. *Manual of Child Psychology*. New York, NY: Wiley; 1946.

Emotions and Social Development: Infants' Recognition of Emotions in Others

Arlene S. Walker-Andrews, PhD

Introduction

Imagine the following scenario:

> A 14-month-old infant plays on the floor with her mother when an unfamiliar person enters. The mother stands up, smiles, extends her hand, and walks over to the stranger. Observing this, the infant loses interest and goes back to her toys.

The infant has shown a skill – social referencing – that illustrates her ability to use expressions and actions to understand events.[1] Had the mother responded with fear or anger in her face, voice, or gestures the child would have acted quite differently. Infants learn to read and understand expressions, and use that information to guide their actions. This skill seems to develop rapidly, starting with a sensitivity to emotions, leading later to an understanding of those emotions. The as-yet-unresolved questions about this process are: What information do younger infants detect in expressions? Can they discriminate various expressions? When can they understand the meanings of those expressions?

To date, most researchers agree that infants begin to "recognize" emotional expressions at about 7 months.[2,3] In some cases, even the 5-month-old shows limited understanding, and there are scattered reports of neonates' responding differentially to expressions.[4,5] But true "recognition" seems to arrive after 6 months of age. Using emotional recognition for social referencing, as described in the scenario, begins at about 8 to 10 months.[1]

In learning to discriminate and understand expressions, infants rely on contextual cues. Broadly defined, these cues include familiar settings, familiar persons, and multimodal (ie, sight AND sound AND touch) and amodal (ie, rhythm, intensity, rate, shape) information. By looking closely at the developing child's responsiveness to emotional expressions in a number of contexts, we can gain understanding of the separate and combined influences of these contexts. The experiments described in the following paper have been recently completed, but data analysis and interpretation are still underway.

Familiarity of Situation: Peek-A-Boo

The peek-a-boo game was used to examine young infants' perception of other people's expressions.[6] Peek-a-boo provides a unique opportunity to examine infants' responses to expressions:

- Parents and infants are familiar with the game

- Infants are attentive and enjoy peek-a-boo

- Infants have specific "expectations" about how the game is played

- Exaggerated expressions can be presented in a familiar context

- Peek-a-boo allows presentation of dynamic expressions to infants

- Infant responses to changes in expressions can be measured

Methods

Forty 4.5-month-old infants were enrolled and randomly assigned to one of four "emotion change" groups. These groups were: sad, anger, fear, and as the control, consistent happy/surprise. The babies were shown three typical happy/surprise peek-a-boos followed by a fourth in which the test expression varied according to group assignment. Each block of trials concluded with a typical happy/surprise. Please refer to Table 1 for an outline of the groups.

In each trial, the experimenter covered her face with a cloth for 3 seconds and called the child's name. She then reappeared for approximately 7 seconds with the target facial expression and said "peek-a-boo" in an affectively matching tone of voice. The experimenter's facial and vocal expressions and the infants' behaviors were filmed for later analysis. To insure consistency and accuracy of facial expressions, the investigator used Ekman and Friesen's technique for portraying facial expressions using specific muscle movements.[7] In

Table 1. The peek-a-boo test

Group	Block 1 trial sequence	Block 2 trial sequence
	1, 2, 3, 4	1, 2, 3, 4
Fear	H, H, H, F, H	H, H, H, F, H
Anger	H, H, H, A, H	H, H, H, A, H
Sad	H, H, H, S, H	H, H, H, S, H
Control	H, H, H, H, H	H, H, H, H, H

H = typical happy/surprise face in a peek-a-boo game, F = fearful face, A = angry face, S = sad face.

addition, the experimenter had a small mirror behind the cloth and another above the baby to monitor her own expressions

The infants' total looking time (TLT) was calculated for each trial. The MAX system (Maximally Discriminative Facial Movement Coding System) was also used to identify the infants' facial expressions.[8]

Results

Infants in the control group of consistent happy/surprise peek-a-boos increased their total looking time (TLT) slightly over the first three to four trials, and then diminished. This finding is consistent with typical visual habituation studies. Infants in the sad group decreased their TLT from that trial forward. Infants in the angry group increased their TLT from that trial forward, including all the typical peek-a-boos that followed. Infants in the fear group increased their TLT the largest extent, but TLT decreased immediately with subsequent typical peek-a-boos, and continued to decrease until the second fear face. Ongoing statistical analysis confirmed these results.

The infants' expressions, using the MAX system, generally showed interest/surprise throughout the experiment. There were very few full-fledged expressions of other discrete emotions. Overall, the mean frequency of interest/surprise increased both times infants saw the sad face. The frequency increased only the first time infants saw fear or anger, and decreased consistently for the control infants. In addition, facial coding for any emotional change increased for sad, fear (to a far lesser degree), and anger. For the control group, the incidence of facial movements decreased.

Table 2. Peek-a-boo results

Group	Total Looking Time	Interest/Surprise Expressions
Fear	Increased for both fear faces	Increased for first fear face
Anger	Increased for all subsequent faces	Increased for first angry face
Sad	Decreased after seeing sad face	Increased for both sad faces
Control	Decreased continuously after 4th trial	Decreased consistently

In general, infants responded differentially to facial/vocal expressions present-ed in the context of a peek-a-boo game. Looking time increased for anger and fear portrayals, and decreased for sad or the control happy/surprise expression. Interest expressions, however, were highest for sad portrayals, and the incidence of facial movement was most apparent for sad portrayals.

Follow-up. A follow-up experiment was conducted in which the peek-a-boo face was held for 14 seconds in order to give infants more time to respond. The results were similar to the first study: decreased looking at consistent happy/surprise peek-a-boos over time; decreased looking at sadness (particu-larly on block 2); increased looking at fear on the first exposure, followed by decreases; increased looking at anger on both trials. Observers also completed global coding of the infants' facial expressions. Infants in the consistent happy/surprise group became more positive throughout the session. In the sad group, the majority became more negative when they saw the sad face. Infants in the anger and fear groups had variable facial expressions. Further analysis of their expressions is ongoing.

Discussion

Results from these two experiments provide evidence that 4-month-old infants can discriminate facial/vocal expressions of anger, fear, sadness, and happy/surprise when presented in a familiar context, and that infants' reac-tions to these expressions are specific. The looking time data confirm prior results for discrimination of static facial expressions and vocal expressions,[9-11] but the infants' own expressions were different than the ones they were exposed to. At this time is unclear whether infants were responding to the facial expressions, vocal expressions, or both.

Familiarity of Person: Matching Faces and Voices

Infants at 5 to 7 months of age can detect common meanings in facial and vocal expressions that allows them to match a happy face with a happy voice or a sad face with a sad voice.[4] Matching experiments often record infants' looking time when they are presented with videotapes of paired facial expressions (eg, sad and happy, angry and happy, happy and neutral) along with an appropriate sound or silence.[12] (For a review see Walker-Andrews: Infants' perceptions of the affordances of expressive behaviors.[13]) In general, 2-month-old infants look at happy expressions regardless of the sounds they hear – they looked at the happy face when it was sound-accompanied 81% of the time, compared to 77% of the time when it was silently projected. However, 5- and 7-month-old infants increase their looking time to any facial expression (happy, sad, angry, neutral) when it is sound-specified. Even when the synchrony relations are disrupted (by delaying the soundtrack 5 seconds; or by occluding the mouth area of the face), infants look proportionately longer to the film that is sound-specified. Moreover, when the facial expressions are presented in either of two orientations (upside down or upright) with a single soundtrack, 7-month-olds only responded to the vocal match when facial expressions are shown in the upright orientation.

Methods

Infants as young as 3 months were presented videotape of either their mother or a stranger depicting happy and sad facial and vocal expressions.[14] During the experiment, infants saw two facial expressions simultaneously for four 25-second trials (the expressions were shown alternately on the right and left sides), accompanied synchronously by a single soundtrack matching one of the facial expressions. Total looking time for each infant on the two expressions was recorded and analyzed.

Results

When infants were presented with videotapes of their mother, they generally looked longer at an expression when it was sound specific (57%) than when it was silent (50%). They looked at the happy expression 67% of the time when it was sound specific, and 52% of the time when it was silent. With sound, the sad face was looked at 48% of the time, but only 33% of the time when silent.

In contrast, infants who were presented with videotapes of the stranger's face and voice did not show a preference. The average looking time was 50% whether or not the expression was accompanied by sound. Individual values for happy were 54% (sound) and 53% (silent); values for sad were 46% (sound) and 47% (silent). Furthermore, infants who were shown their own mothers demonstrated an overall preference for the happy expression.

Discussion

These data show that infants as young as 3 months are able to detect the correspondence between facial and vocal expressions, suggesting that they can understand something about the affective displays of their mothers. There are several potential explanations, none is entirely satisfying. First, infants could be aroused differentially by adult expressions and match their arousal level with what they see and hear; however, infants failed to make intermodal matches between the faces and voices of strangers. They may also have used the temporal synchrony between face and voice; but even with synchronized sound and expressions, infants preferred their mothers over strangers and preferred right-side-up faces to upside-down faces. Ongoing studies of mothers' facial expressions with asynchronous voices among 3-month-olds currently indicates that infants look longer at matching facial/vocal expressions, even when the voice is out of synch.

Multimodal Information for Expressions

Young infants probably require the "whole" emotional expression to appreciate its meaning.[3] That is, infants may first recognize affective expressions as part of a unified multimodal event that has a unique communicative meaning. Faces and voices are typically experienced together, as part of an event that also includes touch and smell. Yet, infants learn to discriminate auditory and visual information, and detect abstract invariants that specify the same emotional meaning. As noted by Flavell[15]:

> In the extralaboratory world people do not present themselves to babies as voiceless or faceless voices.... Moreover, the face and voice are unified in space and time: The voice and the face share the same spatial location, and the face's mouth movements are temporally synchronized. In addition, certain specific faces always co-occur with certain specific voices....

Finally, how each face looks and acts on a given occasion is highly correlated with how its voice sounds; for instance, happy and sad voices usually accompany happy and sad faces, respectively.

In this model, infants detect unimodal information that has the potential to specify the meaning of an expression. They detect acoustic parameters, such as timbre and frequency, that provide information for affect. Even neonates can detect the fundamental frequencies of two different voices and discriminate them, but there is no evidence that this information specifies an emotional nuance to the infant. Likewise, facial feature differences in expressions can be detected several months postnatally. However, this modality-specific information does not allow for recognition of emotions until somewhat later.

Recognition probably first occurs in multimodal contexts. The critical information specifying an emotion is found in the overall dynamic flow, particularly in the invariant patterns of movement and change undergone by facial musculature, body, and voice. Therefore, for infants, dynamic, naturalistic, and multimodal presentations may be the optimal stimuli.[16]

Methods

Sixty 5-month-old infants were visually habituated to a single videotape of a compound stimulus (either a facial/vocal expression of happy or angry, or a dot-light face accompanied by a happy or angry vocal expression) and their total looking time recorded. Once the infant reached a criterion of habituation, one of several changes was made.

Group 1.   Face and Voice Change. These infants were visually habituated to a happy or angry facial expression accompanied by its characteristic, but asynchronous, vocal expression. Once the infant became habituated, she was presented two posttests in which both the face and voice were changed.

Group 2.   Face-Only Change. These infants saw a happy or angry facial expression accompanied by a characteristic synchronous vocal expression. When habituated, the facial expression was switched, but the original voice continued.

Group 3.   Voice-Only Change. These infants saw a happy or angry facial expression accompanied by its characteristic synchronous vocal expression. When habituated, the voice was switched.

Group 4. Dot-Light Face, Voice-Only Change. This group of infants saw a dot-light rendition of a happy or angry facial expression accompanied by its characteristic vocal expression. (Infants will treat a dot-light face as if it were a face.[17] Research with 7-month-olds indicates that infants will show intermodal matching for such facial and vocal expressions.[18]) After the habituation criterion was reached, the vocal expression was switched from happy to angry, or vice versa.

Results

The length of looking time when habituation was broken by the new stimulus was as follows (greatest to least):

1. Both face and voice changed

2. Voice-only change, accompanied by upside-down dot-light face

3. Voice-only change, accompanied by dot-light face

4. Face-only change; voice remained constant

5 & 6 (tie). * Voice-only change; face remained constant

* Control; no change in face or voice

An ANOVA revealed that the overall between-groups effect was significant, and more detailed analysis is being performed.

Discussion

It appears that infants can discriminate: changes in face and voice together; changes in vocal expressions when accompanied by dot-light faces; changes in facial expressions alone. However, they did not discriminate changes in vocal expression when accompanied by a normal fully illuminated face.[18] This difference may be inherent in the study design that could have biased infants' attention to the face or voice. For example, visual attention was used as an index of the infants' looking and listening behavior. Also, the face and voice were asynchronous in all trials, a condition that should have been obvious when infants were presented a fully-illuminated facial expression for habituation. Additionally, the peculiar sight of the dot-light faces may have led to enhanced attention to the vocal expressions. These factors may have combined in interesting ways to produce the infants' patterns of fixation on the dishabituation trials. Further research to clarify these contributions is ongoing.

Summary

In two exploratory studies, 3- to 4-month-old infants seem better able to discriminate and perhaps recognize facial and vocal expressions in familiar contexts. In the first, presenting the expressions to the infants in a familiar situation (the peek-a-boo game); and in the second, presenting the expression in the context of a familiar person (the child's own mother) has led to greater understanding of the infant's sensitivity to emotional expressions.

Studying infants' perceptions of facial and vocal expressions is an important method to learn how infants develop a sense of meaning to the world around them. Our focus has been on the information available to infants, and to determine whether they merely detect that information, discriminate instances of it, and/or respond to it in meaningful ways. In these projects, we are beginning to look at what might be called contextual information, as provided by familiar situations, familiar people, and "redundant" presentations (multimodal renditions of emotional expressions). My suggestion is that as infants' perceptual systems mature, they gain experience with the emotional expressions of those around them; they may then use contextual information to discriminate and understand the meaning of those expressions as "social signals" for their own behavior.[19]

In these three studies, we have begun accruing evidence for young infants' discrimination of emotional expressions in familiar contexts, for familiar persons, and when facial or vocal information are available. By using converging evidence, we can make progress in determining how infants "recognize" emotional expressions as meaningful. That is, when infants respond consistently to specific expressions and when they can detect correspondences between visual and acoustic information, they may begin to use emotional information to guide their own actions.

Acknowledgement

We wish to thank the families whose infants participated in these studies, as well as the research assistants who aided in data collection. The research was supported by National Science Foundation Grant SBR-9408993.

References

1. Klinnert M, Campos JJ, Source J, et al. Emotions as behavior regulators: social referencing in infancy. In: Plutchik R, Kellerman H, eds. *Emotions in Early Development*. New York, NY: Academic Press; 1983;2:57-86.

2. Nelson CA. The recognition of facial expressions in the first two years of life: mechanisms of development. *Child Development*. 1987;56:58-61.

3. Walker-Andrews AS. Infants' perception of expressive behaviors: differentiation of multimodal information. *Psychological Bulletin*. 1997;121:437-456.

4. Walker AS. Intermodal perception of expressive behaviors by human infants. *Journal of Experimental Child Psychology*. 1982;33:514-535.

5. Everhart V, Henry S. Indicators of early empathy: newborns learning the meaning of changes in facial expression within 5 minutes. Paper presented at the International Conference on Infant Studies; 1992; Miami, FL.

6. Montague D. Infants' discrimination of emotional expressions in a peekaboo interaction. Paper presented at the Society for Research in Child Development; 1995; Indianapolis, IN.

7. Ekman P, Friesen W. *Facial Action Coding System*. Palo Alto, CA: Consulting Psychologists Press; 1978.

8. Izard CE. *The Maximally Discriminative Facial Movement Coding System (MAX)*. Newark, DE: University of Delaware; 1979.

9. Young-Browne G, Rosenfeld HM, Horowitz FD. Infant discrimination of facial expressions. *Child Development*. 1977;49:555-562.

10. Walker-Andrews AS, Grolnick W. Discrimination of vocal expression by young infants. *Infant Behavior and Development*. 1983;6:491-498.

11. Walker-Andrews AS, Lennon E. Infants' discrimination of vocal expressions: contributions of auditory and visual information. *Infant Behavior and Development*. 1991;14:131-142.

12. Spelke ES. Infants' intermodal perception of events. *Cognitive Psychology*. 1976;8:553-560.

13. Walker-Andrews AS. Infants' perception of the affordances of expressive behaviors. In: Rovee-Collier CK, ed. *Advances in Infancy Research*. Norwood, NJ: Ablex; 1988;5:173-221.

14. Kahana-Kalman R. *Contextual Effects in Intermodal Perception of Emotional Expressions by Young Infants*. New Brunswick, NJ: Rutgers University; 1997. Dissertation.

15. Flavell JH. *Cognitive Development*. 2nd ed. Englewood Cliffs, NJ: Prentice-Hall; 1985.

16. Dickson L, Walker-Andrews AS. Discrimination of vocal expressions: the effects of context. Paper presented at the Society for Research in Child Development; April 1997; Washington, DC.

17. Kaufmann R, Kaufmann F. The face scheme in 3- and 4-month-old infants: the role of dynamic properties of the face. *Infant Behavior and Development*. 1980;3:331-339.

18. Soken NH, Pick AD. Intermodal perception of happy and angry expressive behaviors by seven-month-old infants. *Child Development*. 1992;63:787-795.

19. Oster H. "Recognition" of emotional expression in infancy. In: Lamb ME, Sherrod LR, eds. *Infant Social Cognition: Empirical and Theoretical Considerations*. Hillsdale, NJ: Erlbaum; 1981:85-125.

Language Development and Emotional Expression

Lois Bloom, PhD

Introduction

The relation of language and emotion in development is most often thought about in terms of how language describes emotional experiences with words that name different feelings. Not surprisingly, therefore, developmental studies of emotion and language have typically described how children acquire emotion labels, like "mad," "happy," "scared."[1-3] However, children typically do not begin to use these words until language development is well underway, at about 2 years of age. Other studies have described how caregivers use emotion words when talking to their infants in the first year. Caregivers are very good, almost from the beginning, at attributing particular emotions to a young infant's cries, whines, whimpers, smiles, and laughs, for example, "what a *happy* baby," "don't be so *sad*," "are you *angry*?"[4,5] However, once infants begin to learn language, mothers are far less likely to name a child's emotion than to talk about the situations and reasons for the child's feelings and what might be done about them.[6,7]

This research emphasis on the words that name emotions has at least these two limitations. First, the number of emotion words in the dictionary is small – at most a few dozen terms for emotions and feeling states – compared to the enormous number of names in a dictionary for objects and actions. Second, the emotional expressions of infants and young children are generally transparent in their emotional meaning. Thus, the label for an emotion is very often redundant with its expression and adds no new information. Given the relatively small number of words for naming feelings and emotions, and the redundancy between emotion words and the expressions they name, understanding how emotion and language are related in early development requires looking beyond just acquisition of specific emotion words.

Studying Language Acquisition in its Developmental Context

The core of development that brings an infant to the threshold of language in the second year is the convergence of emotion; cognition, and social connectedness to other persons.[8,9] Children learn language in the first place because they strive to connect with other persons in order to share what they are feeling and thinking with others. When language begins toward the end of the first year, infants have had a year of learning about the world. The results of their cognitive developments have given children contents of mind – beliefs, desires, and feelings – that have to be expressed because they are increasingly elaborated and discrepant from what other persons can see and hear in the context. Language expresses and articulates the elements, roles, and relationships in mental meanings in a way that a child's smiles, cries, frowns, and whines cannot. Language, then, emerges in the second year out of a nexus of developments in emotion, social connectedness, and cognition.

For the past 10 years, I have been studying how language comes together with the cognitive, emotional, and social developments of the first 3 years of life,[8] with the basic assumption that language acquisition is tied to other developments in a child's life. The knowledge we set out to explain was language: how children learn words in the second year and then learn to combine words for phrases and simple sentences in the beginning of the third year. Early words are fragile, imprecise, and emerge tentatively at the same time that emotional expressions are robust, frequent, and fully functional. We asked, therefore, how these two systems of expression, emotion and language, come together in the second year of a child's development. We looked at both the *content* of developments in emotional expression and language as well as the *process* of their interaction.

The model of development that guided our research, in Fig 1, built on the link between two well-known concepts in psychology: engagement and effort. Knowledge of language is represented here by the tripartite model of language that Peg Lahey and I introduced 20 years ago. Linguistic *form* – sounds, words, and syntax – is only part of language, albeit the part that attracts the most attention. Form necessarily interacts with *content* or meaning, because language is always about something. And form and content interact with the pragmatics of language *use*: Language is used in different situations, for different purposes and functions. Only one or the other of these components, notably form alone, cannot, by itself, be a language – rather language is, necessarily, the convergence of content, form, and use.[10]

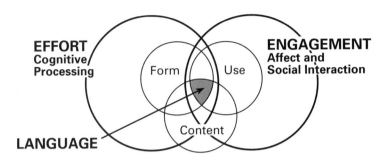

Fig 1. Model of the interaction between engagement and effort for language development.[11]

Engagement embraces the child's emotional and social directedness for learning a language in the first place, while *effort* captures the work it takes to learn a language and the cognitive processes that are required. Language, I have proposed, is acquired in a dialectical tension between engagement and effort that is governed by principles of relevance, discrepancy, and elaboration.[9,11] These principles are responsive to different aspects of a child's development.

Emotion and the Principle of Relevance

Language is learned when the words a child hears are about what the child has in mind – the objects of engagement, interest, and feelings. Word learning is intimately connected to a child's emotional life because infants learn language to talk about and thereby to share those things that they are thinking and feeling: the persons, objects, and events that make up the goals and situations in everyday events and are the causes and circumstances of emotion. The principle of relevance is responsive, in particular, to a child's emotional life and engagement in an interpersonal and physical world.

Social Development and the Principle of Discrepancy

Language has to be learned when what the child has in mind differs from what someone else has in mind and must be expressed in order to be shared. As infants remember past events and anticipate new events, they have beliefs, desires, and feelings about things which other persons cannot yet know. Children will have to acquire a language when caregivers cannot exploit clues from the context for understanding – when the objects of a child's belief, desire, and feeling are not already evident. Thus, the principle of discrepancy is responsive, in particular, to a child's social development and need to sustain social connectedness to other persons.

Cognition and the Principle of Elaboration

The principle of elaboration is responsive to a child's cognitive development. Developments in the symbolic capacity, concepts, and conceptual structure make possible the representations in consciousness that are expressed by language and that are set up by interpreting what other persons say. Children will have to learn more words and, eventually, procedures for sentences, if they are to express and articulate the increasingly elaborated contents of mind made possible by developments in cognition as well as in social and emotional understanding.

In this view of language acquisition, therefore, language is acquired by a child with feelings and thoughts about other persons, a child engaged in dynamic real-life events, a child learning to think about a world of changing physical and psychological relationships, and, most importantly, a child poised to act, to influence, to gain control – in short, a child reaching out and embracing the learning of language for the power of expression it provides.

Developments in Emotion and Language: From First Words to Sentences

We have studied 12 children from mixed racial, ethnic, and religious backgrounds, from 9 months to 2½ years. All were first-born, growing up in different neighborhoods in the greater New York metropolitan area, and their mothers were their primary caregivers throughout the study. We saw the children and their mothers every month in our laboratory playroom and also in their homes (see Bloom[8] for the full description of the study).

Children vary greatly in age of onset and rate of progress in their language learning. The children we studied did, indeed, differ in when they began to say words and in the length of time between their first words and the beginning of sentences. Fig 2 shows the average age and the range in their ages at the time of three language achievements. First Words began to occur at the beginning of the second year. A Vocabulary Spurt was a sharp increase in the number of new words in a child's vocabulary, and occurred toward the end of

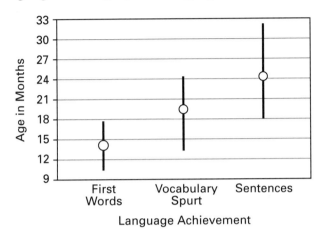

Fig 2. Average age and range of each language achievement in months.[8]

the second year. With the achievement of Simple Sentences, at about 2 years of age, the children were putting words together with an average utterance length of least 1.5 words.[8] However, the children differed in their ages of achievement, as can be seen.

The children also differed in their emotionality – how frequently they expressed emotion (nonneutral expression with positive, negative, or mixed affective tone) – in the period from 9 to 21 months of age. Moreover, the differences among them in emotional expression were related to the differences in their ages at the times of the three language achievements. When measured across time, from 9 to 21 months of age, the children who were *earlier* word learners spent more time in **neutral** affect expression and did not increase in their frequency of emotional expression. However, the children who were later word learners increased in frequency of emotional expression between 9 and 17 months of age instead of learning words early.[12] Moreover, age of language achievement was correlated with the children's expression of emotion and neutral (nonemotional) affect: more time in neutral affect expression predicted earlier age and more frequent emotional expression predicted later age of language achievement.[13]

We concluded that learning words and expressing emotion compete for the limited cognitive resources of the young language-learning child and neutral affect promoted earlier language learning. The two groups of earlier and later word learners did not differ in emotionality at 9 months of age, but the children who began to acquire words somewhat later in the second year increased in their frequency of emotional expression from 9 to 17 months, instead of acquiring words early.

However, development is more than change in relation to chronological age, because age is only an index of the passing of time and reveals nothing about the transformations in structure or function that characterize the *process* of development. Looking at change at times of developmental transition, such as each of the language achievements, was more informative than looking at change only in relation to age alone.[14-16] Therefore, we equated the children for language achievement, and looked more closely at developments in emotional expression in relation to language learning.

First, we looked simply at how often the children said words and how often they expressed emotion (all nonneutral affect expressions) at the two achievements, First Words and Vocabulary Spurt. The frequency of speech increased from First Words to Vocabulary Spurt but this was not surprising, since the Vocabulary Spurt was defined as an increase in new words learned from one month to the next. However, in this same period of time, the children did not express emotion more or less frequently.[17] We have since confirmed this result in a finer analysis, looking at the actual amount of time the children spent talking, expressing emotion, or both talking and expressing emotion at First Words, the Vocabulary Spurt, and the beginning of Sentences.[11] A computer program tallied whether a particular kind of expression (emotion or speech) occurred in any of the 54,000 video frames that made up the first half-hour of each playroom session (1 second of video tape equal to 30 frames). The result is shown in Fig 3 as the percentage of all the frames in a half-hour that contained speech and/or emotional expression, at each of the language achievements.

Again, as with frequency of speech, the amount of time spent talking increased from First Words to Vocabulary Spurt to Sentences, as expected, given how the achievements in language were defined. However, while speech increased, the percentage of time in emotional expression did not change *between the language achievements.* This result meant two things. First, that development in the second year is not simply an increase in overall expressivity (because speech increased but emotional expression did not increase when children were equated for language achievement rather than age). Second, that children do not express emotion less often as words are acquired (which means they are not learning to say words *instead* of

Fig 3. Average percent of time (as percent of video frames) spent in expressing emotion and speaking.[11]

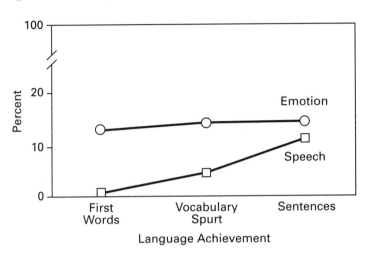

expressing emotion). Children continue to express their feelings through displays of affect, as they learn to say more words in the single-word period and length of utterance increases with the occurrence of simple sentences.

The children said a total of 11,404 words (tokens), consisting of 326 different words (types) in the playroom sessions, from First Words to 1 month after the Vocabulary Spurt.[18] Except for one child who said the words "scared" and "sorry," none of the children's words were names of emotions or feeling states, and the mothers did not report emotion words in the diaries they kept. Reports in the literature of the "early" use of emotion words by English-speaking children have relied on mothers' reporting whether such words ever occur at all, through the use of diaries and checklists, and the youngest children in these studies have typically been older than 2 years.[1-3] The children in our study might have said such words on occasion as well and, if we had explicitly asked their mothers, perhaps they would have reported such words at home. But names for the emotions were not among the words they used in their everyday activities.

Names for the emotions were even rare in the mothers' own speech when they were responding to their children's emotional expressions, and the verb "like" was the most frequent emotion word they used.[6,7] Nevertheless, the children were quite adept at letting others know when they were pleased or distressed. Their mothers, in turn, knew easily enough when their infants were happy, angry, frustrated, or frightened. Thus, consistent with the Principle of Discrepancy, the children did not have to say what their emotions were; they did not need to say they were "happy" or "mad," because their feelings were already evident to other persons. But words were needed to *do* something about their distress, or to achieve and extend their happiness. Consistent with the Principle of Relevance, they were, indeed, learning to talk about those things that were relevant to the objects, causes, and circumstances of feelings, even though they were not learning emotion labels. The children were learning words *to express what their feelings were about* while they continued to express how they were feeling through displays of positive and negative affect.

Effort and Engagement in the Development of Expression

Saying words and expressing emotion put demands on a young child's limited cognitive resources. At a minimum, expressing emotion requires a representation of goals and plans in consciousness, as well as an evaluation of the circumstances in the situation in relation to the representation the child has in mind. Again, at a minimum, saying words requires a mental representation and recall of the words to express and articulate the elements, roles, and relationships in that representation. Evidence of the effort that requirements for the two forms of expression entailed came from looking at both the words the children said and the kind of emotion expressed when both words and emotional expression occurred at the same time.

First, the words the children said with emotional expression were either among their most frequent words or were "old" words that were easiest for them to recall and say. The words children said with neutral expression were relatively newer words, which were presumably less well known and harder to recall and/or say. Thus, the effort of saying new words interfered with the cognitive and affective requirements for emotional expression. Further, when the children expressed emotion at the same time they said words, the emotion was significantly more often positive and of low intensity.[19] Less cognitive "work" is required for positive emotion since a goal has been achieved, and there is no need to construct a plan for removing an obstacle to a goal (as in the case of anger) or for creating a new goal (as in the case of sadness, where the goal is lost).[20]

In addition to developments across time in the second year, we also looked at the actual moments that speech occurred and measured the second-to-second timing relationship between emotional expression and speech in the stream of the children's activity in the playroom. In an earlier analysis,[19] we had assumed that if the effort required for speech and emotional expression competed for a young child's cognitive resources, then we should see the effects of effort in the actual moments in which speech and emotion occurred. Also, it should be easier for children to express emotion and say words at Vocabulary Spurt, when they knew more words, and words came more easily to them, with less effort. In fact, both of these assumptions were confirmed, and the results are shown in Fig 4.

Fig 4. Average difference from baseline rates of emotional expression during speech and in the five 1-second intervals before and after (in standard deviation units), at First Words and Vocabulary Spurt.[19]

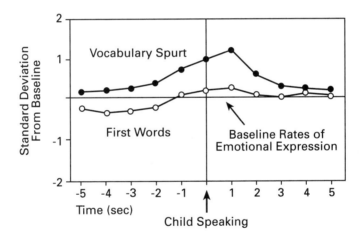

The horizontal line in Fig 4 represents the baseline rate of the behavior that was tracked over time, emotional expression in this case, in relation to a target event, in this case speech. A child's baseline was the likelihood that the child would be expressing emotion at any point in the course of an observation, given how often the child expressed emotion overall (see Fig 3). The vertical line in the figure represents the time interval of the speech target event, from the start of a word to the end of the word (words lasted about 1 sec, on average). The 10 other data points in the figure each represent a 1-sec interval, 5 before the speech event, and 5 after it. The result is the extent to which emotional expression was different from the baseline rate, during speech (the vertical line) and in the 1-sec intervals before and after speech. The children were less likely to be expressing emotion around their First Words (FW), when they were just beginning to learn words, than they were to be expressing emotion around words at the Vocabulary Spurt (VS), when speech presumably required less effort. The dip below baseline before speech at First Words was an indication of the cognitive effort required for speech at the time that words first began. The patterns (shape of the curves around speech) were the same at both First Words and Vocabulary Spurt, but emotional expression was greater than baseline at Vocabulary Spurt, increasing at the time of speech and then decreasing. This result indicated to us that the children were able to integrate the two kinds of expression at Vocabulary Spurt, because by that time saying words required less effort.

These results provided evidence of both engagement and effort. The increased likelihood of emotional expression relative to baseline at VS was interpreted as evidence of *engagement*. The children were learning to talk, in general, about those things that were *relevant* to them, those things they cared about. However, the words they said with emotion were the children's easiest words and emotional expression was most likely to be positive and at low levels of intensity, therefore requiring less *effort*. So there was, in effect, an accommodation between effort and engagement in the timing of speech and emotional expression in the single-word period. Given that most of the emotion the children expressed was positive, the peak in emotional expression immediately after a word recalls the smiles of recognition that have been described in younger infants,[16,21] and smiles following mastery[22] or assimilation after concentrated attention.[23]

Evidence of effort was even more apparent when the children began to say sentences, and this result is shown in Fig 5. At the time the children were working at learning the syntax of language, they were far less likely to express emotion around speech than could be expected from their baseline levels of emotional expression,[11] indicating the effort that the two kinds of expression required. The children were most likely to be expressing neutral affect in the moments around and during their efforts at talking.

However, the results were different for children who were earlier and later syntax learners. The differences between the earlier and later word learners were echoed in these microanalyses of the timing between the two kinds of expression at each of the language achievements. The differences between the groups at the time of the transition to sentences is shown in Fig 6. The

Fig 5. Average difference from baseline rates of emotional expression during speech and in the five 1-second intervals before and after (in standard deviation units), at the time of the transition to multi-word speech.[11]

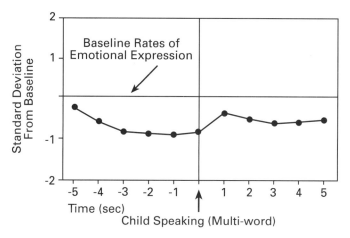

Fig 6. Average difference from baseline rates of emotional expression during speech and in the five 1-second intervals before and after (in standard deviation units), earlier and later learners at Sentences transition.[11]

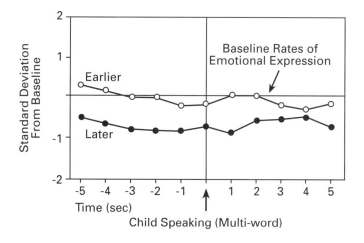

patterns of emotional expression around speech were essentially the same for both groups of children relative to their respective baseline rates of emotional expression, but the children who were older when they began to say sentences expressed substantially less emotion around speech than the children who were younger. The emotional expression of the later syntax learners was substantially below baseline and differed significantly from the emotional expression of the earlier, younger learners, who did not differ from baseline. Children who were learning to say sentences somewhat later, and evidently working harder at language learning, were using their language with more effort than the children who were earlier language learners.

Conclusions

Many questions about the complex developmental relationship between language and emotion remain for further research, but our findings provide some insight into the effort and engagement required by both language learning and emotional expression. We propose that the *heart of language acquisition* is in the dialectical tension between the two psychological components of effort and engagement (shown earlier, in Fig 1).

To begin with, a language will never be acquired without *engagement* in a world of persons, objects, and events – the world that language is about and in which language is used. The concept of engagement embraces the social, affective, and emotional factors that figure in language learning. Other persons and the *social* context are required, because the motivation for learning a language is to express and interpret contents of mind so that child and others can share what each is thinking and feeling (the principle of discrepancy).

Affect and emotional expression are required for establishing intersubjectivity and sharing between child and caregiver before language, and also for motivating a child's attention and involvement with people, objects, and events for learning language. The relevance of adult behavior is assured when adults tune into what a child is feeling and thinking. Language is learned when the words a child hears are about the objects of engagement, interest, and feelings – about what the child has in mind (the principle of relevance). In turn, children use the language they are learning for talking about the things they care about – the objects of their engagement.

Acquiring language requires *effort*, first, for setting up the meanings consciousness that language expresses or that results from interpreting the expressions of others. Second, further effort is required for learning the increasingly complex language needed to express and articulate the increasingly elaborated mental meanings that are made possible by developments in cognition (the principle of elaboration). And, third, effort is also required for coordinating different kinds of behaviors – like talking, expressing emotion, and playing with objects (as described in Bloom et al[11]) – that make up the ordinary activities of a young child's life. Neither speech nor emotional expression occur in isolation – they are always and necessarily embedded in complex events.

In sum, language and emotion are related in complex ways in the process of development. Language is created by a child in the dynamic contexts and circumstances that make up the child's world, and acquiring a language requires both engagement and effort. A child's feelings and emotions are central to engagement with the personal and physical world and determine the relevance of language for learning. And the effect of the effort needed to coordinate cognitive, emotional, and linguistic resources for learning language is to recruit states of neutral affect for attention and processing. Children who began to learn words early spent more time in neutral affect, while children who learned words somewhat later expressed more emotion instead. Effort was also apparent in the timing relation of speech and emotional expression at the transition to sentences, especially for the later language learners.

By the time language begins, toward the end of the first year, emotional expression is already well established and children do not need to learn the names of the emotions in order to tell other people what they are feeling. But they do need to learn the language to tell other people what their feelings are about. Language does not replace emotional expression. Rather, children learn language for expressing and articulating the objects and circumstances of their emotional experiences while they continue to express emotion with displays of positive and negative affective tone.

References

1. Bretherton I, Fritz J, Zahn-Wexler C, Ridgeway C. Learning to talk about emotions: a functionalist perspective. *Child Development.* 1986;57:529-548.
2. Cervantes C, Callanan M. Labels and explanations in mother-child emotion talk: age and gender differentiation. *Developmental Psychology.* 1998;34:88-98.

3. Ridgeway D, Waters E, Kuczaj S. Acquisition of emotion-descriptive language: receptive and productive vocabulary norms for ages 18 months to 6 years. *Developmental Psychology.* 1985;21:901-908.

4. Klinnert M, Sorce J, Emde R, Stenberg C, Gaensbauer T. Continuities and change in early emotional life: maternal perceptions of surprise, fear, and anger. In: Emde R, Harmon R, eds. *Continuities and Discontinuities in Development.* New York, NY: Plenum; 1984:339-354.

5. Johnson W, Emde R, Pannabecker B, Stenberg C, Davis M. Maternal perception of infant emotion from birth through 18 months. *Infant Behavior and Development.* 1982;5:313-322.

6. Data on file, Lois Bloom.

7. Capatides (Bitetti) J. Mothers' socialization of their children's experience and expression of emotion. New York, NY: Columbia University; 1990. PhD dissertation.

8. Bloom L. *The Transition From Infancy to Language: Acquiring the Power of Expression.* Cambridge, MA: Cambridge University Press; 1993.

9. Bloom L. Language acquisition in its developmental context. In: Kuhn D, Siegler R, eds. *Cognition, Perception, and Language. Vol II.* In: Damon W, series ed. Handbook of Child Psychology. New York, NY: John Wiley & Sons; 1997.

10. Bloom L, Lahey M. *Language Development and Language Disorders.* New York, NY: John Wiley & Sons; 1978.

11. Data on file, Lois Bloom.

12. Bloom L, Beckwith R, Capatides (Bitetti) J. Developments in the expression of affect. *Infant Behavior and Development.* 1988;11:169-186.

13. Bloom L, Capatides (Bitetti) J. Expression of affect and the emergence of language. *Child Development.* 1987;58:1513-1522.

14. Connell J, Furman W. The study of transitions: conceptual and methodological issues. In: Emde R, Harmon R, eds. *Continuities and Discontinuities in Development.* New York, NY: Plenum; 1984:153-173.

15. Emde R, Harmon R. Entering a new era in the search for developmental continuities. In: Emde R, Harmon R, eds. *Continuities and Discontinuities in Development.* New York, NY: Plenum; 1984:1-11.

16. McCall R. Smiling and vocalization in infants as indices of perceptual-cognitive processes. *Merrill-Palmer Quarterly.* 1972;18:341-347.

17. Bloom L, Beckwith R, Capatides (Bitetti) J, Hafitz J. Expression through affect and words in the transition from infancy to language. In: Baltes P, Featherman D, Lerner R, eds. *Life-span Development and Behavior.* Vol 8. Hillsdale, NJ: Erlbaum; 1988:99-127.

18. Bloom L, Tinker E, Margulis C. The words children learn: evidence against a noun bias in children's vocabularies. *Cognitive Development.* 1994;8:431-450.

19. Bloom L, Beckwith R. Talking with feeling: integrating affective and linguistic expression in early language development. *Cognition and Emotion.* Reprinted in Izard C, ed. *Development of Emotion-Cognition Relation.* Hillsdale, NJ: Erlbaum; 1989;3:313-342.

20. Stein N, Jewett J. A conceptual analysis of the meaning of basic negative emotions: implications for a theory of development. In: Izard C, Read P, eds. *Measurement of Emotion in Infants and Children. Vol 2.* New York, NY: Cambridge University Press; 1987:238-267.

21. Zelazo P. Smiling and vocalizing: a cognitive emphasis. *Merrill-Palmer Quarterly.* 1972;18:349-365.

22. Sroufe A, Waters E. The ontogenesis of smiling and laughter: a perspective on the organization of development in infancy. *Psychological Review.* 1976;83:173-189.

23. Kagan J, Lapidus D, Moore M. Infant antecedents of cognitive functioning. *Child Development.* 1978;49:1005-1023.

Section 3:
Management of Clinical
Problems and Emotional Care

Abstracts From Section 3. Management of Clinical Problems and Emotional Care

Early Emotional Care for Mothers and Infants

Nadia Bruschweiler Stern, MD

The experiences of most child health professionals give them only partial insight into the complex emotional and behavioral changes brought on by maternity. This chapter describes an approach to clinical management and emotional care based on the principles of: birth as an opportunity for reorganization and change; the meeting of the mothers' "real" and "imagined" babies; appreciation of the infant's strengths; and development of a therapeutic alliance with the mother. Central to this process is the creation of a safe holding environment for the mother, especially mothers of preterm infants.

Colic and Crying Syndromes in Infants

Ronald G. Barr, MD

Colic or excessive crying is one of the most frequent problems presented to pediatricians by new parents. Organic disease accounts for less than 5% of infants presenting with colic syndrome. Colic may be best viewed as a clinical manifestation of normal emotional development, in which an infant has diminished capacity to regulate crying duration.

Environmental Risk Factors in Infancy

Arnold J. Sameroff, PhD

Environment plays an important role in shaping development from the newborn period through adolescence. Many individual environmental risk factors may impinge on development (poverty, mental illness, minority status, and many others), but the most detrimental effects are caused when multiple risk factors act on a single infant. These effects were revealed by The Rochester Longitudinal Study, an ongoing comprehensive investigation of environmental risk factors, summarized in this chapter.

Early Emotional Care for Mothers and Infants

Nadia Bruschweiler Stern, MD

Introduction

This paper describes a perspective on early clinical management and emotional care that evolved from my experience as pediatrician, child psychiatrist, infant developmentalist, and also as a parent.

In pediatrics, our concern is most often the integrity and functioning of the baby's different organ systems. Our focus is on the baby as a unique living organism.

In child psychiatry, the baby is seen linked to his mother as a relational partner, where the mother's representation of him is a determinant of his future. Here we see the baby as a repository of the parent's attributions.

In child development, we try to demonstrate the baby's competencies, preferences, adaptation to his immediate environment, and his stimulus thresholds. We seek to understand what the baby means, who he is as an individual. Here we see the baby as a person.

As parents, we experience the intense new emotions that emerge with the new life – facing the task of keeping the baby alive, answering his needs, regulating the baby's states, and establishing a new relationship, making him *our* baby. Here we see the baby as our own child.[1]

The experiences of each of the child health professions do not prepare a parent, particularly a mother, for the revolution provoked by maternity. Each specialty has a partial view of the baby that can be far removed from the parent's view and experience of their baby.[2] This disparity has led me to an approach that integrates some of these four roles.

Basic Principles

This approach to clinical management and emotional care is based on several basic principles, described in the following paragraphs.

Reorganization and change. Moments of disequilibrium tend to open up a system for reorganization and change. Normal life crises, such as birth, provide such an opportunity. In addition, birth is an early time to conduct preventions or interventions that may be effective later on.

Imagined/real baby. At this crisis point, one of the mother's tasks is to build a representation of her baby that integrates her expectation of the baby in her mind (the "imagined baby") and the "real baby" in her arms. It is preventive and therapeutic to help through this process. This requires attention to both the baby's objective behavior and to the parents' interpretation and reaction to their baby's behavior.

A constructive view. The mother's imagined baby may be seen as potentially problematic. However, it is far more important, but less appreciated, to consider her imagined baby as potentially constructive for the infant's development.

Therapeutic alliance. Fourth, when healthcare professionals have successfully provided a favorable environment for building positive experiences and representations, we enter a privileged psychological position in the parent's mind. We are empowered to act as the professional person to coordinate the management of medical and emotional care. This is important because care is most often fragmented among several subspecialties and disciplines. In this sense, the process of facilitating the mother-infant encounter also creates very early and quickly a special therapeutic alliance that can be put to good use for ongoing emotional and physical development.

The Imagined Baby

Knowing how the "imagined baby" develops in the mother's mind is essential to understand how a mother and caregiver can create a therapeutic alliance.

Long before she gets pregnant, the mother has been building a representation of the child and the family she will have. Depending upon her style, personality, and life experience, these representations can be vague or precise.

The psychological process of preparation for a baby and a future family does not begin at the moment of conception. It has been in preparation since the mother's childhood as seen in doll games, or "Mama and Papa" games, and by the examples of maternal behavior seen in her family and surroundings, among friends, in books, on television, and all of her life's experiences.

During adolescence, genital maturation triggers a sense of her reproductive capacity – to have an infant that you bring into the world. This is part of the adolescent upheaval and leads to the definition of a new identity which includes that of a possible future mother. Marriage or living together makes imminent the possibility of having a baby. This leads to all of the choices relevant to that possibility, such as contraception or planned pregnancy. This developmental process thus begins in childhood and evolves through various phases into adulthood until it becomes intensely active during pregnancy.

While the physical pregnancy is going on in the uterus, the mother experiences simultaneously a mental pregnancy. This mental pregnancy consists of psychological changes that prepare the way for profound changes in her identity within her marriage, her family origin, her professional and social life, and her sense of self. She works upon her image of her baby, of herself as a future mother, of her husband as a future father, of her new nuclear family,

Fig 1. Prenatal perceptions of infant personality.

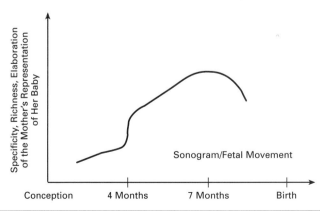

of her baby's role in this family, as the next generation of her family, and many other similar permutations.

This mental work is like a "personality-genesis" that would be the counterpart of the baby's organogenesis. These two simultaneous physical and psychological processes mutually influence one another during the entire pregnancy.

Mother's Representation of the Baby

The richness, elaborateness, and specificity of the mother's representation of her baby increases during the first months of pregnancy. Her sense of her baby makes a big leap around the fourth month, after the first ultrasound and feeling the baby's movements. It continues to grow progressively, reaching a high point around the seventh month. After this summit, the mother's representation of the baby loses some of its richness and specificity; the mother lets it fade and undo itself during the last weeks of pregnancy.[3-7] It is as if the mother has to decrease her precise expectations of the baby in order to prepare for meeting her real baby.

The mother's representation of her baby is not a coherent and complete image of a particular personality. It is the fruit of an exploration of the wishes and fears, past and present, that are woven together over time and integrated with real events that arose during the pregnancy. Conceptually, the mother navigates in her imagination between two groups of representations concerning her baby.

One concerns the wished-for baby: a boy or a girl, good-looking, strong, athletic, charming or beautiful, vivacious, smart, easy tempered. Or a baby who achieves something she had dreamed for herself, one who has characteristics of her hero or heroine.

On the other hand, the same imagination is working upon the feared baby: malformed, weak, trisomic, ugly, troublesome. One who will become violent, alcoholic, or a criminal, just like some member of the family.

In the same way, she explores the idea of who she will be as a mother – thinking of her own mother, of mothers she admires, and of others she despises. She does the same with the father, both her families, and the different areas of her life that are touched by the arrival of her new baby.

All these representations constitute a vast repertoire of experiences in the mother's mind. Some of them will naturally or forcefully emerge when she becomes a mother. But the nature of the perinatal period is such that the social environment can have a great influence by activating representations of the mother's repertoire which then become reality.

The classic notion of "ghosts in the nursery," as revealed during consultation in child psychiatry, has taught us the potentially pathological function that representations of past relationships may have in the present. But there are not only bad ghosts in the nursery, there are good ones too (as well as good fairies). They play an important role as model for the mother for herself and as a positive inspiration for her future.

Around birth, if negative representations of the past are not expressed spontaneously, they should not be asked about. This is because the effect of asking could be the activation of background representations that would not otherwise have come out. These then become vivid in the mother's mind and influence her behavior with her baby, like looking for a previous baby's death in the family, and dwelling on losses and separations.

Looking for the positive by emphasizing baby's strengths provides a means to face the actual difficulties in the baby's behavior. Looking for the mother's representations of a "good mother," those she has experienced as a support in her life, and that give her confidence, may promote the most secure part of her self to enter her relationship with her baby.

Emphasizing the positive also contributes to a supportive emotional environment for the mother. She will feel cared for. This is essential to permit the building of a therapeutic alliance between the mother and care provider in the service of the family's health.

Birth: A Good Time for Intervention

Birth is a moment of disequilibrium in the mother's system. It is the moment when the "imagined baby" meets the "real baby." And it is the moment when the mother's representations and priorities undergo change.

Survival of the baby emerges as the first preoccupation. When her baby is born, she first needs to make sure he is alive, and make him her own at a deep instinctive level. To physically experience the weight of his little body on her, his texture and scent, to feel him, warm and alive. After that, she wants to know that all is going well, that he is anatomically intact and in good health. The physical status of the baby answers this question.

When she has been reassured that her baby is alive and well, the mother seeks to meet this new member of the family as a person. She has put out all of her antennae to perceive *who* is this mysterious baby she has created and carried for so long. She is lying in wait for the slightest indication that might orient her. She will search to appropriate him through physical resemblances: "He has his father's forehead and eyes, but he has my mouth!"; and through his behavioral similarities: "When he is hungry, you've got to be there right away! He is demanding like my father"; or "He sleeps a lot; in my family, we are all great sleepers," and so forth.

The mother has created many different maternal and familial images in her imagination during childhood and more recently while pregnant. These involve her baby as a person, herself as a mother, her early relationship with her baby and later with him as a child, about her husband in his role as a father, to name a few. All of these images are in a suspension, like a cloudy emulsion in a liquid, ready to precipitate out and crystalize during the discovery process when she interacts with her baby. She has long imagined her new baby and latches on to each bit of information that could concern him – or herself as a mother – whether it comes from her baby or from those around them. She is particularly sensitive during this perinatal period and all input may influence her relationship with her baby.

During this phase also, it is necessary to emphasize the very important role of the perinatal team. In the mother's eyes, the maternity staff has an expertise such that whatever they say during these first days will often become indelibly engraved in her mind and can strongly influence her future relationship with her baby by reinforcing either a positive or negative preexisting representation. For example: A mother brought her 4-year-old child for a consultation because he was violent, kicking her with his feet, and she couldn't make him obey her. Among her first words, she said: "Even in the maternity word, a nurse said that he was bad!" Of course, the nurse's declaration didn't make the baby bad, but her words resonated with her fear of having a bad baby. They left their imprint on her image of him, and may have contributed to setting them on the path of the feared baby.

We can direct a mother on the path of the wished-for baby just as easily. It is crucial to realize that even if it is not as visible, in the neonatal period, words can have the same power as narcotic drugs.

Premature Birth

A premature birth occurring around 30 to 32 weeks will not only produce a premature baby, but also a premature mother.

At around 7 months of pregnancy, the mother doesn't yet want to see her real baby. In her imagination, she has a fairly well-defined image of her baby, usually that of a vigorous, active, and gratifying 3-month-old – not a full-term neonate. Unfortunately, with an early birth, she finds herself facing neither a gratifying 3-month-old nor even a solid and well-developed full-term baby. Instead she encounters a baby who is frail, not very pretty, fragile, hyperdependent, and easily overwhelmed – a baby for whom she is in no way prepared. She is a premature and disappointed mother.

Even more, this unfinished and vulnerable baby makes her feel like a mother who has not been able to fulfill her pregnancy and become a real mother. This feeling of incompetence is confirmed by the fact that specialists and sophisticated equipment are needed to care for her baby, and worse – that she can do nothing for him. This feeling of uselessness is reinforced by the physical separation from her baby, who is placed in a neonatal intensive care unit.

She is a mother who is premature, disappointed, and isolated. She experiences herself as vulnerable and having failed. From a psychological point of view, the mother of a premature baby is like a fragile piece of china.

Above all, healthcare professionals should avoid stigmatizing her as a psychiatric case. At the same time, we can help her a great deal by recognizing her vulnerability and helping her to connect with her infant.

Techniques for Emotional Care and Clinical Support

Two basic principles form the intervention for full-term newborns and prematures.

First, we must provide the mother with a safe holding environment from an experienced, accepting, and warm person. For a premature mother, this holding environment must respect the timing of a woman who has been thrown into the role of mother, but is not ready to take it on. This holding environment must gently accompany the mother through her accelerated metamorphosis.

Second, we must recognize that during the perinatal period, the mother is psychologically open to the negative as well as to the positive. We need to make it a constructive crisis by validating her in her new role, and by avoiding all criticism and disqualification.

Therapeutic Alliance

It is important to initially develop a therapeutic alliance with the mother. I do this by explaining how I can help and then asking how she feels. I try to develop it along the lines of a semi-structured interview, looking for the content and quality of the experience she has had.

The interview touches on the delivery – How did it go? Is she pleased with herself? What did she feel when she saw her baby? Was she surprised? What did the baby look like? What did he do?

It touches on the pregnancy – Did anything particular happen? What did the baby feel like? How did he manifest himself? How did she imagine him/her?

Then I ask more general questions like – Are there other babies in the family? Does she have experience with taking care of babies? How does she feel about her new role as a mother? Confident or worried? Will her husband be at home for the first days? Does she have a support system that will be available for help?

Finally, I want to know how she sees her baby now – How does he look physically? How does he behave? What does he do when feeding, sleeping, or bathing? When is he alert? Is he cuddly? When he cries, is he easy or difficult to console?

In summary, I look for the quality of the experience that she had, for her sense of having the baby she expected, her self-confidence in her new role as a mother, her support network. I look for the elements that will help her feel satisfied and confident.

After, never before, a sense of mutual trust has been established, and after I have a sense of the mother's expectations of herself and of her baby, I start to do the Brazelton Neonatal Behavioral Assessment Scale (NBAS) with her at my side.[8] I try to do a complete Brazelton and make comments along the way. Depending on the baby's state and on the mother's needs, I will interrupt the procedure to address her concerns, or give her the baby to comfort or touch.

When the scale is over, I usually place the baby into the mother's arms and start to comment on the exam. I try to answer the concerns she may have evoked earlier on. I comment on the baby's behaviors that confirm her representations or observations (the positive matches). I address the areas where the baby's behavior may present difficulties and help devise strategies to deal with them. When there are negatively distorted perceptions, I try to use the baby's behavior to correct them.

In the case of preterms, I use the Newborn Individualized Developmental Care and Assessment Program (NIDCAP) that Heidi Als has developed as my theoretical reference and practical guide to comment on the infant's behavior periodically during their hospitalization.[9] These comments about the preterm are used in the same spirit as those about a full term's behavior during the Brazelton.

Summary

To facilitate the integration of emotional care and clinical support, I first establish a holding environment and a positive therapeutic alliance. From that privileged position, I attempt to align the mother's vision of the baby with respect to who he really is, and who she really is. This process promotes their attachment and bonding during a very sensitive moment in their lives.

In this approach, the central focus is not on the baby's behavior during the NBAS (the real baby), nor on the mother's representation of her baby (the imagined baby). Rather, the focus is on the specific match between the real and imagined babies. It is this slight but important difference that distinguishes this technique from the original developmental pediatric approach in which the NBAS was used for nonspecific education about the baby's capacities. It also differs from the traditional psychodynamically oriented parent-infant psychotherapy approach, where the mother's representations and their history (the origins of the imagined baby) are the central focus.

This emotional and clinical support adds a new dimension to clinical care. This caring person is someone who acts like a doula during the immediate postnatal period, but a doula who tries to bring about the birth of the baby in the mother's mind and who promotes the birth of the psychological mother.

References

1. Stern DN, Stern-Bruschweiler N. *The Birth of a Mother.* New York, NY: Basic Books; 1998.

2. Stern-Bruschweiler N, Stern DN. The role of the mother's representation of her infant: a perspective on understanding different approaches to disturbed mother-infant relationships. *Infant Health Journal.* 1989;10:3.

3. Ammaniti M. Maternal representations during pregnancy and early infant-mother interactions. *Infant Mental Health Journal.* 1991;12(3):246-255.

4. Ammaniti M, Baumgartner E, Canderoli C, et al. Representations and narratives during pregnancy. *Infant Mental Health Journal.* 1992;13(2):167-182.

5. Fava-Viziello G, Antonioli M, Cocci V, et al. From pregnancy to motherhood: the structure of the representative and narrative change. *Infant Mental Health Journal.*1993;14(1):4-16.

6. Zeanah C, Benoit D, Barton, et al. Representations of attachment in mothers and their one-year old infants. *Journal of the American Academy of Child and Adolescent Psychiatry.* 1993;32(2):278-286.

7. Zeanah C, Keener M, Stewart L, Anders T. Prenatal perception of infant personality: a preliminary investigation. *Journal of the American Academy of Child and Adolescent Psychiatry.* 1985;24(2):204-210.

8. Brazelton TB, Nugent JK. *Neonatal Behavioral Assessment Scale.* Cambridge, MA: MacKeith Press, distributed by Cambridge University Press; 1995.

9. Als H. Developmental care for the very low-birth-weight preterm infant: medical and neurofunctional effects. *Journal of the American Medical Association.* 1994;272:11.

Colic and Crying Syndromes in Infants

Ronald G. Barr, MD

Introduction

Of all infant behavior, crying is perhaps the one most familiar to clinicians. "Colic" or excessive crying is one of the most frequent complaints brought to physicians in the first 3 months.[1] It is associated with maternal anxiety and emotional lability[2]; it often causes premature weaning because mothers think that crying is due to "insufficient milk"[3,4]; it can be the presenting complaint of almost any disease in infants; it rarely, but too often, triggers abuse or even death in infants.[5]

There are four clinical "crying" syndromes in the first year of life:

- colic

- persistent mother-infant distress syndrome

- the temperamentally "difficult" infant

- the dysregulated infant

These four syndromes are challenging to clinicians for at least two reasons. They are all difficult to define, manage, and treat. There is also surprisingly little guidance in the literature about how they may be related to each other.

For researchers studying emotional development, crying is also a central behavior. However, it must be clearly understood that there is a difference between infant *emotions* (or *emotionality*) and *crying behavior*. That is to say we are concerned with the overt, observable behavior of crying rather than the *inferred* negative emotion for which crying may be the overt expression.

To help bridge the gap between infant emotional research and clinical practice, I propose the following: In general, the crying syndromes most clinicians deal with are best understood as *clinical manifestations of normal emotional development* rather than of organic pathophysiological processes. Better understanding of these syndromes will come from both clinical and child development researchers. Clinical research can provide careful, systematic, and controlled descriptions of the clinical syndromes; normative child development research can provide empirical support for the reasons why babies cry.

The following manuscript illustrates these themes with available evidence from clinical, developmental, cross-cultural, and experimental studies regarding the syndrome of *colic*. While this may not do the complete job of making the transition from the probable knowledge of groups of infants to the complete and certain knowledge of individual infants in the clinical context, it may at least allow us to take the first steps across the bridge.

Clinical Crying Syndromes

Colic is defined by excessive crying. Although there are many hypotheses, there is no established etiology (or set of etiologies) for this syndrome.[5] It is usually characterized by the following:

* Timing: It typically begins at about 2 weeks of age and resolves by 4 months. Within the day, crying is concentrated in the late afternoon and evening hours.

* Associated behaviors: The bouts of crying are prolonged and unsoothable, even by feeding. The infant is usually described as having clenched fists, legs flexed over its abdomen, back arching, flushing, a hard distended abdomen, regurgitation, passing of gas, and an active, grimacing, or "pain" faces.

* Paroxysmal crying: The word "paroxysmal" is usually used to describe unpredictability or apparent spontaneity of the crying bouts, unrelated to events in the environment, including soothing attempts by the parents.

Persistent mother-infant distress syndrome refers to a clinical picture in which infants present after the early crying peak at 2 months and show no decrement in amount of crying.[6-8] The infants and families typically have a number of additional "at risk" characteristics. The infants often have disturbances in feeding and/or sleeping, mild developmental delay, and organic risk factors. The parents may have significant psychosocial risk factors, prenatal emotional distress, maternal psychopathology, and postnatal parental conflicts. Although the exact pathogenesis is unknown, Papousek and colleagues propose that the combination of significant parental, infant, and familial risk factors serves to disrupt the normal interactive and co-regulatory behaviors of infants and caregivers ("intuitive parenting").

Temperamentally "difficult" infants refer to one of a number of possible individual differences, characterized by a predisposition to negative affect, poor adaptability, greater intensity of reactions, and unpredictability. Strictly speaking, it does not represent a clinical classification, but rather a normal variant of early development. It is presumed to capture behavioral differences that are primarily constitutional or biological in origin, present early in life, and relatively stable across time and situations, although expressed differently at different developmental stages.[9,10]

Dysregulated infants are those with disturbances in many behavioral domains (affect, feeding, motor activity, and attention) presumably secondary to some central regulatory dysfunction. Clinically, they present in the second half of the first year of life with fussiness, irritability, poor self-calming, intolerance to change, and a hyperalert arousal.[11] The presumed regulatory deficit includes hypo- and hypersensitivity to sensory stimuli in any channel, and possibly an atypical vagal system responsiveness.[12] In the Zero to Three Diagnostic Classification,[13] there are four subcategories of this descriptive clinical syndrome: (a) hypersensitive, (b) underreactive, (c) motorically disorganized-impulsive, and (d) processing-behavior undefined.

Colic as a Clinical Manifestation of Normal Emotional Development

For understandable reasons, clinicians and parents alike have tended to see colic (excessive crying in the first 3 months of life) as a distinct behavioral syndrome probably indicating something wrong with the infant, the caregiver, or the infant-caregiver interaction. After all, when crying continues to *increase* despite the best mothering you can provide, when crying bouts *continue* despite every soothing technique you can think of, and when the infant looks for all the world like it is *in pain*, it is reasonable to think something is "wrong" or "abnormal." The impression that colic is a distinct behavioral syndrome, rather than a manifestation of normal development, may be because the most extreme cases are seen in clinical settings, so that any continuity with normative crying behavior is unlikely to be observed. Also, crying can be the presenting complaint of virtually any organic disease process, so that organic disease will sometimes be found that "explains" the colic syndrome.

However, a number of recent lines of evidence have contributed to a reinterpretation of the behavioral syndrome of colic. This literature is growing rapidly, and has been reviewed recently.[14-18] Only a few examples of each type of evidence will be used here for purposes of illustration.

Organic disease. The first line of evidence is that organic diseases are likely to account for less than 5% of cases of infants presenting with colic syndrome. In a recent review of the literature over the past 30 years, Gormally and Barr reported that: the number of disease entities documented to have caused colic syndrome was fewer than expected; in those diseases that can present as colic syndrome, the prevalence of organic disease as a cause was low; evidence for organic disease was not often very strong or well-documented.[15] Table 1 lists the organic diseases thought to cause colic syndrome, and their judgement of the strength of the evidence supporting it.

Table 1. *Organic etiologies for colic syndrome classified according to strength of evidence that it is causal of colic syndrome*

Strong	Moderate	Weak
Cow's milk protein intolerance	Reflux esophagitis	Lactose intolerance
Isolated fructose intolerance	Infant abuse	Glaucoma
Fluoxetine hydrochloride		CNS abnormalities (Chiari type I malformation)
Infantile migraine		Urinary tract infection

Although this table is based on the best available current evidence, it is possible that the incidence and causes of colic are more numerous than reported. Also, the rarity of organic causes does not make detection of organic disease unimportant. Indeed, it illustrates the difficulty faced by clinicians in identifying those that have an organic etiology from those that do not.

Normal crying behavior. Most, and perhaps all, of the defining clinical manifestations of colic syndrome are also characteristic of the crying behavior of normal infants. For example, the colic crying pattern (late afternoon and evening onset; peak crying at 2 months) is also characteristic of crying behavior in normal infants. The importance of this was actually anticipated by Morris Wessel and colleagues in the 1950s[19] when they wrote that "... the time distribution and frequency of diurnal regularity are similar for the mild fussy periods of the 'contented babies,' and for the more prolonged periods of the 'fussy infants.'" Subsequently, Brazelton documented this early "peak" crying pattern in 80 normal infants from his clinical practice in Massachusetts.[20] The same thing was confirmed about 25 years later in a Montreal study in normal infants.[21] Indeed, most studies with sufficient sample sizes have found a similar pattern.[22]

Cross-cultural and premature studies. !Kung San hunter-gatherers' caregiving practices differ considerably from our own Western industrialized child care practices. These include constant carrying, direct body contact, upright positioning, "continuous" feeding (4 times/hour for 1 to 2 minutes/feed), and contingent responsivity. Compared to Western babies, !Kung San infants cried half as long, but the frequency *and* the 2-month peak were similar.[23] Other studies have contributed convergent evidence for the normality of the early increased crying in the first 3 months.[24-26] In a cohort of relatively well preterms born an average of 8 weeks early, the increase in crying tended to occur at 6 weeks *corrected* age. This was also true for the evening clustering. Furthermore, the timing of the peak was unrelated to a variety of postnatal medical complications, implying that the timing of this pattern was quite resilient to postnatal experience altogether.[27] Similar results have been reported in another study of preterm infants from Ireland.[28]

Colic crying is hard to stop. Compared to normal infants, the crying of infants with colic is relatively difficult to stop once it is started. In a controlled study of infant crying characteristics, those with colic cried for longer than other infants but surprisingly had the same frequency of crying bouts. In short, what *was* different was the length of the crying bouts; it wasn't *that* they cried, but rather that when they cried, they did not stop.[29]

This *dissociation* between frequency and bout length has been observed in normal infants. Among the !Kung San, the crying frequency was the same, but the crying duration was about half of that observed in "separated" Western-style caregiving.[23] This frequency-duration dissociation was also apparent in a randomized controlled trial of increased carrying and holding.[21] When these Western mothers held their infants 3 hours per day they cried about 43% less, but the frequency of crying bouts remained the same. This leads to the not unreasonable hypothesis that infants with colic may cry longer because caregiving maneuvers are not especially effective in helping them regulate their crying. Alternately, they may be receiving less caregiving than they need, or a combination of both.

Hidden regulators. Evidence from a number of experimental studies suggests that, *within* normal caregiving maneuvers, there exist a variety of "hidden regulators" of infant crying behavior. These regulatory principles can operate through at least two pathways, the "contact pathway" and the "nutrient pathway." In everyday life these pathways are often intertwined. Thus, when an infant is fed, both contact and nutrient pathways are being accessed. It is also apparent that they will be accessed more frequently in a !Kung San-style caregiving context than in a Western-style, more separated context.

Increased contact can be powerful in regulating crying behavior. However, recent evidence suggests that nutrient pathways are also impressively effective. Following the lead of Elliott Blass and his colleagues, we have been examining the effectiveness of sucrose tastes in calming crying infants. In our model, infants are observed prior to or after feeding until they cry for 15 consecutive seconds. Then a sucrose taste stimulus (24% or 50%) is provided to the anterior midline of the tongue, and the infant is observed for up to 5 minutes. In newborn infants, the effect is impressive. Crying infants that receive 250 microliters of 24% sucrose solution once stop crying within 10 seconds. Furthermore, relative to a water taste, this reduction in crying is significant for 5 minutes or more.[30] Interestingly, the sucrose effect is still present, but much weaker at 6 weeks of age, the time of peak crying.[30] In sum, both contact and nutrient pathways are likely to be important in regulating crying once it is started.

Access to regulation. Infants with colic (those who cry like normal infants, but once started, continue crying longer) may be different in the extent to which these regulatory processes are accessed, or are able to be accessed. Stated another way, normal regulatory processes inherent in caregiving activity are less effective in them. Two studies are particularly relevant in this regard. The first is a randomized controlled trial of increased carrying as a "treatment" for infant colic.[31] The design was similar to the carrying study with normal infants[21] except that mothers were asked to increase their carrying time by 50%. Despite the increased carrying time in the experimental group, there was no difference from the control group in the amount of crying after treatment started. This suggests that caregiving contact that is an effective crying regulator in normal infants is not as effective in infants with already established colic.

This may also be true for calming systems accessed by nutrient pathways. We compared the responsiveness of crying infants with and without colic to sucrose tastes.[32] Because sucrose tastes are less effective in 6-week-old infants than in newborns, we provided three 250-microliter tastes of 50% sucrose 30 seconds apart in already crying infants. Interestingly, the immediate (first minute) response to sucrose was similar for infants with and without colic, but the calming response continued to be relatively effective up to 4 minutes after the taste in infants without colic, while it was almost completely gone after the first 2 minutes in infants with colic. This suggests that infants with and without colic are equally "reactive" to sucrose taste, but that it is less effective in regulating the crying state in infants with colic.[33] These studies suggest that infants with colic may differ in regard to the ease with which caregiving can access these regulatory processes.

Colic in Terms of Emotion Regulation and Temperament

Findings from the study of emotional development are likely to be important in order to understand these clinical crying syndromes further. Given that these syndromes are described in terms of emotionally salient behaviors, it is surprising that more convergent research has not been done previously.

Three important themes in the field of temperament and emotional regulation are *responsivity, reactivity, and regulation*.[34-36] Responsivity is a term usually used as a superordinate category that refers to three conceptually distinguishable response properties (Table 2). Behaviorally, humans can differ on type and/or the dynamics of response. In infants, type of response usually refers to whether the response is *positive* (smiling) or *negative* (crying).

Table 2. The concept of responsivity

- Type: positive (smiling) or negative (crying) response
- Dynamics: quality, intensity, timing of the response
  - Reactivity: threshold, intensity, time of onset
  - Regulation (or inhibition): duration, rate of recovery

Dynamics refers to the quality, intensity, and timing characteristics of the response. It includes reactivity, as reflected in threshold, intensity, and time of onset; and regulation (or inhibition) as reflected in duration or rate of recovery of response. One of the helpful features of these concepts is that they can be applied to different levels of description (eg, behavior and physiology) of individual responsiveness, even though these different levels may not always act "in association" with each other.

Together these concepts can be used to describe the "transient responsivity hypothesis" of colic syndrome. In this model, infants with colic syndrome will manifest increased responsivity (increased reactivity and/or decreased regulation) compared to infants without colic, but this responsivity will be transient (present at 2 months but absent by 5 months).

Investigating colic syndrome in this way is potentially interesting and valuable for a number of reasons. *First,* it permits the use of measures already available in the temperament and emotional regulation literature to investigate the clinical syndrome. *Second,* this hypothesis differs from the traditional temperament hypothesis which holds that colic is an early manifestation of a stable temperamental predisposition. (The traditional model would predict that infants with colic will show increased responsivity both at 2 and 5 months.) *Third,* stating the hypotheses in these terms permits us to look independently at both behavioral and physiological responsive systems relevant to emotion regulation and temperament. Previous research has been limited by the fact that the mother is reporting both the manifestations of the clinical syndrome and the ratings of temperament. In the case of colic and the "difficult" infant especially, this results in an obvious confound, because crying behavior is defining for both. *Fourth,* using these concepts permits us to make even more specific predictions on the basis of previous clinical findings that can then be subject to empirical verification or rejection.

As an example, we have suggested that infants with colic are not just generally more responsive, rather that they are **normally reactive, but have diminished regulatory capacity.** For example, controlled clinical observation has shown that what differentiates the crying of infants with colic from those without colic is not that they cry, but that they cry longer; that is, the frequency of crying bouts is the same but the bout lengths are longer.[29] Another important observation was the infant's response to sucrose. The initial quieting response to sucrose represents a reactivity to the presence of the stimulus in the mouth, while the duration of the response represents access to a central distress regulation system mediated by endogenous opioid release.[33] These data support the model that infants with colic differ from those without in regard to physiological *regulation,* but not in regard to *reactivity.*

These concepts may be valuable as a way of testing whether or not the four clinical crying syndromes of the first year of life are, or are not, related to each other. On the basis of available clinical descriptions it may be possible to classify crying syndromes in terms of responsivity concepts (reactivity and regulation). These are represented in the Table. For example, we have characterized infants with colic as normally reactive, but poorly regulated. Temperamentally "difficult" infants would likely have increased reactivity AND difficulty with regulation.

Further specification of the hypotheses can be undertaken if one **adds developmental stage** of the infant as well. For example, if the transient responsivity hypothesis for colic syndrome holds, then infants with colic will be characterized by normal reactivity and decreased regulation early, but normal reactivity and normal regulation later. By contrast, infants with difficult temperament would have increased reactivity and decreased regulation both early and later. Infants with regulatory disorders, at least in terms of currently described criteria, would have normal reactivity and regulation early, and increased reactivity and decreased regulation later.

Conclusions

In sum, I have argued that increasingly systematic, careful, and controlled studies of clinical phenomenology are critically important for providing constraints that guide hypothesis testing concerning underlying processes that help to explain these clinical syndromes. In the case of colic, such work has led to a reinterpretation of the syndrome from behavior that primarily reflects distinct pathological (usually gastroenterologically mediated) processes to behavior that primarily reflects normal behavioral (probably central nervous system-mediated) development, except that there is more of it. By bringing core concepts from the study of emotional development to bear on this (and other) clinical crying syndromes, we can generate relatively specific predictions that are subject to empirical test. By so doing, we may be able to dispel some of the "mystery" that is associated with these clinical syndromes, to the benefit both of harried parents and harried clinicians whose calling and responsibility it is both to diagnose and, hopefully, to treat.

References

1. Forsyth BW, Leventhal JM, McCarthy PL. Mothers' perceptions of problems of feeding and crying behaviours. *American Journal of Diseases of Children.* 1985;139:269-272.

2. Miller AR, Barr RG, Eaton WO. Crying and motor behavior of six-week-old infants and postpartum maternal mood. *Pediatrics.* 1993;92:551-558.

3. Forsyth BWC, McCarthy PL, Leventhal JM. Problems of early infancy, formula changes, and mothers' beliefs about their infants. *Journal of Pediatrics.* 1985;106:1012-1017.

4. Cunningham AS, Jelliffe DB, Jelliffe EFP. Breast-feeding and health in the 1980's: a global epidemiological review. *Journal of Pediatrics.* 1992;118:659-666.

5. Barr RG. Colic. In: Walker WA, Durie PR, Hamilton JR, Walker-Smith JA, Watkins JB, eds. *Pediatric Gastrointestinal Disease: Pathophysiology, Diagnosis, and Management.* St. Louis, MO: Mosby; 241-250.

6. Papousek M, von Hofacker N. Persistent crying in early infancy: a non-trivial condition of risk for the developing mother-infant relationship. *Child: Care, Health and Development.* In press.

7. Papousek M, Papousek H. Excessive infant crying and intuitive parental care: buffering support and its failures in parent-infant interaction. *Early Child Development and Care.* 1990;65:117-125.

8. Papousek M, von Hofacker N. Persistent crying and parenting: search for a butterfly in a dynamic system. *Early Development and Parenting.* 1995;4(4):209-224.

9. Goldsmith HH, Buss AH, Plomin R, et al. Roundtable: what is temperament? Four approaches. *Child Development.* 1987;58:505-529.

10. Thomas A, Chess S, Birch H. *Temperament and Behavior Disorders in Children.* New York, NY: University Press; 1968.

11. DeGangi GA, DiPietro JA, Greenspan SI, Porges SW. Psychophysiological characteristics of the regulatory disordered infant. *Infant Behavior and Development.* 1991;14:37-50.

12. DeGangi GA, Porges SW, Sickel RZ, Greenspan SI. Four-year follow-up of a sample of regulatory disordered infants. *Infant Mental Health Journal.* 1993;14(4):330-343.

13. National Center for Clinical Infant Programs. *Diagnostic Classification: 0-3.* Arlington,VA: Zero to Three/National Center for Clinical Infant Programs; 1994.

14. Barr RG. Infant cry behaviour and colic: an interpretation in evolutionary perspective. In: Trevathan W, McKenna JJ, Smith EO, eds. *Evolutionary Medicine.* New York, NY: Oxford University Press; 1995.

15. Gormally SM, Barr RG. Of clinical pies and clinical clues: proposal for a clinical approach to complaints of early crying and colic. *Ambulatory Child Health.* In press.

16. Miller AR, Barr RG. Infantile colic: is it a gut issue? *Pediatric Clinics of North America.* 1991;38(6):1407-1423.

17. Treem WR. Infant colic: a pediatric gastroenterologist's perspective. *Pediatric Clinics of North America.* 1994;41(5):1121-1138.

18. Anonymous. *Colic and Excessive Crying.* Columbus, OH: Ross Products Division Abbott Laboratories; 1977.

19. Wessel MA, Cobb JC, Jackson EB, et al. Paroxysmal fussing in infancy, sometimes called "colic." *Pediatrics.* 1954;14:421-434.

20. Brazelton TB. Crying in infancy. *Pediatrics.* 1962;29:579-588.

21. Hunziker UA, Barr RG. Increased carrying reduces infant crying: a randomized controlled trial. *Pediatrics.* 1986;77:641-648.

22. Barr RG. The normal crying curve: what do we really know? *Developmental Medicine and Child Neurology.* 1990;32:356-362.

23. Barr RG, Konner M, Bakeman R, Adamson L. Crying in !Kung infants: a test of the cultural specificity hypothesis. *Developmental Medicine and Child Neurology.* 1991;33:601-610.

24. St. James-Roberts I, Bowyer J, Varghese S, Sawdon J. Infant crying patterns in Manali and London. *Child: Care, Health and Development.* 1994;20:323-337.

25. Lee K. The crying pattern of Korean infants and related factors. *Developmental Medicine and Child Neurology.* 1994;36:601-607.

26. Alvarez M, St. James-Roberts I. Infant fussing and crying patterns in the first year in an urban community in Denmark. *Acta Paediatrica.* 1996;85:463-466.

27. Barr RG, Chen S, Hopkins B, Westra T. Crying patterns in preterm infants. *Developmental Medicine and Child Neurology.* 1996;38:345-355.

28. Malone A. The crying pattern of preterm infants. *ISSBD Programme.* 1997:4. Abstract.

29. Barr RG, Rotman A, Yaremko J, et al. The crying of infants with colic: a controlled empirical description. *Pediatrics.* 1992;90(1):14-21.

30. Barr RG, Quek V, Cousineau D, et al. Effects of intraoral sucrose on crying, mouthing and hand-mouth contact in newborn and six-week-old infants. *Developmental Medicine and Child Neurology.* 1994;36:608-618.

31. Barr RG, McMullan SJ, Spiess H, et al. Carrying as colic "therapy": a randomized controlled trial. *Pediatrics.* 1991;87:623-630.

32. Barr RG, Young SN, Wright JH, et al. Sucrose quieting in 2-month-old infants with and without colic. *Archives of Pediatrics and Adolescent Medicine.* 1995;149:64. Abstract.

33. Barr RG, Young SN. A two phase model of the soothing taste response: implications for a taste probe of temperament and emotion regulation. In: Lewis M, Ramsay D, eds. *Soothing and Stress.* Hillsdale, NJ: Lawrence Erlbaum Associates; 1997.

34. Rothbart MK, Derryberry D. Development of individual differences in temperament. In: Brown AL, Lamb ME, eds. *Advances in Developmental Psychology.* Hillsdale, NJ:Lawrence Erlbaum; 1987:37-86.

35. Thompson RA. Emotion regulation: a theme in search of definition. In: Fox NA, ed. *The Development of Emotion Regulation: Biological and Behavioral Considerations.* Chicago, IL: University of Chicago Press; 1994:25-52.

36. Barr RG, Gunnar MR. Colic – the transient responsivity hypothesis. In: Barr RG, Hopkins B, Green J, eds. *Crying as a Signal, a Sign, and a Symptom: Developmental and Clinical Aspects of Early Crying Behaviour.* London, England: MacKeith Press; In press.

Environmental Risk Factors in Infancy

Arnold J. Sameroff, PhD

Introduction

The pursuit of happiness is a fundamental right in our society, yet the goal of achieving a sense of satisfaction with one's abilities and achievements is becoming increasingly elusive for large segments of the population. Our interest in emotional development in early childhood is in part a concern that infants and toddlers be happy, but also a concern that this early evidence of mental health will be predictive and continuous with happiness and mental health in later life. Yet over half of today's 10- to 17-year-olds engage in two or more risk behaviors, including unsafe sex, teenage pregnancy, drug or alcohol abuse, school failure, delinquency, and crime – and 10% of these youths engage in all of these risks.[1] To what extent can these problems of later life be attributed to emotional behavior during early childhood, and to what extent must we examine intervening life circumstances as determinants of later emotional behavior?

The roots of these failures are frequently attributed to environmental factors that undermine achievement and mental health.[2] Therefore, attention must be paid to the multiple contexts that support development in the family, the school, and the community, from infancy through adolescence. Moreover, few studies have directly tested the premise that it is continuing environmental adversity that undermines development. Many studies have examined the stability of child characteristics over time, but few have examined continuities of contextual risk. Brooks-Gunn and her associates[3] found the best predictor of competence during early childhood was not the current economic circumstance of the family but the number of previous years that the family had spent in poverty. In the Rochester Longitudinal Study, we too have found long-term continuities in the effects of social risk on children that should improve our understanding of the relative contributions of early emotional behavior and later environmental circumstance on mental health.

Assessing Environments

Despite the nominal interest of developmentalists in the effects of the environment, the analysis and assessment of context has fallen more in the domain of sociology than of developmental psychology.[4-6] The magnitude of a social ecological analysis involving multiple settings and multiple systems[7] has daunted researchers primarily trained to focus on individual behavioral processes. A further daunting factor has been the increasing need to use multicausal models to explain developmental phenomena.[8,9]

To examine the effects of the environment on early emotional behavior and later mental health, we began an investigation of the development of a group of children from the prenatal period through adolescence living in a socially heterogeneous set of family circumstances – the Rochester Longitudinal Study (RLS). During the early childhood phase of the RLS[10] we assessed children and their families at birth, and then at 4, 12, 30, and 48 months of age, both in the home and in the laboratory. During adolescence, we made new assessments of the families when the children were 13 and 18 years old. At each age we evaluated two major indicators of developmental status: the child's cognitive and social-emotional competence. Because many of the families had single parents, we focused our assessments on characteristics of the mother. This approach was taken not because we believed that fathers were unimportant, but because there were too few available for participation in our study.

In the RLS we hypothesized that differences in family socioeconomic status (SES) would produce differences in child behavior. We found these social status effects throughout the first 4 years of life. Children from the poorest families in our sample exhibited the poorest development. They had poorer obstetrical status, more difficult temperaments, and lower developmental test scores at 4 months, less responsivity during the home and laboratory observations at 12 months, and less adaptive behavior in the home and laboratory at 30 and 48 months of age.

At the end of 4 years of development we had discovered the effects of multiple risk factors. On one hand, if the *only* developmental risk for a child was a mother with an emotional problem, *or* who lacked social support, *or* had a low educational level, usually the child was doing fine. On the other hand, if the child had a mother who was mentally ill, *and* poor and uneducated, *and* without social supports, that child was doing poorly. What we learned was the overriding importance of attending to the combination of environmental adversity with the social context of children in order to understand their development. To better understand the role of contextual factors, a more differentiated view of environmental influences needed to be taken. We had to discover what was different about the experience of children raised in different socioeconomic environments.

Environmental Conditions as Developmental Risks

Although SES is the best single variable for predicting children's cognitive competence, and an important, if less powerful, predictor of social-emotional functioning, we decided to add more psychological content to this sociological variable. SES operates at many levels of the ecology of children. It impacts on parenting, parental attitudes and beliefs, their family interactions, and many institutions in the surrounding community. From the data available in the RLS, we searched for a set of variables that were related to economic circumstance but not the same as SES. The factors we chose homed in from distal variables (such as the financial resources of the family) to intermediate variables (like the mother's mental health) to proximal variables (like the mother's here-and-now behavioral interaction with the child).

From the 4-year assessment of the children in the RLS, we chose a set of 10 environmental variables that were correlates of SES but not equivalents.[11] We then tested whether poor cognitive and social-emotional development in our preschool children were a function of the compounding of environmental risk factors found in low-SES groups. The definitions of the 10 environmental risk variables are as follows and detailed in Table 1: (1) history of maternal mental illness, (2) high maternal anxiety, (3) parental perspectives that reflected rigidity in the attitudes, beliefs, and values that mothers had in regard to their child's development, (4) few positive maternal interactions with the child observed during infancy, (5) head of household in unskilled occupations, (6) minimal maternal education, (7) disadvantaged minority status, (8) single parenthood, (9) stressful life events, and (10) large family size.

We found, indeed, that each of these variables was a risk factor. We compared the high-risk and low-risk group for each variable separately. For both the cognitive and mental health outcomes, the low-risk group had higher scores than the high-risk group. Most of the differences were enough to demonstrate the effects for group comparisons, but certainly not enough to detect which specific individuals with the risk factor would have an adverse

Table 1. Summary of risk variables[11]

Risk Variables	Low Risk	High Risk
Mental illness	0-1 psychiatric contact	More than 1 contact
Anxiety	75% least	25% most
Parental perspectives	75% highest	25% lowest
Spontaneous interaction	75% most	25% least
Occupation	Skilled	Semi- or unskilled
Education	High school	No high school
Minority status	No	Yes
Family support	Father present	Father absent
Stressful life events	75% fewest	25% most
Family size	1-3 children	4 or more children

outcome. Although statistically significant differences in outcome are associated with single environmental risk factors, these differences rarely explain large proportions of outcome variance.

Accumulating Risk Factors

In a much-cited study, Rutter[12] argued that it was not any particular risk factor but the number of risk factors in a child's background that led to psychiatric disorder. Psychiatric risk for a sample of 10-year-olds he studied rose from 2% in families with zero or one risk factors to 20% in families with four or more. The six risk factors included severe marital distress, low socioeconomic status, large family size or overcrowding, paternal criminality, maternal psychiatric disorder, and admission of the child to foster care. Another study[13] found similar results relating behavioral disorders in 11-year-olds to a cumulative disadvantage score based on number of residence and school changes, single parenthood, low SES, marital separation, young motherhood, low maternal cognitive ability, poor family relations, seeking marriage guidance, and maternal mental health symptoms.

In the RLS there were significant effects for the single risk factors, but it was clear that most children with only a single risk factor would not end up with a major developmental problem. But how would children growing in environments with many risk factors compare to children growing in environments with very few? We created a multiple risk score that was the total number of risks for each individual family. In the RLS, the range was well distributed between scores of 0 and 8, with one family having as many as 9 risks. When these risk factors were related to the child's intelligence and mental health, major differences were found between those children with few risks and those with many.

The relation between the multiple risk scores and the emotional health can be seen in Fig 1. It is clear that the effect of combining the 10 risk variables was to strongly accentuate the differences noted for the individual scores described above. As the number of risk factors increased, performance decreased for children at 4 years of age. Thus the combination of risk factors resulted in a nearly threefold increase in the magnitude of differences found among groups of children relative to the effect of single variables.[14] Similarly, on an intelligence test, children with no environmental risks scored more than 30 points higher than children with eight or nine risk factors.[11] On average, each risk factor reduced the child's IQ score by 4 points.

Fig 1. Multiple risk by 4-year mental health.

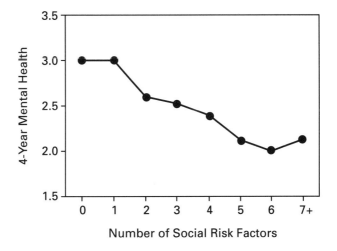

Number of Social Risk Factors

These analyses of the RLS data were attempts to elaborate environmental risk factors by reducing global measures such as SES to component social and behavioral variables. We were able to identify a set of risk factors that were predominantly found in lower SES groups, but affected child outcomes in all social classes. Moreover, no single variable was determinant of outcome. Only in families with multiple risk factors was the child's competence placed in jeopardy.

We found that the following all play a role in the contemporary development of child intelligence test performance and mental health: multiple pressures of environmental stress, the family's resources for coping with that stress, the number of children that must share those resources, and the parents' flexibility in understanding and dealing with their children.

Continuity of Environmental Risk

Studies like the RLS that have explored the effects of environmental risk factors on early development have shown major consequences for children living in multi-problem families. What are the long-term consequences of these early adverse circumstances? Will later conditions alter the course for such children or will early experiences lock children into pathways of deviance? To answer this question we must return to a consideration of data from the adolescent phase of the Rochester Longitudinal Study.

Within the RLS our attention has been devoted to the source of continuities and discontinuities in child performance. We completed further assessments of the sample when the children were 13 and 18 years of age.[15,16] Because of the potent effects of our multiple risk index at 4 years, we calculated new multiple environmental risk scores for each family based on their situation 9 and 14 years later. To our surprise there were very few families that showed major shifts in the number of risk factors across the 9-year intervening period. Between 4 and 13 years, the factor that improved most was maternal education, where the number of mothers without a high school diploma or equivalent decreased from 33% to 22%. The risk factor that increased the most was single parenthood, wherein the number of children being raised by their mothers alone increased from 24% to 41%. On average, however, there was little change in the environments of the children in our sample.

The typical statistic reported in longitudinal research is the correlation between early and later performance of the children. We too found such correlations. Mental health at 4 years correlated significantly with mental health at 13 years. Intelligence at 4 years correlated even more strongly with intelligence at 13 years. The usual interpretation of such numbers is that there are continuities of competence or incompetence in the child. Such a conclusion cannot be challenged if the only assessments are of the children. Fortunately, in the RLS we examined and were also able to correlate environmental characteristics across time. We found a higher correlation between environmental risk scores at the two ages that was as great or greater than any continuity within the child. Whatever the child's ability for achieving higher levels of competence, it was severely undermined by the continuing paucity of environmental support in high-risk contexts and fostered in low-risk contexts. Whatever the capabilities provided to the child by individual factors, the environment acted to limit or expand further opportunities for development.

Because of the very high stability in the number of risks experienced by these families, it was impossible to determine if the effects of early adversity or contemporary risk were having the greater effect on the later behavior of the children. Those children who had been living in high-risk environments at 4 years of age were still living in them at 13 years of age. Moreover, these contemporary high-risk contexts were producing the same negative effects on behavior as the earlier ones had done.

Secular Trends

The thrust of a contextual analysis of developmental regulation is not that individual factors in the child are nonexistent or irrelevant, but that they must be studied in a context larger than the single child. The risk analyses discussed so far have implicated parent characteristics and the immediate social conditions of family support and life event stress as important moderators of healthy psychological growth in the child. To this list of risks must be added changes in the historical supports for families in a given society. The importance of this added level of complexity was emphasized when we examined secular trends in the economic well-being of families in the United States.

At 4 years we had divided the sample into high-, medium-, and low-risk groups based on the number of cumulative risks: 0 or 1 in the low-risk group, 2 or 3 in the medium-risk group, and 4 or more in the high-risk group. We found that 22% of the high-risk group had IQs below 85, whereas none of the low-risk sample did. Conversely, 59% of the low-risk group had IQs above 115 but only 4% of the high-risk sample did.

After the 13-year assessment we made the same breakdown into high-, medium-, and low-risk groups and examined the distribution of IQs within risk groups. Again we found a preponderance of low IQ scores in the high-risk group and a preponderance of high IQ scores in the low-risk group, indicating the continuing negative effects of an unfavorable environment. But strikingly, the number of children in the high-risk group with IQs below 85 had increased from 22% to 46%, more than doubling. If our analysis was restricted to the level of the child and family, we would hypothesize that high-risk environments operate synergistically to further worsen the intellectual standing of these children during the period from preschool to adolescence, placing them in a downward spiral of increasing incompetence.

An alternative hypothesis was that society was changing during the 9 years between the RLS assessments. In a study completed by the House of Representatives Ways and Means Committee[17] it was found that between the years 1973 to 1987, during which time we were doing this study, the average household income of the poorest fifth of Americans fell 12% while the income of the richest fifth increased 24%. Elder[4] has made a strong case for attending to major changes in society as determinants of the life course for growing children. His work centered on the Great Depression of the 1930s. Similar effects seem to be apparent in our own times.

Protective Factors and the Search for Resiliency

When studies are successful in identifying protective factors, the issue is raised of identification on an individual basis of resilient (or protected) individuals. Ideally, one would like to identify a substantial subset of children who by any measure of competence were doing better than average, despite the adversity they faced in daily life. We selected a high-risk subsample of children who had four or more environmental risks to determine the characteristics of those who were doing better than expected. Only 3 of the 50 high-risk children were above the total sample mean on our 13-year child outcome measures; but all 3 had also improved in their risk status. They had been in the highest risk category at 4 years of age, but by 13 years were doing better. Thus, it is unclear whether the more favorable outcomes in these children were due to protective factors or to a lessening of risk.

When we examined the whole RLS sample to see what the consequences were for children moving from high (4 or more) to low (0 or 1) environmental risk (or from low to high risk) we found striking effects. The group that changed from high risk at 4 years to low risk at 13 years improved in mental health. In contrast, the group that changed from low risk at 4 years to high risk at 13 years showed a decline in mental health. These findings make a strong case for the powerful effects of environmental risks on the children. Unfortunately, such changes in number of risk factors is not common. We discussed above the stability of risk factors from early childhood to adolescence. Only one child was in the group that went from high to low risk and there was only one child in the group that went from low to high risk. Stability rather than change appeared to be the rule.

There are many who argue that children do poorly in conditions of poverty because they don't have individual characteristics that would promote resilience, overcome challenge, and eventuate in productive work and family life. By identifying characteristics of children who achieve despite adverse circumstances, some people hope that we could instill those characteristics in other children to help them overcome environmental adversity. In contrast, others hold the position that environmental risks are so pervasive that opportunities do not exist for positive development even if the child does have excellent coping skills. Is it possible that, despite social adversity, children with high levels of personal resources are able to overcome minimal resources at home and in the community to reach levels of achievement comparable to children from more highly advantaged social strata?

So far the presentation of our data has focused on issues of environmental adversity and neglected individual factors that may permit children to overcome disadvantage. At this point we can turn to an examination of individual factors in the child, including emotional behavior during infancy. From the Rochester data collected during the first year of life, we created a multiple competence score for each child during infancy that included a number of emotional indices. The infant risk score included 12 factors – Brazelton neonatal test scores, easy temperament scores, and Bayley Infant Behavior Rating scores. We then divided the sample into low-, medium-, and high-competence groups of infants and examined as outcomes the 4-year IQ and social-emotional functioning scores that I have previously mentioned.

There was no relation between infant emotion scores and 4-year mental health, especially when compared to the effects of the contemporaneous

Fig 2.　Relation of early social environmental risk to 4-year mental health scores for high and low competence infants.

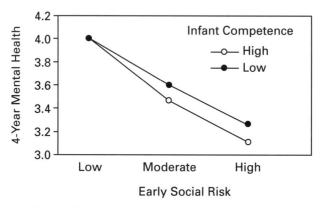

infant environmental multi-risk scores described earlier (see Fig 2).　However, there is a general feeling that infant developmental scales may be weak predictors because they assess different processes than are captured by later mental health and personality assessments.　Perhaps if we move up the age scale we can determine whether characteristics of these children at 4 years of age contribute to adolescent achievements at our 18-year assessment.　We divided the 4-year-olds into high and low mental health groups.　We then compared these groups on how they did at 18 years on their mental health assessment (see Fig 3).

Fig 3.　Relation of 4-year social environmental risk status to 4-year mental health scores for high and low competent infants.

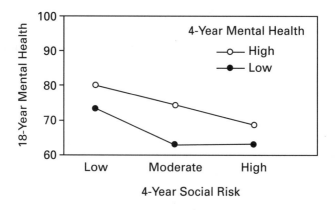

Although as a group the high mental health 4-year-olds were doing better at 18 years than the low mental health group, when we controlled for environmental risk, the differences between children with high and low levels were small when compared to the differences in performance between children in high- and low-risk social environments. Moreover, in each case, high competent children in high-risk environments did worse than low competent children in low-risk environments.

Perhaps at 4 years mental health is still too ephemeral to resist the negative consequences of adverse social circumstance. Would competent children at 13 years succeed where competent children at 4 years had failed? How would they stack up at our 18-year assessments of mental health? To find out, we divided the sample of children into a high and low mental health group based on their assessments at 13 years of age and examined their 18-year behavior (see Fig 4).

Fig 4. *Relation of 13-year social environmental risk status to 18-year mental health scores for 13-year-olds in high and low mental health groups.*

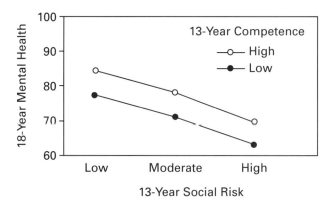

Again, in each case when we controlled for environmental risk we found that the highly competent children in personality or intelligence do far less well than we would expect. Those groups of children with earlier high levels of competence living in conditions of high environmental risk did worse than similar groups in low-risk conditions, but even more to the point, did worse than low competent children in low-risk environments. The negative effects of a disadvantaged environment seem to be more powerful contributors to the emotional health of the child at every age than the prior personality characteristics of the child.

Summary

Our findings from the RLS reveal that single environmental or child risk factors alone may have statistically significant effects on emotional development, but these differences are small in comparison with the effects of the accumulation of multiple negative influences that characterize high-risk groups. There are many successful adults who were raised in poverty and unsuccessful ones who were raised in affluence. There are many healthy and happy adults who come from broken homes, and there are many unhappy ones who were raised by two parents.

The important implication is that a focus on single characteristics of individuals (like resourcefulness or intelligence) or families (like welfare or marital status) can never explain more than a small proportion of variance in normal behavioral development involving a wide variety of environments. But major differences do emerge when comparisons are made between groups of children with many risk factors and those with only a few. To truly appreciate the determinants of competency requires that attention be paid to a broad constellation of ecological factors in which these individuals and families are embedded.

We have indicated that there are many environmental risk factors associated with poor developmental outcomes. Our analyses of the effects of environmental risk on development have focused on the negative side of each variable. This was intentional in that we were trying to find a way to identify those infants who are likely to be the most troubled and truly in need of intervention. These risk factors can be found in all socioeconomic strata but are most concentrated in areas of poverty. There may be social consequences of this research if changes can be made in the number of risk factors experienced by families. In the natural course of time in the sample we studied, there were few such changes. High-risk families remained high risk and low-risk families remained low risk.

In the introduction to this chapter I contrasted a concern with the current and future happiness of infants. The conclusion from our work is that the future happiness of children is only minimally related to their behavior during infancy. The current and future social context is a major developmental determinant with the power to foster or hinder later emotional well-being. The study of the social ecology of children must be a central concern of professionals hoping to understand and promote the emotional development of children.

References

1. Dryfoos JG. Adolescents at risk: a summation of work in the field: programs and policies. *Journal of Adolescent Health.* 1991;12:630-637.

2. Zigler E, Taussig C, Black K. Early childhood intervention: a promising preventative of juvenile delinquency. *American Psychologist.* 1992;47:997-1006.

3. Brooks-Gunn J, Duncan GJ, Klebanov PK, Sealand N. Do neighborhoods influence child and adolescent development? *American Journal of Sociology.* 1993;99(2):353-395.

4. Elder GH, Jr. Families, kin and the life course: a sociological perspective. In: Parke RD, ed. *Review of Child Development Research: The Family.* Vol 1. Chicago, IL: University of Chicago Press; 1984.

5. Kohn M, Schooler C. *Work and Personality: An Inquiry Into the Impact of Social Stratification.* Norwood, NJ: Ablex; 1983.

6. Mayer SE, Jencks C. Growing up in poor neighborhoods: how much does it matter? *Science.* 1989;243:1441-1445.

7. Bronfenbrenner U. *The Ecology of Human Development.* Cambridge, MA: Harvard University Press; 1979.

8. Sameroff AJ. Developmental systems: contexts and evolution. In: Kessen W, ed. *History, Theories, and Methods.* Vol I of Mussen PH, ed. *Handbook of Child Psychology.* New York, NY: Wiley; 1983: 237-294.

9. Sameroff AJ. General systems theories and developmental psychopathology. In: Cicchetti D, Cohen D, eds. *Developmental and Psychopathology.* Vol 1. New York, NY: Wiley; 1995:659-695.

10. Sameroff AJ, Seifer R, Zax M. Early development of children at risk for emotional disorder. *Monographs of the Society for Research in Child Development.* 1982;47;Serial No. 199.

11. Sameroff AJ, Seifer R, Barocas R, et al. Intelligence quotient scores of 4-year-old children: social environmental risk factors. *Pediatrics.* 1987;79:343-350.

12. Rutter M. Protective factors in children's responses to stress and disadvantage. In: Kent MW, Rolf JE, eds. *Primary Prevention of Psychopathology. Vol 3. Social Competence in Children.* Hanover, NH: University Press of New England; 1979:49-74.

13. Williams S, Anderson J, McGee R, Silva PA. Risk factors for behavioral and emotional disorder in preadolescent children. *Journal of the American Academy of Child and Adolescent Psychiatry.* 1990;29:413-419.

14. Sameroff AJ, Seifer R, Zax M, Barocas R. Early indicators of developmental risk: the Rochester Longitudinal Study. *Schizophrenia Bulletin.* 1987;13:383-393.

15. Sameroff AJ, Seifer R, Baldwin A, Baldwin C. Stability of intelligence from preschool to adolescence: the influence of social and family risk factors. *Child Development.* 1993;64:80-97.

16. Baldwin AL, Baldwin CP, Kasser T, et al. Contextual risk and resiliency during late adolescence. *Development and Psychopathology.* 1993;5:741-761.

17. Passell P. Forces in society and Reaganism, helped by deep hole for poor. *The New York Times.* July 16, 1989;1;20.

Section 4:
Emotional Care of
the At-Risk Infant

Abstracts From Section 4. Emotional Care of the At-Risk Infant

Behavioral Outcomes in Low-Birth-Weight Infants

Cecelia McCarton, MD

Low-birth-weight infants are at increased risk for behavioral and emotional problems. The Infant Health and Development Program was the first multi-site randomized clinical trial designed to evaluate the efficacy of intense pediatric and family support on reducing developmental and behavioral problems in low-birth-weight, premature infants. The major findings of this and other studies are presented in this chapter.

Emotional Characteristics of Infants Associated With Maternal Depression and Anxiety

M. Katherine Weinberg, PhD & Edward Z. Tronick, PhD

Infants as young as 3 months are able to detect depressive behavior in their mothers. Depressed mothers are sufficiently different from nondepressed mothers in affect and interaction that the social, emotional, and cognitive functioning of their infants are compromised. This chapter reviews current findings on the effects of maternal depression and psychiatric illness on infants.

Early Interventions for Infants of Depressed Mothers

Tiffany Field, PhD

Infants of mothers who remain depressed for 1 year following birth have a distinct profile of behavioral, physiological, and biochemical dysregulation. Their mothers also have a distinct profile that can be used to target those in need of interventions. These interventions may include mood induction, massage therapy, interaction coaching, and natural buffers such as nonde-pressed fathers and caregivers.

Behavioral Outcomes in Low-Birth-Weight Infants

Cecelia McCarton, MD

Introduction

In the last decade, the survival rate for low-birth-weight (LBW) infants has increased markedly,[1] raising questions about their subsequent health and development. A number of studies have found that LBW infants are at increased risk for developmental delay[2] and for a variety of medical complications in infancy compared with their normal-birth-weight counterparts.[3] At later ages, LBW children tend to have lower scores on tests of cognitive functioning[4,5] are more prone to difficulties in behavioral adjustment,[4,6,7] and are at risk for having learning problems and poor academic achievement,[8] even when cognitive test scores are normal.[9,10] The risk of cognitive deficits is present for all birth weights 2500 g or less, although the risk increases as birth weight decreases.[4,11,12] The likelihood of adverse developmental and scholastic outcomes also is greater in the face of socioeconomic disadvantage[13-15] – itself a risk factor for LBW and prematurity – and this places many LBW premature infants at dual risk from both biologic and environmental factors.[16,17]

This paper will focus on only one developmental aspect of LBW infants: behavior. The primary questions to be explored are:

- Are LBW infants at increased risk for the development of emotional and behavioral problems?

- What are the behavioral problems seen in LBW children?

- Is there a role for intervention?

Review of Behavioral Outcome Studies in LBW Infants

Half a century ago, prematurely born children were already described as suffering from "... restlessness, nervousness, fatigability which resulted in distractibility and disturbed concentration ...".[18] Research on this population has been rather unsystematic, limited, and atheoretical.[19] Buka, Lipsitt, and Tsuang published an excellent review summarizing the recent world literature on the emotional and behavioral development of LBW infants born since 1960.[20] In looking at six studies of LBW infants as a group (without comparison subjects), they concluded that LBW infants have an increased risk for the subsequent development of behavioral difficulties.[21-26] Behaviors such as inattention, impulsivity, and hyperactivity were described in some of the studies. No clear consensus could be drawn regarding the role of social class and "neurologic soft signs" in contributing to these behaviors.

Another series of longitudinal studies in which LBW infants were compared to a control population also supported the hypothesis that LBW infants had more emotional and behavioral problems and extreme aspects in temperament.[27-34] Variables associated with poor behavioral outcomes included extreme prematurity (birth weight <1500 g), male gender, low social class, and the stage of pregnancy at which slow head growth began. Behavioral disturbances included hyperactivity, short attention span, less adaptability, more intensity, and higher thresholds to sensory stimuli. Only one study found the children less active, shyer with classmates, and maintaining more contact with adults.[27]

Six large cohort studies from prescribed geographic regions compared the behavioral development of an LBW subset of the cohort to that of the normal-weight members. Again, the consensus was that LBW infants displayed a higher risk of developing behavioral problems. The primary abnormal outcomes were described as hyperactivity and attention deficit. The associated factors included social class and intrauterine growth retardation.[7,35-39]

The only longitudinal report of behavioral outcomes extending to 29 years of age showed no significant differences in the rate of psychiatric disorders for normal and LBW infants (Buka, Tsuang, Lipsitt, 1990, unpublished).

The Role of Intervention: Infant Health and Development Program (IHDP)

Recognizing that LBW infants and perhaps certain subpopulations of LBW infants are at increased risk for emotional and behavioral problems provides opportunities for early detection and intervention. The following is a description of a family-based educational curriculum and family support program that can be effective in reducing behavioral problems in LBW children.[40]

The IHDP is the first multisite, randomized clinical trial designed to evaluate the efficacy of combining early child development and family-support services with pediatric follow-up in reducing developmental, behavioral, and other health problems in LBW premature infants (birth weight <2500 g; gestational age ≤37 weeks). The intervention protocol and the specific curricula used were adapted for LBW infants from two longitudinal studies of successful early intervention with socially disadvantaged normal-birth-weight children.[41,42]

Patients and Methods

Eight medical institutions serving diverse demographic populations in different geographical locations were selected through a national competitive review.

Sample. All infants born in participating hospitals who weighed <2500 g at birth and had completed ≤37 weeks of gestation were eligible for the entire study.[40,43,44] In addition, the families of the children had to live within a specified distance from the intervention site and be able to speak English. Children with major anomalies or other specified conditions who were better assisted in other programs were excluded. The primary analysis group comprised 985 infants.

The research design included stratification by eight sites and two birth-weight groups (infants weighing 2001 to 2500 g, designated *heavier,* and those weighing <2000 g, designated *lighter*). One third of the sample came from the heavier and two thirds from the lighter group. To minimize the cost of the study, subjects within each weight group were randomly allocated: one third to the intervention group and two thirds to the follow-up (or control) group.

Program description. The program was initiated on the infants' discharge from the neonatal nursery and continued until 36 months of age, corrected for prematurity. Infants in the intervention and control groups participated in the same pediatric follow-up, which comprised medical, developmental, and social assessments, with referral for pediatric care and other services as indicated. The services exclusively for the intervention group consisted of: home visits, attendance at a child-development center, and parent group meetings. All services were provided free to the families.

Home visits. The protocol specified weekly home visits for the first year and biweekly visits thereafter. The home visitor provided health and developmental information and family support and implemented two specific curricula. One curriculum emphasized cognitive, linguistic, and social development via a program of games and activities for the parent to use with the child. The second curriculum involved a systematic approach to help parents manage self-identified problems.

Child development centers. Beginning at age 12 months and continuing until corrected age 36 months, the intervention children attended the center 5 days per week. The teaching staff continued to implement the curriculum of learning activities used by the home visitors and tailored the program to each child's needs and developmental level. Teacher-child ratios were 1:3 for children aged 12 to 23 months and 1:4 for those aged 24 to 36 months; class sizes were six and eight children, respectively. Each site provided transportation in IHDP-operated vans to any child who needed it.

Parent groups. Beginning at age 12 months, bimonthly parent-group meetings provided information on child rearing, health and safety, and other parenting concerns, as well as some degree of social support.

Assessment of behavioral competence. Behavior competence was assessed using two behavior-problem scales. At the 24- and 36-month visits, mothers reported on behavior problems using the Behavior Checklist, an adaptation of the 60-item Behavior Screening Questionnaire,[45,46] which consists of 21 questions used to produce a 12-item score. The items are scored using a three-point Likert scale.[46,47] The total score was used. At the 36-month visit, mothers also completed the Child Behavior Checklist for Ages 2-3.[48,49] A three-point Likert scale is used for 99 items. Mothers were read the items by the interviewers to control for possible differences in reading ability. A total-problem raw score was used. Higher scores indicate more behavior problems in both scales.

Videotaping procedure. For the mother-child interaction study, three types of interactions were videotaped at 30 months using a standardized protocol: an 8-minute free-play period, a clean-up period, and three different problem-solving tasks based on previous research by Matas et al.[50] On each of the three tasks, the child works to obtain a toy contained in a Plexiglas apparatus. The videotaping continues for each task until the child solves the problem or 6 minutes have elapsed, whichever occurs first. The first task (the fixed lever) was relatively easy and was used as a warm-up task. Data are reported here for the second task (the rake box), which was expected to be moderately diffi-cult for the child and to require the mother's assistance for solution. In the rake task, the child must connect two sticks to make one long stick, insert it into a narrow opening at one end of a flat Plexiglas box, and take a small toy from the box.

Results

Child behavioral competence – primary analysis. The average score on the Child Behavior Checklist was significantly lower for the intervention group than for the follow-up group, with higher scores indicating more reported behavior problems (Table 1).[40] Although the difference between study groups was small, the adjusted odds for having a score above 63, the cut point above which scores are correlated with clinically evident behavior problems,[48,49] were 1.8 times greater in the follow-up group (95% confidence interval, 1.2 to 2.9). The actual percentages were 18.8% for the follow-up group and 13.9% for the intervention group.

Secondary analysis. The multiple regression analysis indicated significant main effects of several initial status variables. Higher scores (suggestive of more behavior problems) were associated with being African-American or Latino, with being male, and with lower maternal age and education level. Controlling for these variables, there was a significant effect of the inter-vention (adjusted Effect Size = −.20, P = .003). The only variable that had a significant interaction with the intervention was maternal education

Table 1. Behavioral competence –
Infant Health and Development Program[40]

	Control Group (n = 547) mean (sd)	Intervention Group (n = 338) mean (sd)	Effect Size (P)
Child behavior checklist (age 2-3 years)	47.2 (20.5)	43.7 (19.1)	−18 (.006)

(P = .009). With college-educated mothers, there seemed to be little difference between the control and intervention groups, whereas with mothers with less education, those in the intervention group reported fewer behavior problems.

Thus, the intervention may have helped these mothers become better informed about age-appropriate behaviors and consequently report fewer behavior problems; it may have taught them more effective techniques for behavior management; or it may have altered the children's behavior.

Brooks-Gunn and colleagues further analyzed these data and found that in terms of behavioral competence the intervention was most efficacious in African-American children whose mothers had not graduated from high school.[51]

Specific Maternal Characteristics Influenced by Intervention

Recent studies suggest that intervention programs can be effective in teaching mothers to interact and communicate better with their children. For example, interventions have influenced parental involvement, acceptance, and stimulation.[52-54] Others have found increased maternal involvement and vocalizations and improvements in expressiveness, contingent responsivity, game playing, and quality of assistance.[55-57] Numerous studies have also demonstrated that intervention programs can be effective at teaching mothers to be more responsive and less directive in their interactions with their children.[58-60] Research has also found that intervention improves turn-taking behaviors.[58-60] Mahoney and Powell reported that other maternal affective characteristics (warmth and enjoyment) were less responsive to intervention coaching.[61]

The importance of mother-child interaction for child development is substantiated in numerous studies. These early interactions appear to be especially important for LBW premature infants. Researchers have turned to intervention programs in hopes of facilitating infants' early interaction and developmental outcomes. Although intervention programs have proven effective in improving the developmental consequences of LBW premature infants, few studies have actually measured the effects of intervention on the quality of mother-child interaction, and thus little is known about their influence on dyadic exchanges.

Spiker and colleagues focused on enhancing maternal interactive behavior and child social competence in LBW premature infants. They rated multiple maternal variables, child variables, and dyadic variables based on an 8-minute videotape that had free play and a structured learning task at the 30-month IHDP visit.[57]

Significant effects were seen on six out of eight ratings (Table 2). Intervention mothers had higher ratings on quality of assistance; intervention children had higher ratings on persistence and enthusiasm, on overall competence and involvement, as well as lower ratings on percentage of time off task; intervention dyads were rated as more synchronous.[57]

Additional research was pursued in determining the effects of IHDP on the quality of maternal interactive behavior. It is important to remember that the IHDP aimed at having an impact on both the parent and the child. The IHDP curriculum included activities to assist parents in teaching their children. It provided information to parents on child management, child development, appropriate expectations for children, and the importance of providing a rich array of experiences to children. Parents were also provided general social support and were assisted in developing problem-solving skills,

Table 2. Maternal and child behaviors –
Infant Health and Development Program[57]

	Control mean (sd)	**Intervention** mean (sd)	**P value**
Maternal ratings:			
Supportive presence	4.0 (1.5)	4.2 (1.5)	NS
Quality of assistance	3.3 (1.5)	3.6 (1.5)	.05
Child ratings:			
Persistence	3.2 (1.0)	3.5 (1.0)	.01
% time off task	0.19 (.2)	0.14 (.2)	.01
Enthusiasm	4.2 (1.4)	4.5 (1.3)	.05
Overall child	3.2 (.9)	3.4 (1.0)	.01
Dyadic ratings:			
Overall experience	3.2 (1.0)	3.3 (1.0)	NS
Mutuality	2.7 (1.0)	3.0 (.95)	.01

both of which are factors that seemed likely to make the parents more accepting, effective, and thoughtful managers of their children. IHDP also included a highly enriched day-care experience for children that was aimed at enhancing the child's intellectual language and social competence.

Wheeden used the free-play portion of the 30-month mother-child videotaped IHDP sessions to explore maternal characteristics.[62] The means and standard deviations for each of the 12 maternal behaviors examined are presented in Table 3.[57] Mothers in the intervention group showed more expression and enjoyment toward their children than did mothers in the follow-up group. They demonstrated more positive affect and fondness toward their children. Intervention mothers seemed more aware of their children's activities and interests and responded more consistently and appropriately to their children's behavior. Furthermore, they showed more encouragement of their children's sensorimotor and cognitive development, and they provided their children with a larger repertoire of types and approaches toward toys. Also, intervention mothers were more successful in engaging their children in play interactions and displayed more acceptance and approval of their children during interactions.

Table 3. Maternal interactive ratings (mean)[57]

Maternal Behavior	Total Sample mean (sd)	Intervention mean (sd)	Control mean (sd)	*P* value
Expressiveness	2.83 (.76)	3.08 (.75)	2.67 (.73)	<.001
Enjoyment	2.88 (.77)	3.05 (.74)	2.78 (.77)	.002
Warmth	2.33 (.84)	2.55(.86)	2.18 (.80)	<.001
Sensitivity	3.22 (.98)	3.49 (.92)	3.05 (.98)	<.001
Responsivity	2.98 (.95)	3.22 (.99)	2.83 (.98)	<.001
Achievement	3.38 (.86)	2.73 (.87)	2.16 (.78)	<.001
Inventiveness	2.26 (.64)	2.38 (.63)	2.18 (.64)	.008
Praise	1.75 (.90)	1.85 (.90)	1.68 (.89)	NS
Effectiveness	3.11 (.82)	3.28 (.74)	2.00 (.85)	.004
Pace	3.03 (.70)	3.01 (.61)	3.04 (.75)	NS
Acceptance	2.83 (.78)	3.00 (.73)	2.73 (.79)	.003
Directiveness	3.32 (.86)	3.23 (.77)	3.37 (.90)	NS

Although significant differences were found in many components of maternal interactive behavior, achievement orientation was the factor that most differentiated mothers in the intervention group from those in the follow-up group. This finding is meaningful in that the IHDP was designed to improve the developmental outcomes of LBW premature infants. Although improving mother-child interaction was a component of the curriculum, the primary focus was on the child. It is possible that mothers whose children received the IHDP intervention program, compared with those whose children did not receive the intervention, were aware of this focus on improving children's developmental outcomes. Accordingly, mothers in the intervention group might have attempted to encourage their children's learning and development to a greater extent than did mothers in the follow-up group who were not aware of the focus of IHDP.

Finally, these findings suggest that an intervention program primarily designed to improve the developmental consequences of LBW premature infants was also effective in influencing specific aspects of maternal interactive behavior. Qualitative differences were seen in domains not directly targeted by the IHDP curriculum, suggesting that the intervention had many avenues of influence on the children and families. It is likely, for example, that topics and issues discussed during the home visits and parent-group meetings, such as children's developmental milestones and child-rearing guidance, served to enhance maternal awareness and contribute to the higher ratings of maternal interactive behaviors.

Alternatively, it is possible that the effects of the IHDP intervention were mediated by the impact on and improvements in the children. Because a major focus of the IHDP was on the child, it is possible that the intervention children may have been more cooperative and involved social partners and more advanced cognitively, which may have affected their synchrony with their mothers.[57]

Summary

This study demonstrates that LBW infants, as a group, are at increased risk for emotional and behavioral problems. A comprehensive educational and developmental intervention program such as the IHDP was successful not only in improving the behavioral competence of LBW infants at 3 years of age but also in influencing maternal characteristics and mother-child interactions.

Once the intervention ended, however, the differences in behavioral performance disappeared. Follow-up studies of the IHDP cohort through 5 and 8 years of age showed no difference in behavioral competence between the follow-up and intervention groups.

In the 1960s, a number of theorists suggested that the first years of life were of extraordinary importance in remediating the academic disadvantages often observed among poor and ethnic-minority children.[63,64] Moreover, in some cases a more radical suggestion was made: that disadvantaged children could possibly be "inoculated" against their disadvantages by providing them with enrichment experiences in the first years of life. It was implied that, like inoculations against infectious diseases, these enrichment inoculations might provide long-lasting protection.

The results of the IHDP call into question the notion that providing enriching experiences in the first few years of life can protect children against biological disadvantages for extended periods of time. As Zigler[65] has stated, it is unrealistic to expect 1 year of center-based intervention, in the case of Head Start, or even several years of such intervention, to offset totally the experiences of children living in difficult and impoverished family circumstances or receiving low-quality care.[66] It seems likely that interventions to improve the long-term behavioral performance of biologically vulnerable children will have to extend beyond age 3 years to attain maximum effectiveness during the school years. Further research is required to determine the most effective type, timing, and intensity of intervention services for biologically vulnerable children.

References

1. McCormick MC. The contribution of low birth weight to infant mortality and childhood morbidity. *New England Journal of Medicine.* 1985;312:82-90.

2. Shapiro S, McCormick MC, Starfield BH, et al. Relevance of correlates of infant deaths for significant morbidity at 1 year of age. *American Journal of Obstetrics and Gynecology.* 1980;136:363-373.

3. Hack M, Blanche C, Rivers A, Fanaroff AA. The very low birth weight infant: the broader spectrum of morbidity during infancy and early childhood. *Journal of Developmental and Behavioral Pediatrics.* 1983;4:243-249.

4. Drillien CM. *The Growth and Development of the Prematurely Born Infant.* Edinburgh, Scotland: E & S Livingstone; 1964.

5. Broman SH, Nichols PL, Kennedy WA. *Pre-school 10: Prenatal and Early Developmental Correlates.* Hillsdale, NJ: Lawrence Erlbaum Associates Inc; 1975.

6. Escalona SK. Babies at double hazard: early development of infants at biological and social risk. *Pediatrics.* 1998;70(5):670-676.

7. Neligan GA, Kolvin L, Scott DM, Garside RF. *Born Too Soon or Born Too Small.* London, England: Spastics International Medical Publications (Clinics in Developmental Medicine, No. 61); 1976.

8. Scott DT. Premature infants in later childhood: some recent follow-up results. *Seminars in Perinatology.* 1987;11:191-199.

9. Klein NK, Hack M, Breslau N. Children who were very low birth weight: development and academic achievement at nine years of age. *Journal of Developmental Behavior Pediatrics.* 1989;10:32-37.

10. Nobel-Jamieson CM, Lukeman D, Silverman M, Davies PA. Low birth weight children at school age: neurological, psychological and pulmonary function. *Seminars in Perinatology.* 1982;6:266-273.

11. McBurney AK, Eaves LC. Evolution of developmental and psychological test scores. In: Dunn HG, ed. *Sequelae of Low Birthweight: The Vancouver Study.* Philadelphia, PA: JB Lippincott; 1986:54-67.

12. Dunn HG. Neurological, psychological and ophthalmological sequelae of low birthweight. In: Dunn HG, ed. *Sequelae of Low Birthweight: The Vancouver Study.* Philadelphia, PA: JB Lippincott; 1986:1-22.

13. Escalona SK. Babies at double hazard: early development of infants at biologic and social risk. *Pediatrics.* 1982;70:670-676.

14. Francis-Williams J, Davies PA. Very low birth-weight and later intelligence. *Developmental Medicine and Child Neurology.* 1974;16:709-728.

15. Hoy EA, Bill JM, Sykes DH. Very low birth-weight: a long-term developmental impairment? *International Journal of Behavioral Development.* 1988;11:37-67.

16. Sameroff AJ, Chandler MJ. Reproductive risk and the continuum of caretaking casualty. In: Horowitz FD, Hetherington EM, Scarr-Salapatek S, Siegel GM, eds. *Review of Child Development Research.* Chicago, IL: The University of Chicago Press; 1975;4:187-244.

17. Parker S, Greer S, Zuckerman B. Double jeopardy: the impact of poverty on early child development. *Pediatric Clinics of North America.* 1988;35:1227-1240.

18. Benton AL. Mental development of prematurely born children. *American Journal of Orthopsychiatry.* 1940;10:719-746.

19. Koop CB. Risk factors in development. In: Harth M, Campos JJ, eds. *Handbook of Child Psychology.* 4th ed, vol 2. New York, NY: John Wiley & Sons; 1983:1081-1188.

20. Buka SL, Lipsitt LP, Tsuang MT. Emotional and behavioral development of low birthweight infants. In: Friedman SL, Sigman MD, eds. *The Psychological Development of Low Birthweight Children.* Norwood, NJ: Ablex Publishing Corp; 1992:187-214.

21. Escalona SK. Social and other environmental influences on the cognitive and personality development of low birthweight infants. *American Journal of Mental Deficiency.* 1984;88:508-512.

22. Smith L, Sommer FF, Von Terchner S. A longitudinal study of low birthweight children: reproductive, perinatal, and environmental precursors of developmental status at three years of age. *Seminars in Perinatology.* 1982;6:294-304.

23. Hertzig ME. Neurologic "soft" signs in low-birthweight children. *Developmental Medicine and Child Neurology.* 1981;23:778-791.

24. Rickards AL, Ford GW, Kitchen WH, et al. Extremely low-birthweight infants: neurological, psychological, growth and health status beyond five years of age. *Medical Journal of Australia.* 1987;147:476-481.

25. Steiner ES, Sanders EM, Phillips ECK, Maddock CR. Very low birthweight children at school age: comparison of neonatal management methods. *British Medical Journal.* 1980;281:1237-1240.

26. Astbury J, Orgill A, Bajuk B. Relationship between two-year behavior and neurodevelopmental outcome at five years of very low-birthweight survivors. *Developmental Medicine and Child Neurology.* 1987;29:370-379.

27. Bjerre I, Hansen E. Psychomotor development and school adjustment of 7-year-old children with low birthweight. *Acta Paediatrica Scandinavia.* 1976;65:88-96.

28. Calame A, Fawer CL, Claeys V, et al. Neurodevelopmental outcome and school performance of very-low-birth-weight infants at 8 years of age. *European Journal of Pediatrics.* 1986;145:461-466.

29. Dunn HG, Crichton JU, Grunau RVE, et al. Neurological, psychological and educational sequelae of low birth weight. *Brain Development.* 1980;2:57-67.

30. Grigoroiu-Serbanescu M. Intellectual and emotional development and school adjustment in preterm children at 6 and 7 years of age: continuation of a follow-up study. *International Journal of Behavioral Development.* 1984;7:307-320.

31. Hertzig ME, Mittleman M. Temperament in low birthweight children. *Merrill-Palmer Quarterly.* 1984;30:201-211.

32. Parkinson GE, Wallis S, Harvey D. School achievement and behavior of children who were small-for-dates at birth. *Developmental Medicine and Child Neurology.* 1981;23:41-50.

33. Portnoy S, Callias M, Wolke D, Gamsu H. Five-year follow-up study of extremely low-birthweight infants. *Developmental Medicine and Child Neurology.* 1988;130:590-598.

34. Breslau N, Klein N, Allen L. Very low birthweight: behavioral sequelae at nine years of age. *Journal of the American Academy of Child and Adolescent Psychiatry.* 1988;27:605-612.

35. McGee R, Silva PA, Williams S. Perinatal, neurological, environmental and developmental characteristics of seven-year-old children with stable behavior problems. *Journal of Child Psychology and Psychiatry.* 1983;25:573-586.

36. Nichols PL, Chen TC. *Minimal Brain Dysfunction: A Prospective Study.* Hillsdale, NJ: Erlbaum; 1981.

37. McCormick MC, Gortmaker SL, Sobol AM. Very low birth weight children: behavior problems and school failure in a national sample. *Journal of Developmental and Behavioral Pediatrics.* 1989;10:266.

38. Cohen P, Velez CN, Brook J, Smith J. Mechanisms of the relation between perinatal problems, early childhood illness, and psychopathology in late childhood and adolescence. *Child Development.* 1989;60:701-709.

39. Buka SL, Lipsitt LP, Tsuang MT. Birth complications and psychological deviancy: a twenty-five year prospective inquiry. *Acta Paediatrica Japonica.* 1988;30:537-546.

40. Infant Health and Development Program. Enhancing the outcomes of low-birthweight, premature infants: a multi-site, randomized trial. *Journal of the American Medical Association.* 1990;263:3035-3042.

41. Ramey CT, Bryant DM, Sparling JJ, Wasik BH. Educational interventions to enhance intellectual development: comprehensive daycare versus family education. In: Harel S, Anastasiow N, eds. *The 'At-Risk' Infant: Psycho/Socio/Medical Aspects.* Baltimore, MD: PH Brookes Publishing Co; 1985:75-85.

42. Ramey CT, Campbell FA. The Carolina Abecedarian Project: an educational experiment concerning human malleability. In: Gallagher JJ, Ramey CT, eds. *The Malleability of Children.* Baltimore, MD: PH Brookes Publishing Co; 1987:127-139.

43. Constantine NA, Kraemer HC, Kendall-Tackett KA, et al. Use of physical and neurologic observations in assessment of gestational age in low birth weight infants. *Journal of Pediatrics.* 1987;110: 921-928.

44. Constantine WL, Haynes CW, Spiker D, et al. Recruitment and retention in a clinical trial for low birth weight, premature infants. *Journal of Developmental Behavior Pediatrics.* 1993;14:1-7.

45. Richman N, Graham PJ. A behavioural screening questionnaire for use with three-year-old children: preliminary findings. *Journal of Child Psychology and Psychiatry.* 1971;12:5-33.

46. Richman N, Stevenson J, Graham PJ. *Preschool to School: A Behavioral Study.* London, England: Academic Press; 1982.

47. Richman N. Behavior problems in pre-school children: family and social factors. *British Journal of Psychiatry.* 1977;131:523-527.

48. Achenbach TM, Edelbrock CS, Howell CT. Empirically based assessment of the behavioral/emotional problems of 2- and 3-year old children. *Journal of Abnormal Child Psychology.* 1987;15:629-650.

49. McConaughy SH, Achenbach TM. *Practical Guide for the Child Behavior Checklist and Related Materials.* Burlington, VT: University of Vermont, Department of Psychiatry; 1988.

50. Matas L, Arend R, Sroufe LA. Continuity of adaptation in the second year: the relationship between quality of attachment and late competence. *Child Development.* 1978;49:547-556.

51. Brooks-Gunn J, Klebanov PK, Liau FR, Spiker D. Enhancing the development of LBW premature infants: changes in cognition and behavior over the first three years. *Child Development.* 1993;64: 736-753.

52. Barrera M, Kitching K, Cunningham C, et al. A 3-year early home intervention follow-up study of low birthweight infants and their parents. *Topics in Early Childhood Special Education.* 1990;10:14-28.

53. Barrera M, Rosenbaum P, Cunningham C. Early home intervention with low-birth weight infants and their parents. *Child Development.* 1986;57:20-33.

54. Bromwich R, Parmelee A. An intervention program for pre-term infants. In: Field TM, Sostek A, Goldberg A, Shuman H, eds. *Infants Born At-Risk: Behavior and Development.* New York, NY: Spectrum; 1979:389-411.

55. Minde K, Shosenberg B, Marton P, et al. Self-help groups in a premature nursery – a controlled evaluation. *Behavioral Pediatrics.* 1980;96(5):933-940.

56. Widmayer S, Field T. Effects of Brazelton demonstrations for mothers on the development of preterm infants. *Pediatrics.* 1981;67(5):711-714.

57. Spiker D, Ferguson J, Brooks-Gunn J. Enhancing maternal interactive behavior and child social competence in LBW, premature infants. *Child Development.* 1993;64:754-768.

58. Baskin C, Umansky W, Sanders W. Influencing the responsiveness of adolescent mothers to their infants. *Zero to Three.* 1987;18(2):7-11.

59. Beckwith L. Interventions with disadvantaged parents of sick preterm infants. *Psychiatry.* 1988;51:242-247.

60. Girolametto L. Improving the social-conversational skills of developmentally delayed children: an intervention study. *Journal of Speech and Hearing Disorders.* 1988;53:156-167.

61. Mahoney G, Powell A. Modifying parent-child interaction: enhancing the development of handicapped children. *The Journal of Special Education.* 1988;22(1):82-96.

62. Wheeden CA. *The Effects of a Comprehensive Early Intervention Program on the Quality of Maternal Interactive Behavior With Low Birth Weight, Premature Infants.* PhD thesis. University of Miami, Coral Gables, Florida; 1995.

63. Bloom BS. *Stability and Change in Human Characteristics.* New York, NY: John Wiley & Sons Inc; 1964.

64. Hunt JM. *Environment and Experiences.* New York, NY: Roland Press; 1961.

65. Zigler EF. Early childhood intervention: promising preventative for juvenile delinquency. *American Psychologist.* 1992;47:997-1006.

66. Hayes CD, Palmer JL, Zaslow ME. *Who Cares for America's Children? Child Care Policy for the 1990s.* Washington, DC: National Academy Press; 1990.

Emotional Characteristics of Infants Associated With Maternal Depression and Anxiety

M. Katherine Weinberg, PhD & Edward Z. Tronick, PhD

Introduction

Tronick[1] has argued that even very young infants are exquisitely sensitive to the emotions of their caregivers. This emotional sensitivity is critical to our understanding of normal and abnormal emotional development in children and how maternal depression and anxiety disorders affect children's development. In a paradigmatic study, Cohn and Tronick[2] asked nondepressed mothers to simulate a depressed interaction with their 3-month-old infants. With only minimal instruction, mothers had little difficulty in acting depressed. They spoke in a monotone, expressed little or no facial affect, hardly touched their infants, and interacted at a greater than usual distance from their infants. The infants reacted dramatically when exposed to just 3 minutes of simulated depression. The infants looked away from the mothers and became distressed and wary. Their affect cycled among states of wariness and disengagement. They made brief solicitations to the mother to resume her normal affective state. Importantly, the infants continued to be distressed and disengaged from the mother even after the mother resumed normal interactive behavior. Clearly, infants as young as 3 months are able to detect maternal affective states. They react with well-organized emotional displays that are related to the affect expressed by their mothers. These experimental findings led us to hypothesize that the affective and interactive states of infants would be disturbed by maternal depression and anxiety.

Effects of Maternal Depression and Anxiety on Infant Functioning

Research on the effects of maternal depression on infant outcome, reviewed by Weinberg and Tronick[3] and other investigators[4,5] indicates that in each communicative domain – face, voice, and touch – the quantity, quality, and timing of depressed mothers' social and affective behavior is distorted in ways that contrast sharply with the behavior of nondepressed mothers and that these affective characteristics compromise infant social, emotional, and cognitive functioning.[6,7]

Maternal subsets. The research also suggests that the behavior of depressed mothers is heterogeneous. Several researchers have found that some depressed mothers' behavior and affect appear quite normal, whereas the behavior and affect of mothers with similar levels of depressive symptomatology are compromised.[7-11] Cohn and Tronick,[10] for instance, found that some depressed mothers are disengaged and withdrawn when interacting with their infants. These withdrawn mothers engage in little play, talk only rarely to their infants in the "babified" register of motherese, and show flat and sad affect. Other mothers are more intrusive. They express anger to their infants and interfere with their infants' activities. Still another subset of mothers are able to pull themselves together and interact positively with their infants. Campbell et al[12] have argued that the ability to muster the energy to engage in positive mother-infant interactions and to derive pleasure from these interchanges may be one marker of who will or will not show a chronic course of depression.

Infant functioning. Maternal depression affects infant functioning.[3] The infants of depressed mothers have difficulties engaging in object and social interactions as early as 2 months of age.[13] These infants, compared to control infants, look less at the mother, engage less with objects, show less positive and more negative affect, lower activity levels, and greater physiological reactivity as indexed by higher heart rate and cortisol levels.[5] They show compromises in their ability to regulate their affective and behavioral states. These regulatory dysfunctions appear as early as the newborn period,[14] suggesting that there are prenatal effects of maternal depression on the infant's regulatory capacities. Importantly, the infants' affective states are specifically related to their mothers' style of interaction. Thus Cohn and Tronick[10] found that the infants of withdrawn depressed mothers spent most of their time crying and fussing, whereas the infants of the intrusive depressed mothers avoided looking and interacting with their mother. The infants of the emotionally and socially positive depressed mothers behaved similarly to control infants. This suggests that the social emotional interactive style that the infants are exposed to may be more critical than the mothers' diagnosis per se.

At 1 year of age, many infants of depressed mothers show poorer performance on developmental tests such as the Bayley Scales of Infant Development and Piagetian object tasks, suggesting that even at this age these children are beginning to be at risk for cognitive compromises.[15-17] Furthermore, there is some indication that these infants have an insecure attachment to the mother, especially if the mother's illness is severe and chronic.[18] Beeghly et al,[19] however, found no differences in infant attachment security. They did find that infants of mothers with a pregravid history of depression were significantly harder to classify and more likely to exhibit odd or unexpected patterns of affect, a finding that deserves further attention. Insecure attachment has been related to a number of difficulties, including conduct disorders and behavior problems during the preschool and later school periods, and has been suggested as an environmental mechanism for the occurrence of familial psychopathology.

Thus, there is evidence that exposure to maternal depressive symptomatology or depression compromises infant social, emotional, and cognitive functioning. These compromises continue to be observed in the older children of depressed mothers. At later ages, these children exhibit a range of problems including difficulties in school, poor modulation of affect, conflict with peers and parents, and increased rates of psychiatric problems including depression.[4,20,21]

Panic disorder and anxiety. There is a paucity of research on the effects of maternal anxiety disorders on infant functioning, and the literature has focused almost exclusively on the effects of panic disorder. Nonetheless, like the research on depression it appears that maternal anxiety has powerful developmental effects. Adult patients with panic disorder rate their parents as having engaged in dysfunctional parenting, particularly overprotectiveness and lack of care.[22,23] These studies, however, suffer from their exclusive reliance on retrospective self-reports. Patients often are searching for the causes of their problems and may attribute a more negative value to these relationships than they in fact warrant.[22]

Only a handful of studies have evaluated the children of parents with panic disorder and none of these studies have focused on infants under 1 year of age. The studies have found higher rates of behavioral inhibition in these children.[24-26] Furthermore, inhibited older children have been found to be more likely than uninhibited children to evidence higher rates of multiple anxiety disorders than normal controls based on maternal interview data.[27] Thus behavioral inhibition in children may be a precursor to anxiety disorders in later life. The children of mothers with panic disorder also have higher rates of insecure attachment to the mother.[26,28] An astounding 80% of the preschool children in a study by Manassis et al[28] were classified as insecurely attached, with 65% judged disorganized. Furthermore, based on parental interviews, Weissman et al[29] found that 6- to 7-year-old children with a parent with panic disorder were three times more likely than controls to experience anxiety disorders. Taken together, this research indicates that the children of mothers with panic disorder may be at risk for developing anxiety disorders themselves, particularly in the presence of attachment difficulties and inhibited temperamental characteristics, as has been suggested by Manassis and her colleagues.[26]

Importance of study methodology. Several of the studies evaluating the impact of maternal anxiety on child functioning have suffered from methodologic problems including small sample sizes, no comparison groups, and lack of blindness to the mothers' psychiatric status. Several of the studies have also relied on maternal reports of child psychopathology, either parental interviews or parental ratings on measures such as the Child Behavior Checklist (CBCL). The extent to which these reports are biased by the parental disorder is unknown because parents with psychopathology may exaggerate symptoms in their children or be less tolerant of child symptomatic behavior and therefore more likely to underestimate problems.[29] Studies employing direct observations of these children and paying particular attention to methodologic details are needed to evaluate the effects of maternal anxiety on the infants' and children's functioning.

Most of the studies evaluating the effects of depression or anxiety on maternal and infant functioning have not explored the effect of treatment. The studies have used community samples of women who typically have not sought treatment. Although self-reported symptomatology of, for example, depressive symptoms is common during the postpartum period and the prevalence rate of postnatal depression is around 10%, treatment utilization is low.[12,30] Women who seek treatment may therefore represent an extreme group at higher risk than women who do not seek treatment. Although untreated women from the community may be more representative than women who seek treatment, focusing on untreated mothers from the community begs the issue of whether treatment has a mitigating effect on maternal and infant functioning. Few studies have included women in treatment and results from these studies are equivocal and contradictory. For example, Lyons-Ruth et al[17] found no differences in infant attachment in a high social risk sample of depressed treated mothers and nondepressed controls. By contrast, Teti et al[18] found higher rates of insecure attachment in a treated depressed group, particularly in chronically impaired women. Similar results have been reported by Manassis et al,[28] who found greater insecure attachment and disturbances in a sample of anxious mothers in treatment and their children. Thus there is a need for longitudinal observational studies to evaluate the socio-emotional functioning of women with a psychiatric illness who are in treatment, as well as the functioning of their infants.

Furthermore, very few studies have evaluated the relation between mothers' self-reported functioning, their observed interactive behavior with their infants, and the infants' socio-emotional functioning. Teti and colleagues[31,32] found that the quality of depressed mothers' caretaking behavior was related to their perceptions of their maternal competence. Thus the poorer the mothers' feelings of self-efficacy in the mothering role, the poorer their interactions with their infants. Frankel and Harmon[33] further found that within a depressed group of mothers, mothers in remission showed improvement in self-reported functioning but continued to show interactional difficulties with their 3-year-old children. These kinds of data may have significant implications for psychiatry because they suggest that mothers' self-evaluations are not always concordant with their behavior. Thus there is a need to ask mothers how they are feeling and to observe their interactions with their infants if the goal is to understand maternal and child socio-emotional functioning.

Ongoing Study of Maternal Psychiatric Illness and Infant Functioning

At the Child Development Unit at Boston's Children's Hospital, in collaboration with Drs Lee Cohen and Debra Sichel at the Massachusetts General Hospital, we are conducting an ongoing study designed to evaluate the relations between maternal self-reported functioning and direct observations of maternal and infant socio-emotional behavior in a group of mothers in treatment. In this preliminary study, the treated psychiatric group consisted of 30 mothers with a pregravid clinical diagnosis of panic disorder (PD, 37% of sample), major depressive disorder (MDD, 43% of sample), or obsessive-compulsive disorder (OCD, 20% of sample). Mothers were diagnosed using the Structured Clinical Interview for DSM-III Axis I Disorders (SCID)[34] and were treated at and recruited from the Perinatal Psychiatry Clinical Research Program (PPCRP) at MGH. The majority of the mothers were treated with psychotropic medication. Sixty-eight percent of the mothers were maintained on medication during some part of their pregnancy. During the postpartum period, 48% of the mothers were treated with psychotropic medication and an additional 40% with psychotropic medication and therapy. Furthermore, 40% of the sample breastfed while on medication. Thus a majority of the infants were exposed during pregnancy and/or the postpartum period to psychotropic medication, the most common of which were clonazepam, tricyclic antidepressants (nortriptyline, desipramine, imipramine), and fluoxetine.

A limitation of this study is that the treated psychiatric group is a mixed group of mothers with different diagnoses. When the study is completed, the MDD, PD, and OCD groups will be disaggregated in order to determine if there is a differential effect of diagnosis on maternal and infant functioning. Disaggregation will permit us to address the question of whether different maternal psychiatric conditions are associated with specific effects on the infant or with more general effects such as those observed in nonpsychiatric samples (eg, medically ill or maritally dissatisfied mothers and their infants[35,36]). It is our hypothesis that maternal and infant affective behavior will vary by diagnostic status primarily along the dimensions of withdrawal and vigilance. Although specificity is one of the most important issues in the field of high-risk research,[37] few studies have evaluated what outcomes are unique to a specific diagnostic group. When the sample is complete, we will also evaluate the effects of different kinds of treatment and psychotropic medication on maternal and infant functioning. This too is an important issue that remains largely unexplored.

The second group of mothers was a control group drawn from the community. These mothers were recruited from the maternity wards of Boston hospitals. The group consisted of 30 mothers with no documented depressive symptomatology on the Center for Epidemiologic Studies-Depression Scale (CES-D)[38] or clinical diagnosis on the Diagnostic Interview Schedule-Version III Revised (DIS-III-R).[39]

Mothers and infants in both groups met a set of low-risk social and medical criteria (eg, age over 21, living with the infant's father, at least a high school education, healthy mother and infant). Many developmental studies have included very-high-risk samples of mothers and infants. Risk factors known to affect maternal and infant functioning (eg, teen parenthood, poverty, illness) confound and obscure the effects of psychiatric status, making it difficult to disentangle the effects of psychiatric illness from other factors. In this study, given the low-risk sample characteristics, the mothers may be seen as having accumulated protective factors that would mitigate against finding effects of their diagnostic status on their and their infants' functioning. For example, paternal support and involvement is protective of both maternal and infant functioning.[40] A needed study is one which covers a range of high to low social and medical risk factors. Such a study would permit an evaluation of the relative contribution of maternal psychiatric illness among other factors that are related to compromises in maternal and infant functioning.

Maternal Self-Reported Functioning

To evaluate the mothers' perceptions of their own functioning, mothers completed several measures designed to assess depressive symptomatology (using the CES-D), current psychiatric symptoms (using the Symptom Checklist-90-Revised, SCL-90-R)[41] and maternal self-esteem (using the Maternal Self-Report Inventory, MSI).[42] Mothers in the treated psychiatric group reported feeling as well as control mothers on these measures, suggesting that treatment was effective.

When the pattern of responses on these questionnaires was compared to those of a community group of mothers with high levels of depressive symptoms (on the CES-D) who had not sought treatment and who were participants in another research project, an interesting pattern emerged. The untreated community group with high levels of depressive symptoms reported significantly more psychiatric symptoms than the treated psychiatric group. The untreated community mothers also felt that they were less prepared for taking care of their baby than the mothers in the treated psychiatric group. Interestingly, the treated psychiatric mothers and untreated community mothers reported equally high levels of anxiety, suggesting that for both groups the experience of becoming a new mother may have been more stressful than for control mothers.

These data suggest that mothers with a psychiatric illness who are in treatment perceive themselves as functioning well. By contrast, depressed mothers from the community who do not receive treatment reported significant psychological distress and poor functioning. This raises the question of what to do with mothers in the community who are distressed and symptomatic but who typically do not seek help. An effort will need to be made to screen and identify these women. One possible setting might be at well-baby visits, since pediatricians and nurse practitioners routinely come in contact with mothers during the postpartum period. A collaborative effort between the pediatric and psychiatric communities may need to be established to provide pediatric providers with tools for identifying psychiatric illness and with treatment site referrals for identified mothers.

Mother-Infant Interactions

To evaluate whether there were differences in maternal and infant interactive social-emotional behavior, mothers and infants were videotaped in the laboratory of the Child Development Unit at Boston's Children's Hospital at 3 months postpartum. The infants were videotaped in Tronick et al's[43] Face-to-Face Still-Face paradigm, which included a 2-minute face-to-face play interaction with the mother preceding and following a 2-minute still-face episode during which the mother was unresponsive to the infant. In addition, the infants were videotaped during a 2-minute face-to-face play interaction with an unfamiliar female research assistant.

Contrasted to normal face-to-face play (during which mothers are instructed to play with the baby as she would at home), the still-face distorts the mothers' behavior. During the still-face mothers are asked to look at the baby but not to touch, smile at or talk to the infant. The mothers' *en face* position and eye contact signal the infants that social interaction is forthcoming while their expressionless face and lack of response communicate the opposite. The mothers are saying "Hello" and "Good-bye" at the same time and remain expressionless even after attempts by the infants to reinstate the interaction.

The still-face has been used extensively to evaluate young infants' communicative abilities, sensitivity to changes in maternal behavior, and capacity to regulate affective states.[44,45] For example, Gianino and Tronick[46] found that infants who experienced frequent repairs (corrections) of minor interactive errors (eg, misreading of cues) during mother-infant face-to-face play were likely to solicit their mothers' attention during the still-face. Infants who experienced fewer repairs were more likely to turn away and become distressed. Gianino and Tronick concluded that infants who routinely experience repairs have a representation of themselves as effective in making repairs and of their mother as responsive and sensitive. These data have implications for the infants of depressed mothers who are exposed to periods of maternal unavailability or prolonged interactive errors that are not easily repaired. Infants of depressed mothers would be expected to react with more disengagement to the still-face than the infants of nondepressed mothers.

The infants were also videotaped interacting with an unfamiliar female research assistant. This episode was included because of work by Field et al[47] suggesting that negative interactive patterns of infants of depressed mothers generalize to the infants' interactions with an unfamiliar adult. Specifically, Field et al found that infants of depressed mothers showed similar compromises whether they were interacting with their mother or a stranger and that the stranger performed less optimally with these infants than with the infants of controls. These data suggest that infant affect and behavior are not simply immediate byproducts of the adult partner's interactive style but possibly reflect broader representations of interactions.

The infants' and mothers' behaviors and facial expressions were coded microanalytically second-by-second from videotapes using Tronick and Weinberg's Infant and Maternal Regulatory Scoring Systems (IRSS and MRSS,[48,49] also see[50] for a description of these systems) and Izard and Dougherty's AFFEX system.[51] These systems have been very effective at picking up subtle changes in infant and maternal behavior. For example, few studies using global scoring systems or rating scales have been able to demonstrate gender differences in infant behavior before 1 year of age. Weinberg et al,[52] using the IRSS and AFFEX systems, found that 6-month-old boys of nondepressed mothers were more emotionally reactive during social interaction with their mother than girls. The boys' greater emotional reactivity, as indexed by crying and fussing, facial expressions of anger, and attempts to distance themselves from the mother by arching their backs and turning and twisting in the infant seat, suggested that they had greater difficulty regulating affective states on their own and that they needed to rely more on maternal scaffolding than girls. Recently, Weinberg[53] has found similar gender differences in the infants of depressed mothers. Male infants were more demanding social partners and depressed mothers had greater difficulties providing their sons with the regulatory help that they needed. In this way, a cycle of mutual interactive problems between mothers and sons became established, with the mothers showing more anger and the sons showing less positive affect.

Mothers in the treated psychiatric group evidenced a number of interactional difficulties with their infants even though they reported feeling well on the questionnaire measures. Compared to controls, mothers in the treated psychiatric group talked less to their infants, touched their infants less, and were less likely to share their infants' focus of interest. The mothers in the treated psychiatric group were also more likely to perceive the interaction negatively (as reflected in comments such as "You don't like me," "I bore you," or "You don't want to play with me"), loomed more often into the infant's face, which is often invasive and disruptive, and showed more anger to their infants. These interactional difficulties are consistent with those reported in prior research on depressed typically untreated mothers' interactions with young infants.

The infants of the treated psychiatric mothers reacted differently to the still-face and the stranger than the infants of control mothers. They were less interested, expressed more anger and sadness, and tended to fuss and cry more. During their interaction with the stranger, these infants were also less likely to vocalize to the stranger.

We also evaluated the strangers' reactions to the infants in the treated psychiatric and control groups. The stranger interaction is interesting because the stranger is unbiased. The stranger has never seen the baby before and is blind to the infant's and mother's background. Thus the stranger is influenced only by the infant's ongoing behavior during the interaction. The strangers were more disengaged with the infants of the treated psychiatric mothers than with the infants of control mothers. Of particular interest was the minimal amount of time they spent touching these infants. They also avoided using touches that are often arousing and somewhat intrusive such as tickles. Furthermore, the strangers maintained a greater physical distance from these infants than from control infants and when they tried to elicit the attention of these infants, they did so by using distal elicits such as hand waving. It is likely that the strangers were disengaged because they were picking up cues from the infants that the infants did not want to play with them (ie, these infants were less likely to invite interaction by smiling and vocalizing). It is also possible that the strangers may have perceived these infants as more emotionally vulnerable than controls and more likely than controls to become overstimulated and overwhelmed and to start crying or fussing if they played with them in a more animated manner. Both interpretations suggest that the infants in the treated psychiatric group brought something to the interaction which served to compromise their interactions with the stranger.

Conclusions

Our work indicates that maternal psychiatric illness has an effect on mothers' and infants' social and emotional functioning even though the mothers have been in treatment and report feeling well. When asked to complete self-report measures assessing psychiatric symptoms and maternal self-esteem, mothers in the treated psychiatric group consistently perceived themselves as doing well. A notable exception was a higher level of anxiety. However, how well the mothers said they were doing did not always accurately reflect their interactions with their infants. The mothers in the treated psychiatric group demonstrated a number of interactional difficulties similar to those reported in prior research evaluating the interactive behavior of untreated mothers. These findings may have significant implications for treatment because they suggest that mothers' self-evaluations are not always concordant with their behavior. Although the mothers feel better, their behavior with their infants is still compromised. This is consistent with work by Weissman and Paykel[54] demonstrating that even after an acute psychiatric episode is over, mothers continue to show parenting problems.

The mothers' self-perceptions also did not reflect how their infants were doing. These infants' emotional functioning was disturbed. They were angrier and sadder and more disregulated by crying and fussiness. During the still-face they reacted more negatively and with the unfamiliar adult they were also more negative. Furthermore, the finding that the strangers were more disengaged when interacting with these infants suggests that these infants brought something to the interaction which served to compromise their interactions with individuals other than their mother. Thus these infants' emotional disturbance is detectable by our objective coding and by the "natural" sensitivities of an unfamiliar adult. Moreover, we believe that the infants' emotional reactivity may negatively affect the mothers' behavior and become part of a self-reinforcing cycle.

The mothers' and infants' interactive history may be one explanation for the infant findings. However, there are other factors that contribute to infant outcome. Just a partial list includes biological and genetic predisposition and in utero exposure to psychotropic medication. At this point of our understanding, it is difficult to pinpoint the relative contribution of each of these factors.

The data may also reflect the fact that treatment of these mothers did not include an infant component. In many cases, the infant is the "forgotten patient." By excluding the infant in the treatment process, clinicians may not fully address the potential exacerbating effect of the birth of a child on the mother's psychiatric status. Furthermore, by treating mothers in isolation, clinicians miss the opportunity to address developmental difficulties that may lead to later psychiatric problems in a child who may be already genetically vulnerable to psychiatric illness. The results of this study suggest that clinicians should be aware of mother-infant interactional difficulties and be alert to the fact that these difficulties emerge early in the child's life. Including the infant in the therapeutic process may help alleviate mothers' concerns about their infant's development and feelings of guilt and worry that they are not doing everything they should to foster the child's development. The infant who does well can become a therapeutic ally and increase mothers' sense of competence as a parent. Moreover, directly addressing mother-infant interactional difficulties with the mother will also benefit the infant by improving the mother-child relationship.

Acknowledgments

The research was supported in part by funding from the Prevention Research Branch of the National Institute of Mental Health, National Institutes of Health (RO3 MH52265 awarded to M. Katherine Weinberg; RO1 MH45547 and RO1 MH43398 awarded to Edward Z. Tronick). The author wishes to thank Lee Cohen, MD for his comments on the manuscript as well as Lee Cohen, MD and Deborah Sichel, MD, who referred mothers and infants to the Child Development Unit. Portions of this paper were presented at the American Psychiatric Association Annual Meeting, New York, New York, May 4-9, 1996, and in Weinberg MK, Tronick EZ. The impact of maternal psychiatric illness on infant development. *Journal of Clinical Psychiatry.* 1998;59(suppl 2):53-61.

References

1. Tronick EZ. Emotions and emotional communication in infants. *American Psychologist.* 1989;44: 112-119.

2. Cohn JF, Tronick EZ. Three-month-old infants' reaction to simulated maternal depression. *Child Development.* 1983;54:185-193.

3. Weinberg MK, Tronick EZ. Maternal depression and infant maladjustment: a failure of mutual regulation. In: Noshpitz J, ed. *The Handbook of Child and Adolescent Psychiatry.* New York, NY: Wiley and Sons; 1996.

4. Downey G, Coyne JC. Children of depressed parents: an integrative review. *Psychological Bulletin.* 1990;108:50-76.

5. Field T. Infants of depressed mothers. *Infant Behavior and Development.* 1995;18:1-13.

6. Cohn J, Campbell SB, Matias R, Hopkins J. Face-to-face interactions of postpartum depressed and nondepressed mother-infant pairs at 2 months. *Developmental Psychology.* 1990;26:15-23.

7. Field T, Healy B, Goldstein S, Guthertz M. Behavior-state matching and synchrony in mother-infant interactions of nondepressed versus depressed dyads. *Developmental Psychology.* 1990;26:7-14.

8. Radke-Yarrow M. A developmental study of depressed and normal parents and their children. *Society for Research in Child Development.* 1987. Abstract.

9. Cohn JF, Matias R, Tronick EZ, et al. Face-to-face interactions of depressed mothers and their infants. In: Tronick EZ, Field T, eds. *Maternal Depression and Infant Disturbance. New Directions for Child Development, No. 34.* San Francisco, CA: Jossey-Bass; 1986:31-44.

10. Cohn JF, Tronick EZ. Specificity of infants' response to mothers' affective behavior. *Journal of the American Academy of Child and Adolescent Psychiatry.* 1989;28:242-248.

11. Lyons-Ruth K, Zoll D, Connell D, Grunebaum HU. The depressed mother and her one-year-old infant: environment, interaction, attachment, and infant development. In: Tronick EZ, Field T, eds. *Maternal Depression and Infant Disturbance. New Directions for Child Development, No. 34.* San Francisco, CA: Jossey-Bass; 1986:61-82.

12. Campbell SB, Cohn JF, Meyers T. Depression in first-time mothers: mother-infant interaction and depression chronicity. *Developmental Psychology.* 1995;31:349-357.

13. Campbell SB, Cohn JF. Prevalence and correlates of postpartum depression in first-time mothers. *Journal of Abnormal Psychology.* 1991;100:594-599.

14. Zuckerman BS, Bauchner H, Parker S, Cabral H. Maternal depressive symptoms during pregnancy and newborn irritability. *Developmental and Behavioral Pediatrics.* 1990;11:190-194.

15. Murray L. The impact of postnatal depression on infant development. *Journal of Child Psychology and Psychiatry.* 1992;33:543-561.

16. Murray L, Kempton C, Woolgar M, Hooper R. Depressed mothers' speech to their infants and its relation to infant gender and cognitive development. *Journal of Child Psychology and Psychiatry.* 1993;34:1083-1101.

17. Lyons-Ruth K, Connell DB, Grunebaum HU. Infants at social risk: maternal depression and family support services as mediators of infant development and security of attachment. *Child Development.* 1990;61:85-98.

18. Teti DM, Gelfand DM, Messinger DS, Isabella R. Maternal depression and the quality of early attachment: an examination of infants, preschoolers, and their mothers. *Developmental Psychology.* 1995;31:364-376.

19. Beeghly M, Nelson KM, Olson KL, et al. Maternal depression and infant attachment in a low risk cohort. Scientific Proceedings of the 42nd Annual Meeting of the American Academy of Child and Adolescent Psychiatry. 1995;11:97. Abstract.

20. Gelfand DM, Teti DM. The effects of maternal depression on children. *Clinical Psychology Review.* 1990;10:329-353.

21. Rutter M. Commentary: Some focus and process considerations regarding effects of parental depression on children. *Developmental Psychology.* 1990;26:60-67.

22. Faravelli C, Panichi C, Pallanti S, et al. Perception of early parenting in panic and agoraphobia. *Acta Psychiatrica Scandinavica.* 1991;84:6-8.

23. Silove D, Parker G, Hadzi-Pavlovic D, et al. Parental representations of patients with panic disorder and generalized anxiety disorder. *British Journal of Psychiatry.* 1991;159:835-841.

24. Cohen LS, Sichel DA, Dimmock J, Rosenbaum JF. Behavioral outcome in infants of mothers presenting to a perinatal psychiatry clinic. *American Psychological Association.* 1993. Abstract.

25. Rosenbaum JF, Biederman J, Gersten M, et al. Behavioral inhibition in children of parents with panic disorder and agoraphobia: a controlled study. *Archives of General Psychiatry.* 1988;45:463-470.

26. Manassis K, Bradley S, Goldberg S, et al. Behavioral inhibition, attachment and anxiety in children of mothers with anxiety disorders. *Canadian Journal of Psychiatry.* 1995;40:87-92.

27. Biederman J, Rosenbaum JF, Hirshfeld DR, et al. Psychiatric correlates of behavioral inhibition in young children of parents with and without psychiatric disorders. *Archives of General Psychiatry.* 1990;47:21-26.

28. Manassis K, Bradley S, Goldberg S, et al. Attachment in mothers with anxiety disorders and their children. *Journal of the American Academy of Child and Adolescent Psychiatry.* 1994;33:8:1106-1113.

29. Weissman MM, Leckman JF, Merikangas KR, et al. Depression and anxiety disorders in parents and children: results from the Yale Family Study. *Archives of General Psychiatry.* 1984;41:845-852.

30. O'Hara MW, Zekoski EM, Phillips LH, Wright EJ. Controlled prospective study of postpartum mood disorders: comparison of childbearing and nonchildbearing women. *Journal of Abnormal Psychology.* 1990;99:3-15.

31. Teti DM, Gelfand DM. Behavioral competence among mothers of infants in the first year: the mediational role of maternal self-efficacy. *Child Development.* 1991;62:918-929.

32. Teti DM, Gelfand DM, Pompa J. Depressed mothers' behavioral competence with their infants: demographic and psychosocial correlates. *Development and Psychopathology.* 1990;2:259-270.

33. Frankel KA, Harmon RJ. Depressed mothers: they don't always look as bad as they feel. *Journal of the American Academy of Child and Adolescent Psychiatry.* 1996;35:289-298.

34. Spitzer RL, Williams JBW, Gibbon M. *Structured Clinical Interview for DSM-III-R.* New York, NY: Biometrics Research Department, New York State Psychiatric Institute; 1988.

35. Sameroff AJ. The social context of development. In: Eisenberg N, ed. *Contemporary Topics in Developmental Psychology.* New York, NY: Wiley; 1987:273-291.

36. Lyons-Ruth K. Broadening our conceptual frameworks: can we reintroduce relational strategies and implicit representational systems to the study of psychopathology? *Developmental Psychology.* 1995;31:432-436.

37. Seifer R. Perils and pitfalls of high-risk research. *Developmental Psychology.* 1995;31:420-424.

38. Radloff L. The CES-D scale: a self-report depression scale for research in the general population. *Journal of Applied Psychological Measure.* 1977;1:385-401.

39. Robbins L, Cottler L, Keating S. *NIMH Diagnostic Interview Schedule, Version III, Revised.* St Louis, MO: Washington University Department of Psychiatry;1991.

40. Crnic KA, Greenberg MT, Ragozin AS, et al. Effects of stress and social support on mothers and premature and full-term infants. *Child Development.* 1983;54:209-217.

41. Derogatis LR. *SCL-90-R Administration, Scoring, and Procedures Manual II.* Towson, MD: Clinical Psychometric Research; 1983.

42. Shea E, Tronick EZ. The maternal self-report inventory: a research and clinical instrument for assessing maternal self-esteem. *Theory and Research in Behavioral Pediatrics.* 1988;4:101-141.

43. Tronick EZ, Als H, Adamson L, et al. The infant's response to entrapment between contradictory messages in face-to-face interaction. *Journal of the American Academy of Child Psychiatry.* 1978;17:1-13.

44. Tronick EZ, Cohn JF. Infant-mother face-to-face interaction: age and gender differences in coordination and the occurrence of miscoordination. *Child Development.* 1989;60:85-92.

45. Weinberg MK, Tronick EZ. Infant affective reactions to the resumption of maternal interaction after the Still-Face. *Child Development.* 1996;67:905-914.

46. Gianino A, Tronick EZ. The mutual regulation model: the infant's self and interactive regulation, coping, and defense. In: Field T, McCabe P, Schneiderman N, eds. *Stress and Coping.* Hillsdale, NJ: Erlbaum; 1988:47-68.

47. Field T, Healy B, Goldstein S, et al. Infants of depressed mothers show "depressed" behavior even with nondepressed adults. *Child Development.* 1988;59:1569-1579.

48. Tronick EZ, Weinberg MK. The Infant Regulatory Scoring System (IRSS) (Children's Hospital and Harvard Medical School). 1990. Unpublished, available from senior author.

49. Tronick EZ, Weinberg MK. The Maternal Regulatory Scoring System (MRSS) (Children's Hospital and Harvard Medical School). 1990. Unpublished, available from senior author.

50. Weinberg MK, Tronick E. Beyond the face: an empirical study of infant affective configurations of facial, vocal, gestural, and regulatory behaviors. *Child Development.* 1994;65:1503-1515.

51. Izard CE, Dougherty L. *A System for Identifying Affect Expressions by Holistic Judgements (AFFEX).* Newark, DE: University of Delaware, Instructional Resources Center; 1980.

52. Weinberg MK, Tronick EZ, Cohn JF, Olson K. Gender differences in emotional expressivity and self-regulation during early infancy. *Developmental Psychology.* In press.

53. Weinberg MK. Gender differences in depressed mothers' interactions with their infants. *International Conference on Infant Studies.* Providence, RI. 1996. Abstract.

54. Weissman MM, Paykel ES. *The Depressed Woman: A Study of Social Relationships.* Chicago, IL: University of Chicago Press; 1974.

Early Interventions for Infants of Depressed Mothers

Tiffany Field, PhD

Introduction

Infants of mothers who remain depressed for a year following birth show a distinct profile of behavioral, physiological, and biochemical dysregulation. Their mothers also have a profile that can be used to identify those mothers who are likely to remain depressed and to target high-risk mother-infant dyads in need of intervention. This chapter of *New Perspectives in Early Emotional Development* reviews data on identifying mothers who remain depressed; dysregulation in infants of depressed mothers; and interventions, both brief and intensive.

Recent research suggests the following:

- Maternal depression can negatively affect infants as early as the neonatal period, implicating prenatal effects of maternal depression.

- Infants show a profile of "dysregulation" in their behavior, physiology, and biochemistry that may be due to prenatal exposure to a maternal biochemical imbalance.

- These effects are compounded by the disorganizing influence of the mother's interaction behavior.

- Depressed mothers have two predominant interaction styles, withdrawn or intrusive, that seem to have differential, negative effects on their infants because of inadequate stimulation and arousal modulation.

- Nondepressed caregivers such as fathers may buffer these effects because they provide more optimal stimulation and arousal modulation.

- Interventions that are mood altering for the mothers and arousal reducing for the infants (eg, music and massage therapy) make them more responsive to interaction coaching and improve their interactions.

The interventions we have been studying may be effective because 1) they induce a better mood state in the mothers (and alter right frontal EEG, a marker of depression) and lower stress hormone (norepinephrine and cortisol) levels; 2) they reduce sympathetic arousal in the infants; and 3) reduced sympathetic arousal leads to improved responsiveness, greater availability to interaction coaching, and improved interactions.

Depressed Mothers

Of the depressed mothers we studied, 70% had chronic depression that persisted during the infants' first 6 months of life. These infants showed delays in growth and development at 12 months.[1] Physiological/biochemical markers for the mothers' chronic depression included relative right frontal EEG activation[2]; low vagal tone and serotonin (5HIAA); and elevated norepinephrine and cortisol levels.[3] Measurement of these variables at 3 months accounted for 51% of the mothers' continuing depression at 6 months (with mothers' right frontal EEG activation alone explaining 31% of the variance).

Because infants whose mothers remained depressed at 6 months had growth and developmental delays at 1 year, it is important to identify those mothers for intervention purposes. In our sample, a simple EKG, EEG, and urine analysis (for cortisol, norepinephrine, and serotonin) could explain more than half the variance in the mothers' continuing depression. These measures could also be used to identify those mother-infant dyads needing early intervention.

Newborns of Depressed Mothers

Infants of depressed mothers appeared to have profiles of dysregulation as early as the neonatal period. These profiles are characterized by:

- Limited responsivity on the Brazelton scale[4,5]; excessive indeterminate sleep[6]; elevated stress hormone (norepinephrine and cortisol) levels in the neonatal period[3]

- Right frontal EEG activation at 1 week,[6] 1 month,[7] and 3 months[2]; stability in these patterns from 3 months to 3 years[8]

- Limited responsivity to facial expressions[9]; lower vagal tone; signs of neurological delays at 6 months

- Less social referencing at 9 months[10]

- Limited play and exploratory behavior[11]; inferior Bayley scores[1]; delayed growth at 12 months[1]

Evidence for physiological dysregulation in infants of depressed mothers has been noted as early as 1 week of age and is characterized by relative right frontal EEG activation, lower vagal tone, and less mature sleep patterns.[8]

Disturbed Sleep/Wake Behavior

In our studies at the Touch Research Institute, newborns of depressed mothers showed inferior performance on the Brazelton scale for orientation (particularly on inanimate items), depression, and robustness, and they demonstrated more stressed behavior[4,12] (see Table 1). They also showed excessive indeterminate sleep (sleep that is difficult to code), which is disconcerting given the findings of Sigman and Parmelee suggesting an inverse relationship between the amount of indeterminate sleep during the neonatal period and IQ scores at 12 years.[13] Finally, they were less attentive and less expressive when exaggerated faces were modeled for them and their looking behavior and mimicry were recorded.[12]

Table 1. Means for newborn variables

	Newborns of depressed mothers (n=47)	Newborns of nondepressed mothers (n=36)
Brazelton scores		
Orientation	4.8	5.6*
Inanimate auditory	5.5	6.9**
Inanimate auditory and visual	4.4	5.4*
Depression	3.3	2.3*
Robustness	5.0	5.8*
Indeterminate sleep	19.3	2.7***
Norepinephrine	141.2	58.4***

*$P<.05$; **$P<.01$; ***$P<.001$.

Sympathetic Activation

During the neonatal period both the depressed mothers' and their infants' stress hormones (norepinephrine and cortisol) were significantly elevated. Differences continued across the first several months.[3,14]

Fetuses of Depressed Mothers

The need to identify chronically depressed mothers during pregnancy and evaluate the behavior of their fetuses was highlighted in a report by Field and colleagues. In this study the newborns' biochemical profiles matched their mothers' prenatal biochemical profiles.[2] During the third trimester of pregnancy, the depressed mothers' norepinephrine and cortisol levels were elevated and their dopamine levels were lower than those of nondepressed mothers. Assays of their newborns' catecholamine and cortisol levels suggested that they also had elevated norepinephrine and cortisol and depleted dopamine levels.

In a subsequent study, we identified chronically depressed mothers during the third trimester of pregnancy. Again, their catecholamine and cortisol levels were assayed, and a similar pattern was noted. Their fetuses' ultrasounds were evaluated for activity levels and responses to vibrotactile stimuli. The fetuses of the depressed mothers were less active; they had weaker responses to vibration; and their weight was estimated to be significantly lower.

Infants of Depressed Mothers

Right Frontal EEG Activation

Assessments of EEG asymmetry in mothers and infants revealed a pattern that is noted in chronically depressed adults, namely more right frontal EEG activation and less left frontal activation (in both the mothers and their infants) when the infants were 3 months old,[15] 1 month old,[16] and even as young as 1 week of age.[6] Right frontal EEG at 1 month was also related to indeterminate sleep patterns and negative affect in the neonatal period[6] (see Fig 1). That the depressed mothers showed relative right frontal EEG activation is not surprising, but the appearance of this pattern as early as 1 week in their infants was very unexpected, given the supposed plasticity of brain

Fig 1. Frontal asymmetry of 1-month-old infants of depressed and nondepressed mothers.

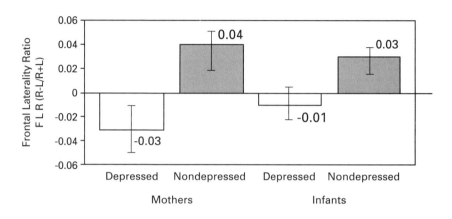

development during the first several months of life. In addition, this pattern appeared to be stable in infants of depressed mothers, at least from 3 months to 3 years of age.[8]

Depressed Vagal Tone

Lower vagal tone has been reported for 6-month-old infants of depressed mothers.[15] Specifically, a developmental increase in vagal tone that occurred between 3 and 6 months for infants of nondepressed mothers did not occur for the infants of depressed mothers. Lower vagal tone at 6 months also correlated with fewer vocalizations during interactions and less optimal neurological ratings, suggesting diminished autonomic development and control in infants of depressed mothers. Lower vagal tone has also been noted in 3-month-old infants of depressed mothers during their interactions with their mothers or nondepressed strangers.[17]

Vagal tone could be responsive to contextual factors such as stress and changes in attention during interactions, and these factors could be different for infants of depressed and nondepressed mothers. For example, depressed mothers are notably less expressive, and their infants may become agitated in their attempts to elicit more expression. Whether the differences are neuroregulatory or reflect different demands in the interaction situation is unclear. The absence of a developmental increase in vagal tone in infants of depressed mothers could relate to cumulative effects of maternal depression, including the continuing elevated norepinephrine levels noted in these infants.

Another complex finding emerged in a study in which both facial expressions and vagal tone were recorded.[15] Here, interest and joy expressions were significantly correlated with vagal tone in infants of nondepressed mothers; however, infants of depressed mothers had more negative behaviors (including gaze aversion, and sad or angry expressions) and were also positively correlated with vagal tone. At 6 months, vagal tone was significantly lower and behavioral responses to facial expressions were slower in the infants of depressed mothers.[15] Although the significance of lower vagal tone is not entirely understood, higher vagal tone is typically associated with better performance on attention and learning tasks.

Laboratory Studies of Affect Perception/Production

In affect perception/production studies at the Touch Research Institute, we have learned that:

- Depressed mothers exhibit fewer positive faces and fewer animated faces and voices.[18]

- Infants of depressed mothers produced more sad and angry faces and showed fewer expressions of interest.[19] They also showed a preference for sad faces/voices (greater looking time at videotaped models looking and sounding sad),[20] which might relate to sad expressions being more familiar to them. They also displayed less accurate matching of happy facial expressions with happy vocal expressions.[12]

- The absence of a relationship between infant facial expressions and vagal tone in infants of depressed mothers suggests biobehavioral uncoupling that might derive from the infants' excessive vigilance in emotional situations.[19]

  Later at 1 year, during a "mother holding doll" situation, infants of depressed mothers showed less protest behavior.[21]

Developmental delays. By 12 months, more infants of depressed mothers had neurological soft signs and showed less exploratory behavior, lower Bayley Mental and Motor scale scores, and lower weight percentiles.[1]

Chronic depression markers used to identify highest risk. In our 6-month longitudinal study (138 depressed dyads, 84 nondepressed dyads), regression analyses yielded several reliable markers of the mothers' chronic depression 6 months postpartum.[14] These included right frontal EEG activation at 3 months, lower vagal tone and serotonin (5HIAA), and elevated norepinephrine and cortisol levels during the neonatal period.

Longitudinal follow-up. In our longitudinal follow-up sample at 3 years, 75% of the mothers with high scores on the Beck during the neonatal period still had elevated Beck scores. Their preschool-aged children continued to show interaction problems, and on the Children's Behavior Checklist they scored in the clinical range for externalizing and internalizing factors.[22] They also had elevated cortisol levels and were considered vulnerable by their mothers. Early infancy predictors that may contribute to this perceived vulnerability included the ratings of the infants' interactions with strangers and their heart rate variability at 3 months.[23] In a follow-up on stability of relative right frontal EEG activation, 3-month-old infants with right frontal EEG continued to have the same pattern at 3 years.[8] The 3-year-olds with relative right frontal activation also were more inhibited in strange object/strange person situations, and they showed nonempathetic behavior during their mothers' display of distress (crying).

Effective Interventions

Natural Buffers of the Depressed Mothers' Negative Effects (Fathers and Nursery School Caregivers)

Natural buffers in the environment for infants of depressed mothers included putative fathers/boyfriends[24] and nursery school teachers.[25] Infants of depressed mothers received better interaction ratings with their nondepressed fathers (see Table 2) and their nursery school teachers than with their mothers. Fathers can also help overcome the negative effects of depression, as improvement is noted when infants of depressed mothers interact with their fathers.[24] The fathers showed more positive facial expressions and vocalizations than mothers, and, in turn, the infants showed more positive facial expressions and vocalizations when interacting with their fathers. These data suggest that nondepressed fathers and nondepressed nursery teachers can compensate for the negative effects of depressed mothering.

Table 2. *Mean interaction ratings of infants (n=26) with nondepressed fathers and depressed mothers* [24]

	Father		Mother		
	M	SD	M	SD	*P*
Parent interaction behaviors					
State	2.5	(0.5)	2.1	(0.3)	<.005
Physical activity	1.6	(0.5)	1.7	(0.7)	NS
Head orientation	2.9	(0.3)	2.9	(0.3)	NS
Gaze behavior	2.8	(0.4)	3.0	(0.0)	NS
Silence during infant gaze aversion	1.9	(0.8)	1.7	(0.8)	NS
Facial expressions	2.4	(0.7)	1.8	(0.4)	<.01
Vocalizations	2.6	(0.9)	1.5	(0.5)	<.001
Infantized behaviors	2.0	(0.7)	1.8	(0.8)	NS
Contingent vocalizations	2.2	(0.4)	2.0	(0.9)	NS
Game playing	2.0	(0.9)	1.3	(0.6)	<.05
Summary score	2.3	(0.2)	1.9	(0.3)	<.005
Infant interaction behaviors					
State	2.8	(0.5)	1.8	(0.7)	<.001
Physical activity	2.3	(0.9)	2.5	(0.5)	NS
Head orientation	2.0	(0.7)	2.0	(0.6)	NS
Gaze behavior	2.7	(0.5)	2.1	(0.7)	<.05
Facial expressions	2.8	(0.6)	1.7	(0.5)	<.001
Fussiness	2.2	(0.9)	1.9	(0.7)	NS
Vocalizations	2.3	(0.8)	1.5	(0.5)	<.005
Summary score	2.4	(0.4)	1.9	(0.4)	<.005

Gender-of-parent effect: $F_{(8.15)} = 3.86$, $P<.01$; Wilks's lambda = .32.

The Touch Research Institute study on switching mothers, which asked whether depressed infants improved when interacting with nondepressed mothers and whether depressed mothers showed more responsive behavior with infants of nondepressed mothers, yielded very few group differences.[26] The infants' "depressed" behavior generalized to the nondepressed mother, possibly because interacting with strangers was stressful for the infant.[17] Interestingly, depressed mothers did not negatively affect the infants of nondepressed mothers, suggesting that normal infants might be less vulnerable to unresponsive interaction behavior than the infants of depressed mothers.

Massage Therapy for Infants

Massage therapy was an effective intervention for the infants of depressed mothers. In contrast to rocking, massage therapy contributed to more organized sleep patterns, more positive interaction behaviors, and greater weight gain.[26] Forty full-term 1- to 3-month-old infants born to depressed adolescent mothers were given 15 minutes of either massage or rocking on 2 days per week for 6 weeks. Compared with rocked infants, massaged infants spent more time in active alert and active awake states, cried less, and had lower salivary cortisol levels, suggesting lower stress. Immediately after the massage, the infants spent less time in an active awake state, suggesting that massage therapy may be more effective than rocking for inducing sleep. During the 6-week period, the massage-therapy infants gained more weight, showed greater improvement on emotionality, sociability, and soothability temperament dimensions, and had greater decreases in stress hormones (norepinephrine, epinephrine, and cortisol) and increased serotonin levels (see Table 3).

Table 3. Means for variables measured at beginning and end of study period for massage therapy and rocking group infants

| | Massage Therapy (n=20) | | Rocking (n=20) | | |
	Day 1	Day 12	Day 1	Day 12	*P*
Weight (lb)	14.7$_a$	16.3$_b$	14.9$_a$	15.4$_a$	.001
Formula intake	7.0$_a$	8.4$_a$	8.0$_a$	10.8$_a$	NS
Temperament					
Emotionality	13.7$_a$	12.2$_b$	13.6$_a$	13.0$_a$	.05
Activity	17.9$_a$	17.6$_a$	16.4$_a$	16.0$_a$	NS
Sociability	18.5$_a$	19.9$_b$	19.1$_b$	18.4$_a$	.05
Soothability	16.5$_a$	18.5$_b$	15.8$_a$	15.6$_a$	.05
Persistence	16.5$_a$	16.7$_a$	16.1$_a$	16.8$_a$	NS
Food adaptation	14.1$_a$	13.4$_a$	14.1$_a$	13.9$_a$	NS
Interaction rating	2.3$_a$	2.6$_b$	2.2$_a$	2.2$_a$	.05
Biochemical variables (ng/mL)					
Norepinephrine	245.3$_a$	119.7$_b$	195.0$_a$	180.0$_a$	.05
Epinephrine	21.5$_a$	10.6$_b$	16.0$_a$	23.6$_a$	.05
Serotonin (5-HIAA)	944.9$_a$	1,427.9$_b$	1,001.5$_a$	1,132.4$_a$	.05
Cortisol (urine)	1,382.9$_a$	656.4$_b$	1,225.4$_a$	1,016.8$_a$	.05

Note: Different letter subscripts (a's and b's) denote significant differences at *P*≤.05 revealed by post hoc comparisons. For emotionality, norepinephrine, epinephrine, and cortisol, lower values are optimal. For sociability, soothability, interaction rating, and serotonin, higher values are optimal.

Mood-Induction Interventions for Mothers

For the mothers, music therapy[27] and massage therapy[26] sessions were extremely effective short-term interventions. Chronically depressed adults have relative right frontal EEG activation that remains when their behavioral symptoms are in remission, suggesting that this pattern would be difficult to alter. However, after only 20 minutes of music (in this instance rock music), 10 out of the 12 depressed mothers showed an attenuation of right frontal EEG activation, moving towards symmetry or towards left frontal EEG activation (see Fig 2). The two adolescents whose EEG pattern did not change claimed that they did not enjoy the rock music. When their favorite music (classical) was played, they too experienced a shift toward symmetry.

Although it is not clear how prolonged these effects may be, it was surprising that the relative right frontal EEG activation, thought to be a marker of chronic depression, could be altered by only 20 minutes of music. Both types of therapy led to attenuated right frontal EEG activation.[26] These results were surprising, since EEG had been considered unalterable in adults and frontal EEG is a marker of chronic depression.[28] However, more recent PET data on blood flow suggest that frontal cortex activity might reflect a difference in mood state, while differences in the amygdala might reflect chronicity.

Fig 2. Attenuation of right frontal EEG activity during and following music mood induction.

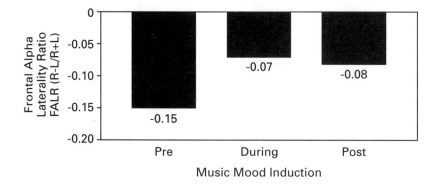

Interaction Coaching

Studies have shown that imitation and attention-getting instructions are effective in improving mothers' interaction behaviors. Mothers became more animated when trying to get their infants' attention, and more sensitive to their infants' signals when imitating them. The infants, in turn, became more responsive.[29] In a subsequent study, we noted that interventions were differentially effective with different (withdrawn/intrusive) depressed mothers.[30] Interventions were most effective when tailored to the mother's style; for example, using imitation with an intrusive mother was effective in "slowing her down."

Lifestyle Intervention Study

Mothers and infants were followed for their first 6 months to assess the infants' development and identify potential markers in the first 3 months that predicted chronic depression in the mothers.[14] The markers were then used to identify a second sample of chronically depressed mothers who received an intervention composed of social/educational/vocational rehabilitation, mood induction (including relaxation therapy, music mood induction, massage therapy, and interaction coaching), and daycare for their infants.

Although the intervention mothers continued to have higher depression scores than the nondepressed mothers, their interaction behavior became significantly more positive and their biochemical values and vagal tone normalized (or approximated the values of the nondepressed control group) (see Table 4). The infants in the intervention group also showed more positive interaction behavior, better growth, fewer pediatric complications, and normalized biochemical values; by 1 year, they had superior Bayley Mental and Motor scores. Thus, chronically depressed mothers could be identified and were offered a relatively cost-effective intervention that attenuated the typical delays in growth and development. Finally, although there was limited success in modifying depressed mothers' relatively flat facial and vocal expressions,[17] we were able to increase their touching behavior. This in turn improved the mothers' mood state and interaction behavior, as well as their infants' interaction behavior.[31]

Table 4. Six-month outcome variables following intervention[30]

	Groups			
	Depressed Control (n=40)	**Depressed Intervention (n=40)**	**Nondepressed Intervention (n=40)**	***P***
Maternal interview				
Beck Depression				
Inventory	13.0$_a$	10.9$_b$	6.5$_c$	.05
DISC dysthymia (%)	22.7$_a$	14.3$_b$	0.0$_c$	.05
Background stress	20.5$_a$	21.3$_a$	22.3$_a$	NS
Interaction ratings				
Mother	2.0$_a$	2.3$_b$	2.5$_b$	.01
Infant	2.0$_a$	2.4$_b$	2.5$_b$	.05
Interactions (% time)				
Mother negative	14.8$_a$	6.8$_b$	10.3$_b$	.05
Mother neutral	43.2$_a$	27.2$_b$	33.9$_b$	.01
Mother positive	41.9$_a$	66.1$_b$	55.6$_b$	.005
Infant negative	5.9$_a$	3.9$_b$	3.0$_b$	.05
Infant neutral	69.6$_a$	64.9$_a$	62.5$_b$	NS
Infant positive	21.6$_a$	31.2$_b$	34.5$_b$	.05
Infant physical measures				
Vagal tone	2.9$_a$	4.7$_b$	3.8$_b$	.05
Weight	8,048.9$_a$	9,211.0$_b$	11,982.7$_c$	.05
Length	67.2$_a$	67.1$_a$	67.9$_a$	NS
Head circumference	42.4$_a$	42.1$_a$	43.7$_a$	NS
Neurological	69.7$_a$	69.8$_a$	68.3$_a$	NS
Pediatric complications	101.5$_a$	109.4$_b$	119.1$_b$	.05

Note: Different letter subscripts denote significant differences between means.

Acknowledgments

We wish to thank the infants and parents who participated in these studies, as well as the research assistants who helped with the data collection. This research was supported by an NIMH Research Scientist Award (#MHOO331) to Tiffany Field. Please send reprint requests to Tiffany Field.

References

1. Field T. Infants of depressed mothers. *Development and Psychopathology.* 1992;4:49-66.

2. Field T, Fox N, Pickens J, et al. Right frontal EEG activation in 3- to 6-month-old infants of "depressed" mothers. *Developmental Psychology.* 1995;31:358-363.

3. Lundy BL, Jones N, Field T, et al. Prenatal depressive symptoms and neonatal outcome. Data on file, Touch Research Institutes.

4. Abrams SM, Field T, Scafidi F, Prodromidis M. Maternal "depression" effects on infants' Brazelton Scale performance. *Infant Mental Health Journal.* 1995;16:231-235.

5. Lundy BL, Field T, Cuadra A, et al. Mothers with depressive symptoms touching newborns. *Early Development and Parenting.* 1996;5:124-130.

6. Jones NA, Field T, Fox NA, et al. Newborns of depressed mothers are physiologically less developed. Data on file, Touch Research Institutes.

7. Jones N, Field T, Fox NA, et al. EEG asymmetry in one-month old infants of depressed mothers. *Development and Psychopathology.* 1997;9:491-505.

8. Jones NA, Field T, Fox NA, et al. EEG stability in infants/children of depressed mothers. *Child Psychiatry and Human Development.* 1997;28(2).

9. Field T, Pickens J, Fox N, et al. Facial expressions and EEG responses to happy and sad faces/voices by 3-month-old infants of depressed mothers. *British Journal of Developmental Psychology.* In press.

10. Pelaez-Nogueras M, Field T. Social referencing in infants of depressed mothers. Data on file, Touch Research Institutes.

11. Hart S, Field T, del Valle C. Depressed mothers' one-year old infants play less. Data on file, Touch Research Institutes.

12. Lundy BL, Field T, Pickens J. Newborns of mothers with depressive symptoms are less expressive. *Infant Behavior & Development.* 1997;19:419-424.

13. Sigman M, Parmelee A. Twelve-year follow-up of premature infants. Paper presented at the American Academy for the Advance of Sciences Meeting in San Francisco, January, 1989.

14. Field T, Pickens J, Prodromidis M, et al. Targeting depressed mothers and infants for early intervention. *Adolescence.* 1998. In press.

15. Field T, Pickens J, Fox N, et al. Vagal tone in infants of depressed mothers. *Development and Psychobiology.* 1995;7:227-231.

16. Jones NA, Field T, Davalos M. Massage attenuates right frontal EEG asymmetry in one-month-old infants of depressed mothers. Data on file, Touch Research Institutes.

17. Field T, Healy B, Goldstein S, et al. Infants of depressed mothers show "depressed" behavior even with non-depressed adults. *Child Development.* 1988;59:1569-1579.

18. Raag T, Maphurs J, Field T, et al. Moderately dysphoric mothers behave more positively with their infants after completing the BDI. *Infant Mental Health Journal.* 1997;18:161-172.

19. Pickens J, Field T. Facial expressivity in infants of "depressed" mothers. *Developmental Psychology.* 1993;29:986-988.

20. Pickens J, Field T. Responses to happy and sad face-voice stimuli by infants of depressed mothers. Data on file, Touch Research Institutes.

21. Hart S, Field T, DelValle C, Letourneau M. Infants protest their mothers' holding an infant-size doll. Data on file, Touch Research Institutes.

22. Field T, Lang C, Martinez A, et al. Preschool follow-up of infants of dysphoric mothers. *Journal of Clinical Child Psychology.* 1996;25:272-279.

23. Bendell D, Field T, Yando S, et al. "Depressed" mothers' perceptions of their preschool children's vulnerability. *Child Psychiatry and Human Development.* 1994;24:183-190.

24. Hossain Z, Field T, Pickens J, et al. Infants of depressed mothers interact better with their nondepressed fathers. *Infant Mental Health Journal.* 1994;15:348-357.

25. Pelaez-Nogueras M, Field T, Cigales M, et al. Infants of depressed mothers show less "depressed" behavior with their nursery teachers. *Infant Mental Health Journal.* 1995;15:358-367.

26. Field T, Grizzle N, Scafidi F, et al. Massage therapy for infants of depressed mothers. *Infant Behavior and Development.* 1996;19:107-112.

27. Field T, Martinez A, Nawrocki T, et al. Music shifts frontal EEG in depressed adolescents. *Adolescence.* 1997. In press.

28. Henriguez JB, Davidson RJ. Regional brain electrical asymmetries discriminate between previously depressed and healthy control subjects. *Journal of Abnormal Psychology.* 1990;99:22-31.

29. Pickens J, Field T. Attention-getting vs. imitation effects on depressed mother-infant interactions. *Infant Mental Health Journal.* 1993;14(3):171-181.

30. Malphurs J, Field T, Larrain CM, et al. Altering withdrawn and intrusive interaction behaviors of depressed mothers. *Infant Mental Health Journal.* 1996;17:152-160.

31. Pelaez-Nogueras M, Field T, Pickens J, et al. Depressed mothers' touching increases infants' positive affect and attention in still-face interactions. *Child Development.* 1996;67:1780-1792.

Section 5:
Communicating With Parents and Community Involvement

Abstracts From Section 5. Communication With Parents and Community Involvement

Teaching Parents About Infant Temperament

William B. Carey, MD

Parents need to understand temperament because it has an impact on their daily interactions with their children. The essential messages for parents should be that: temperamental traits are real; they are important for both child and parent; they are best managed by accommodation, not confrontation or attempts to change them. Parents can be reached at all professional contacts throughout childhood, including the newborn nursery, well-child visits, and when the child enters preschool or daycare.

Talking With Parents About Emotional Development

Matthew E. Melmed, JD

Parents play a central role in their children's emotional and overall development. In order to provide the most developmentally sound environment, professionals need to effectively communicate the fine points of research and clinical studies. This chapter details many strategies for reaching parents; perhaps the most important lessons are to be culturally sensitive, be positive, be relevant, and speak clearly.

International Perspectives in Early Emotional Development

Robert J. Haggerty, MD

This chapter provides a unique look at development – the lessons highly industrialized nations can learn from the rest of the world. Thailand, for example, created a comprehensive child development program through integration of health, education, economic development, social welfare, and community involvement. The program was proven to improve developmental outcomes that included IQ and nutritional status.

Teaching Parents About Infant Temperament

William B. Carey, MD

Introduction

Primary care physicians, whether pediatricians or family doctors, can play a major role in the positive mental health of their patient families. An essential part of this process is teaching parents about their children's temperaments.

Why Teach Parents?

Information on Temperament Is Essential

Primary care professionals should make a special effort to impart information on temperament to parents because of its impact on parents, their children, and the daily interactions between them. This teaching should be expanded and enriched as basic education for child rearing.

To Combat the Prevalent Misinformation

This education is also necessary to combat misinformation about child development that still clouds the diagnostic and therapeutic thinking both of professionals and parents. We have generally escaped from the radical environmentalism of the 1930s and 1940s, the one-sided view that claimed that all behavioral development, for better or worse, is the result of the direct impression of the environment on the blank slate of the child. That model clearly has not fit with the accumulating experience of most seasoned observers. Meanwhile, however, the 1980s and 1990s have seen a popular swing to the opposite extreme of blaming a great deal of behavioral problems on some putative abnormalities of the child's central nervous system (CNS), in particular on a widely diagnosed condition called attention-deficit/hyperactivity disorder. This highly problematic diagnostic term has become the dumping ground for a great variety of childhood behavioral concerns, the majority of which have no demonstrated evidence or even reasonable suspicion of the assumed CNS malfunction.

With the prevailing fashion of ascribing behavioral concerns to either a noxious environment or a disabled nervous system, little or no room is left for the important role of the child's temperament. Proponents of those two extreme views have attempted to dispose of these normal variations in several ways. One tactic has been to maintain that these traits do not exist at all but are merely the "perceptions" of distraught mothers. This argument was highly popular in the 1970s and 1980s but is heard less frequently today. Others have argued that, even if there were such a phenomenon as temperament, parents are too emotionally involved to report on it accurately. Still others have promoted the contention that it does not matter whether parents or others rate it adequately or not, because temperament is insignificant anyway. One eminent child psychiatrist told me about 10 years ago that it is all right for nurses and pediatricians to play around with the idea of temperament, but that no reputable mental health expert should take it seriously. On the other hand, of equal disservice to parents and children is the current error of attempting to eliminate temperament differences by pathologizing them. That is, to recognize them but to attribute them to either parental mismanagement or CNS abnormalities in the child. Thus, misunderstandings and misinterpretations of temperament have been rampant.

Parents May Not Learn Otherwise

In view of the great importance of temperament differences and the distressing amount of misinformation about them in both professional and popular circles, the need for accurate education of parents is enormous. Without a well-conceived and vigorously executed plan of instruction, the parents of today will continue to face their challenging task without the valuable knowledge that is available to help them; instead they will be burdened by a deadening weight of popular but unsubstantiated theories.

These are the reasons we should teach parents about temperament. Herein I offer suggestions about topics professionals should discuss with parents, and some thoughts as to when, where, how, and by whom this vital service can be accomplished.

What to Teach?

The essential message of a temperament-education program for parents should be that these traits are real; that they matter extensively for parents and children; and that they can be managed by accommodation, but not by confrontation or trying to change them.

The most practical definition calls temperament "behavioral style," the "how" of behavior, or the characteristic way that the individual experiences and responds to the internal and external environment.[1] Therefore, it has components of both emotion and behavior, and both must be described here. While mood and intensity are predominantly emotional dimensions, others, such as activity, persistence, and adaptability, are best understood as observable behavioral reactions.

Temperament Is Real

Despite popular misinformation to the contrary, temperament differences in children are real. The research evidence is abundant, and the clinical and personal experience of every observant professional should leave no doubt that these differences are not merely the imaginings of overstressed mothers. The only basic controversies in describing temperament are how best to divide this indivisible phenomenon into several dimensions and whether clusters or single traits are more descriptive. A full review of these matters is beyond the scope of this paper but is readily available elsewhere.[2-4] That these phenomena are variously viewed now, and may be regarded differently in years to come, in no way diminishes the basic fact that temperament exists.

My personal preference has been for the nine dimensions of Thomas and Chess and their New York Longitudinal Study because of their uniquely clinical derivation and their record of widespread practical use. They are: activity, regularity, initial approach/withdrawal, adaptability, intensity, mood, persistence/attention span, distractibility, and sensory threshold.[1,3] Although some researchers and clinicians like to use the New York Longitudinal Study clusters of difficult, easy, and slow-to-warm-up, for me considering the nine characteristics separately has proven to be more informative and more clinically valuable.

About half of temperament has a genetic origin, with the remaining half still awaiting attribution to the other possible sources of the psychosocial environment, the nonhuman environment, and the child's physical condition. The stability of temperament appears to be low in the early days and weeks of life but increases by 2 to 3 years and becomes stronger at least into middle childhood.

Temperament Matters

Not only are temperament differences real, but they matter considerably for parents and children. The child's behavioral style affects both the way parents feel about themselves and the way they function as parents. For example, agreeable, flexible infants are likely to make their parents feel happy, competent, and successful. Irritable, inflexible infants, on the other hand, have been shown to influence adversely their parents' self-esteem, satisfaction as parents, marital harmony, mood, and decisions about when to return to work. Similarly, the way parents function in their role as caregivers, in supplying the physical, developmental-behavioral, and socialization needs of their children, is clearly altered by the kind of child they were given to work with. Some children are far harder, and others far easier, to protect, stimulate, guide, love, and socialize.

Children's temperament differences matter for themselves in practically every aspect of their life adjustment. Some physical problems, such as accidents and abuse, are more likely to occur to certain types of children. The outcome of many illnesses is affected by the child's response to the stress the illness has induced. The rate of developmental progress is to a small but significant degree accelerated or delayed by temperament differences. A "poor fit" between the child's temperament and the values and expectations of the caregivers is one of the commonest sources of parent-child interactional distress and of reactive behavior problems in children. Several traits, including persistence/attention span and adaptability, will be of major importance for scholastic achievement as soon as the child starts school.

Thus, children's temperament matters in a multitude of ways for the parents, the children, and the interactions between them. These effects are all part of our current knowledge and should be included in any program of education of parents.

How to Handle Temperament

The third component of a temperament education program is how to handle it. Once identified, temperament differences should be accommodated to minimize unnecessary stresses without making concessions to the necessary goals of child rearing. Denying that temperament exists is doomed to failure. Trying to work against it will only generate more stress and make matters worse. Attempting to change it, at least in infants, should be avoided. Perhaps irregular sleeping or eating patterns can gradually be encouraged to be more rhythmical, but little else seems possible at present. As children grow older, into the preschool and school periods, they will often learn how to moderate temperamental traits that are disruptive for harmonious human relationships. These alterations include diminishing the intensity of expressed feelings or curbing the impulse to withdraw from new social contacts. In the infancy period, however, recognition of the temperament pattern and accommodating it to make a better fit are the main lessons for parents to learn. Although the basic information needed by parents may be extensive, it is readily available in publications through a library or bookstore.[5-8]

Teaching: When, Where, and by Whom?

When and where should parents learn about temperament, and who should teach them? The simple answer is that all professional contacts throughout childhood should have appropriate components of understanding and mastery of this kind of anticipatory guidance.

Newborn Nursery – Learning to Individualize Care

Prenatal visits serve mainly to begin the doctor-parent relationship, and generally are not concerned with issues of infant behavior. In the newborn nursery, however, there is a real baby, and discussions of infant states and traits are no longer just theoretical.

Contemporary research has demonstrated considerable variation in newborn reactivity, and tests such as the Newborn Behavioral Assessment Scale (NBAS) and its derivatives have made it possible to document them. Whether determined by a formal test such as the NBAS or by the skilled observations of experienced pediatric nurses or physicians, the particular pattern of infant behavior revealed by the newborn can be identified and demonstrated to the parents and its optimal management discussed. Although the postpartum hospital stay has been greatly curtailed by the cost-cutting measures of managed care, it is still possible to initiate parents into the process of "reading" their baby's needs. This involves observing carefully how the infant functions and responds to various stimuli, estimating what these clues tell about the infant's state and needs, and then providing the most suitable care. Although current research indicates that behavioral differences in newborn infants have little correlation with behaviors a few weeks later, it is important for parents to develop skill in understanding their child's behavioral cues.

Well-child Visits – Facilitating Early Adaptation

In most industrialized nations, infants are taken to health-maintenance visits with a pediatrician, family doctor, or nurse. During these encounters a multitude of concerns are covered, including feeding, growth, development, behavior, illness, and immunizations. In addition to directing parents to pertinent literature on temperament, primary medical caregivers can themselves provide information and practical examples of how temperament matters. For example, some infants are more irritable, cry louder and longer, and are less soothable than others. Some infants do not get hungry regularly nor like to try new foods. Predictable sleep patterns are not easily established in some but seem to come naturally to others. Available books do cover these issues, but nothing teaches as well as a knowledgeable clinician, especially when pointing out that a specific behavior is probably evidence of the child's temperament – something that can be accommodated by the parents, but cannot easily be changed.

Day-care – An Adjustment Challenge but a Chance for Independent Observations

These days, many children begin day-care outside the home when they are still infants. The temperament of some will result in a rapid and smooth transition from the home to the new environment, while for others it becomes a transient obstacle to the challenge of adaptation. These variations in response should be recognized for what they are, differences in reactive style, and not simply evidence of the quality of the child's prior life experience or of the skill of the day-care workers.

These issues aside, the placement of the infant in day-care can have a valuable educational function for the parents. Outside observers, who watch the infant during the day, may be able to give the parents some perspective on their child. Well-trained and experienced workers are in a position to support or modify the impressions parents may have formed about the individual style of their child. However, unskilled workers can be a confusing or even harmful source of misinformation, such as when one of them told the parents of a bright and inquisitive but somewhat timid 3-year-old girl that she was "not curious," because she did not rapidly enter a new play activity.

Differentiating Temperament, Behavioral Disorders, and Misperceptions

As children pass through infancy and into early childhood, their parents and outside caregivers frequently develop concerns about the normality of their behavior. Dealing with these situations is a particularly rich opportunity for teaching parents about temperament.

Temperament itself. When an infant displays traits such as persistence, sensitivity, timidity, low adaptability, high activity, irregularity, irritability, low soothability, or any of the other common variations, we should help the parents identify the behavior as temperament and not misread it as something abnormal. We should not be surprised that this confusion is so common, given the prevalence of the current practice of ascribing normal behavioral traits to poor parental management or to a disabled CNS. This kind of parent education is probably the greatest unexploited opportunity to improve mental health services in current primary care. A relatively brief supplement to professional education concerning these matters could initiate a shift in this direction and make a profound difference in the quality of medical care.

Behavioral problems or disorders. Dysfunctional behavior can come from any one or a combination of three main sources: noxious environments, intrinsic abnormalities such as learning disabilities, or a "poor fit" between the normal temperament of the child and his environment.

Recognizing that a behavioral disturbance involves the child's temperament can help the clinician and parents understand why the child reacted to a situation that may have left other children unperturbed, and it aids in setting realistic goals for intervention efforts. An effective solution reduces unnecessary conflict and stress in the parent-child interaction. An improved fit between infant and environment allows the reactive problem to diminish and disappear. Because the child's temperamental predisposition cannot be altered, however, a second step is necessary: learning from the experience – about the child's temperament, the role it has played in the current disturbance, and the possibility that it might do so again in the future.

For example, in colic there is usually nothing wrong with either the infant's physical condition or the parents' emotional state but rather a mismatch between a sensitive, irritable infant and parental handling that is not yet sufficiently tuned in to the infant's specific needs. Successful management improves the fit, reduces excessive crying, and educates the parents about the infant's temperament. Failure to learn from the experience frequently leads to sleep disturbances in the second 6 months of life.

Misperception. Behavioral concerns also arise from parental misperceptions. A parent may regard a normally active child as "hyperactive" or an average toddler as "stubborn" either from misunderstanding or because the parent's own problems deprive him or her of reasonable judgment. This situation calls for supplying information about normal child development or professional help for the parent. Harmonious parent-child relations will be enhanced by assisting the family to establish a clearer, more objective view of the child's actual temperament profile.

Physical Problems – Predispositions and Influence on Outcomes

Primary healthcare physicians for children spend about half of their time dealing with minor illnesses, but few seem to have recognized what a golden opportunity this affords for teaching parents about temperament. Temperament plays a significant part in the causation of some physical problems and can be a powerful element in the outcome of others.

There is a clear contribution of temperament in such widely diverse conditions as accidents, abuse, failure to thrive, obesity, and recurrent abdominal pains and headaches. How do we use this information? For example, if a temperamentally irritable and intense infant is becoming overweight because the parents are feeding him every time he cries, a reasonable intervention would consist of recognizing the aversive behavioral pattern, understanding it, and learning to deal with it by means other than excessive feedings. Similar steps can be taken in comparable situations to help the parents avoid destructive interaction patterns that will damage their children's health, such as respecting a child's timidity when it is a factor in recurrent abdominal pain.

The way an infant or child responds to the stress and discomfort of an illness, regardless of its cause, affects the way parents and medical personnel rally to the child's care. The attention provided is likely to reflect not just the illness itself but also parental and professional impressions of the severity based to some extent on the child's reactive behavior. It is easy to be persuaded that an infant who screams loudly and for a long time with an ear infection is worse off than the one who mildly, briefly, and patiently responds to the pain. Yet, the severity of the ear infection often bears little relationship to the amount of complaining. We cannot doubt that infants and children who complain more forcefully will probably get their parents' attention sooner and come to medical care more rapidly and more often. When parents and the child's physician consider the reaction pattern of the infant in the diagnosis and plan of care, the overall management should be better able to avoid the extremes of too much and too little attention and arrive at the more appropriate intermediate level.

Preschool and School Performance – An Underappreciated Area of Temperament Effects

A discussion of temperament in preschool and elementary school is beyond the scope of this paper. Nevertheless, several temperamental traits, particularly persistence/attention span and adaptability, have been shown to have a major impact on scholastic achievement in elementary school as measured by standardized tests even after factoring out IQ scores. This information is discussed in greater detail elsewhere.[2,4] When studies are performed to evaluate task performance in the second year of life, a similar relationship is likely to be revealed. Persistence gets things done at all ages. Parents usually recognize this fact, but in toddlers they may be more impressed by their persistence at forbidden than at approved activities.

Reactions to Crises – Partially Shaped by Temperament

At all ages, children are confronted by a variety of crises, such as sibling birth and parental separation and divorce. In the first years of life, their reactions tend to be primarily regression in development and disruption of physiological functions such as sleep and eating rather than the open expression of feelings seen in older children. Explanations of these reactions usually emphasize the importance of the nature and degree of exposure to the traumatic event; the quantity and quality of parental support; and the age and gender of the affected child.

Unfortunately, the contribution of the child's temperament has been largely overlooked in discussions of crisis reactions. The quality and magnitude of the child's response may be as strongly affected by preexisting temperament as by parental support, age, gender, or other factors. A convincing available example is that the reaction to a younger sibling's birth is better predicted by existing temperament than by the preparations by the parents or the timing of the birth. Clinicians can help parents anticipate and understand these reactions by taking temperament into consideration.

Methods of Teaching Parents

Three clear opportunities exist for clinicians to teach parents about children's temperament:

- **Anticipatory guidance.** General discussions about temperament can occur at various times when parental knowledge needs to be augmented. These discussions can be supplemented by various available resources (see resources list).

- **When specific advice is needed.** On some occasions, general discussions are not enough, and parents need to know the child's individual temperament profile and receive specific advice based on that. This step is indicated when parents or other caregivers are concerned about the child's behavior, whether or not evidence of a dysfunctional reaction has emerged. The aim is to clarify the contribution of the child to the troublesome interaction. Parent-child interactions can be understood and handled better by parents and professionals who gain this perspective.

  Perhaps the best way of developing such a profile is by using one of the standardized questionnaires for parents or teachers (see resources list). No convincing case has been made, however, for routine testing of all children with these scales or any others at any fixed point by physicians or teachers. For routine use or with lesser degrees of concern, sufficient data can be obtained by brief but appropriately focused parent interviews.

- **When a functional disturbance has developed.** In this instance, knowledge of the child's contribution can be helpful in resolving the problem.

Who Teaches Parents? – The Strategic Position of Physicians in Infancy

Healthcare planners agree that parents should take their infants and children to some sort of well-child checkups or health maintenance visits. During the course of nine recommended encounters in the first 2 years, the parent and child meet with the physician, nurse, and support staff. These medical personnel are thus in a unique position to talk about infant temperament. (Professional caregivers may also be able to contribute.) Mental health professionals like psychologists and psychiatrists, and even social workers, generally have little contact with parents during the first 2 years of the child's life and, therefore, minimal opportunity to educate parents.

One must question how well this function is being carried out by medical personnel presently given this opportunity. The opportunity is probably being squandered by professionals who do not cherish this part of their calling or who, although interested, have not acquired sufficient knowledge themselves to be effective at the job. The most obvious solution is to broaden greatly the education of physicians and nurses at the graduate, postgraduate, and continuing medical education levels.

Parent education is not limited to that which is taught face-to-face by professionals. It can be accomplished largely through an array of self-teaching mechanisms: books, tapes, and self-help groups. The ever-growing Internet has started to dispense some pertinent information in this area, but quality controls are completely lacking. Professionals can help parents select material that is scientifically reliable and avoid the well-intentioned speculation of self-appointed experts.

Summary and Conclusions

Parents need to learn more about children's temperament. Understanding temperament is important for optimal growth and development, but parents are exposed to a great deal of conflicting misinformation.

The major lessons about temperament are these:

- Inborn differences in behavioral style are real

- These differences matter to parents and children in a multitude of ways

- They are best managed by accommodation to reduce unnecessary stress rather than by working against them

Informed professionals can provide parents much-needed instruction about temperament. In the first 2 years of life a variety of opportunities exist for pediatricians and other medical professionals to reach parents. Unfortunately, these opportunities are often underutilized.

Clinicians who revise their diagnostic and therapeutic practices to include dealing with temperament and teaching parents will undoubtedly feel a marked increase in intellectual stimulation and professional satisfaction.

Resources for Teaching Parents

For books, please review the Reference section.

Professionals

Temperament Measurement Techniques

- Parent-report questionnaires (Both sources provide the same scales and offer manual and computer scoring methods.)

    a) Behavioral/Developmental Initiatives, Suite 131, 1316 West Chester Pike, West Chester, PA 19382-6425. Tel: 800-BDI-8303; Fax: 610-296-1325; e-mail: 74261.444@compuserve.com.

    b) Behavioral/Developmental Initiatives, Suite 104, 13802 North Scottsdale Road, Scottsdale, AZ 85254. Tel: 800-405-2313; Fax: 602-494-2688; e-mail: bdi@primenet.com.

- Teacher-report questionnaires

    Pro-Ed Publishers, 8700 Shoal Creek Boulevard, Austin, TX 78757 Tel: 512-451-3246

Parents

Videotapes

- California Department of Education: *Flexible, Fearful, or Feisty: The Temperaments of Infants and Toddlers.* PO Box 944272, Sacramento, CA 94244-2720

- Kaiser-Permanente Health Plan, Audio-Visual Department, 1950 Franklin Street, Oakland, CA 94612. A series of four tapes on infant temperament.

Information on How to Start Self-Help Groups

- Center for Human Development, Temperament Program, 1100 K Avenue, LaGrande, OR 97850

- Kurcinka MS. *Raising Your Child Workbook.* New York, NY: Harper Collins; 1998.

- The Temperament Project c/o Variety Child Development Centre, 9460 140th Street, Surrey, British Columbia, V3V 5Z4, Canada

- Web Site: http://www.b-di.com

References

1. Chess S, Thomas A. *Temperament in Clinical Practice*. New York, NY: Guilford; 1986.
2. Carey WB, McDevitt SC. *Coping With Children's Temperament. A Guide for Professionals*. New York, NY: Basic Books; 1995.
3. Chess S, Thomas A. *Temperament: Theory and Practice*. New York, NY: Brunner/Mazel; 1996.
4. Kohnstamm GA, Bates JE, Rothbart MK, eds. *Temperament in Childhood*. New York, NY: Wiley; 1989.
*5. Carey WB, Jablow MM. *Understanding Your Child's Temperament*. New York, NY: Macmillan; 1997.
*6. Chess S, Thomas A. *Know Your Child*. New York, NY: Basic Books; 1987. Republished: New Brunswick, NJ: Jason Aronson; 1996.
*7. Kurcinka MS. *Raising Your Spirited Child*. New York, NY: HarperCollins; 1991. Reissued 1998.
*8. Turecki S, Tonner L. *The Difficult Child*. New York, NY: Bantam Books; Revised 1989.

* Recommended for parents.

Talking With Parents About Emotional Development

Matthew E. Melmed, JD

Introduction

Parents play a central, critical role in influencing young children's emotional and overall development. Clearly, researchers and clinicians who wish to promote children's healthy emotional development have a stake in conveying their scientific and practical wisdom to parents. This paper will address how we can do that effectively – how scientists and professional practitioners can talk *with* parents in ways they can understand, and how to use our knowledge to effect better outcomes for young children.

Special Significance of Parent Audiences

For this discussion, let us accept that positive emotional developmental outcomes for young children depend greatly on parents. We know that parents have the motivation and the opportunity – through a continuing, intense emotional relationship and through their influence on the child's environment – to shape children's development. They are also often the first to sense that a problem may exist, and they are key figures in addressing such problems whether through changes in their interactions, through professional intervention, or both. By changing parents' knowledge and attitudes, building their self-confidence, and guiding their child-rearing behaviors, one can have a major impact on children's emotional and overall developmental outcomes.[1-7]

The Social Context for Infants and Toddlers

We all understand that parenting is an enormously tough job. Today more than ever, parents from all walks of life need educational and emotional support – of varying kinds and degrees – to do it well. Many professionals have found creative, effective ways to translate their research and clinical knowledge into meaningful educational and emotional support for parents –

through one-on-one clinical work, community-based services, and print and broadcast media.

Still, the task of successful parenting appears daunting, especially when one thinks about families with infants and toddlers who are confronting multiple risks to their children's healthy development. Over the past generation, there has been a steady rise in conditions that potentially undermine the ability of parents from all walks of life to provide the responsive, nurturing care that is the foundation for healthy emotional development. Today's families are more likely to have less time with their babies and toddlers, to be struggling to make ends meet, or to lack access to trusted sources of personalized support and information for parenting. Confounding these problems are changes in family structure, increased rates of divorce and teenage pregnancy, maternal depression, and the horrors of child abuse and neglect.

Although national statistics tell us something about the emotional environment of infants and toddlers, major aspects of the lives of young children are sparsely sampled or ignored altogether in data gathering by the government. This is especially true with regard to parental knowledge and attitudes about the early years. That is why my organization, ZERO TO THREE: National Center for Infants, Toddlers and Families, earlier this year commissioned a national research study among parents of children under 3 years of age to determine what parents know and believe about early childhood development, where they go for information and support, and how receptive they are to new information on child development.

Results of Field Research on Parents' Knowledge and Attitudes

Our intent was to obtain information that could help create a strategic communication campaign targeting parents. Experts tell us that to be successful, mass communications must be tailored to the beliefs and concerns of one's target audience.[8] Consequently, if professionals want to talk to parents of young children, we must first discover how to reach parents "where they are" in terms of their present knowledge and attitudes about early development and child rearing.

Parents are a comparatively new audience for ZERO TO THREE's communications efforts, which for 20 years have focused primarily on professionals from various disciplines concerned with infant/family health and development. In 1996, our board of directors recognized that with the broad array of new knowledge emanating from many fields and growing national attention to the "zero-to-three" age group, there was a tremendous opportunity to capture parents' interest and a clear role for ZERO TO THREE in coordinating, translating, and communicating research and practice-based knowledge to parents in ways that would bolster their child-rearing efforts.

Our research began with a series of eight focus groups held in four cities, with mothers and fathers from a broad range of ages, incomes, and educational backgrounds. These focus groups yielded key insights into parents' knowledge and concerns and helped shape the development of a national poll of more than 1,000 parents, designed to quantify these findings. ZERO TO THREE hired the market research firm of Peter D. Hart Research Associates to conduct an in-depth telephone survey among a representative nationwide sample of mothers, fathers, and legal guardians of children aged 3 years and younger. The survey included supplemental "oversample" interviews of African-Americans and Latinos, which were then weighted back into the sample in their proper proportions according to U.S. Census figures. The survey, conducted in Spring 1997, was funded by the Teresa & H. John Heinz III Foundation and has a margin of error ±3.5%.

Chief Findings

ZERO TO THREE's survey and focus groups confirm that *parents of young children today face daunting challenges and pressures* and offer us important insights into the nature and extent of their needs for information and support. A review of some of our main research findings which suggest barriers and opportunities for effective communication with parents follows.

Parents' Information Deficit

A chief finding of the survey is that most parents' knowledge of child development is limited. This significant information deficit emerged as a fundamental barrier to better parenting for many. Although parents recognize that they have an important influence on their infants' and toddlers' overall development, they do not fully understand how specific parenting practices shape their children's social, emotional, and intellectual development.

Most parents grasp certain fundamental concepts about early child development – for instance, that babies are learning from the moment they are born, that babies are communicating before they use words, and that what a child experiences from birth to age 3 can influence his or her ability to do well in school. Many parents, however, are confused or hold misconceptions about other important concepts. For example, many parents did not know that:

- **Parents' and caregivers' interactions with babies and toddlers can influence children's intellectual abilities.** One in four parents thought babies are born with set levels of intelligence, which cannot be increased or decreased by how parents interact with them. Focus group participants shared this belief that intellect is virtually all nature, rather than nurture, referring to the level of intelligence a child can achieve with such terms as "hard-wired" and "innate ability."

- **Stimulation isn't always good for babies.** Eighty-seven percent of parents thought that the more stimulation a baby receives, the better off he or she is. This is of particular concern given that all the attention on early brain development may make some parents feel driven to do more to stimulate their babies' brain development.

- **Too many changes in caregivers can have a negative impact on a child's development.** Half of all parents surveyed thought that the more caregivers a child has before age 3, the better that child will be at adapting and coping with change. This also held true in focus groups, where we saw that the suggestion that consistency or limited numbers of caregivers was a "hot button" issue that made some parents – particularly those with multiple childcare arrangements – uncomfortable, guilty, or nervous. A mother in a Boston focus group stated this plainly: "I hope [having a limited number of caregivers is] not that important, because my child's on her third. Just don't tell me I'm wrong." In fact, we found that differences in how parents perceive children's exposure to multiple caregivers may need to be reframed as a cultural difference rather than lack of knowledge, per se.

Although parents believe they have the most influence on a young child's *emotional development* (which was defined in the survey as "the ways he/she expresses moods and feelings like contentment, happiness, sadness, or fear"), they say they know least about this domain of development. Parents also report that they do not fully understand how to tell if their children's social, emotional, and intellectual development is on track. For example, as shown in Fig 1:

- Only 38% feel totally sure they can tell if their children's *emotional* development is healthy and about right for their age.

- 37% feel this way about milestones of *social* development.

- 44% feel they can tell if *intellectual* development is on track.

Fig 1. Parents' response to the question:

How sure do you feel that you know how to tell if your child's development is healthy and about right for his/her age?
(% who feel totally sure)

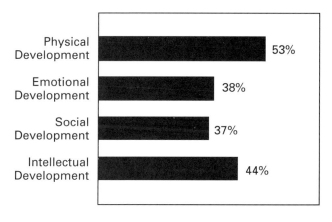

Ref: ZERO TO THREE, Key findings from a Nationwide Survey Among Parents of Zero-to-Three Year-Olds. Washington, DC: ZERO TO THREE and Peter D. Hart Research Associates; 1997.

Challenges of Parenthood

As these information gaps suggest, new parenthood is a time of learning, self-doubt, and worry, as well as of joy and wonderment. A majority of parents struggle to fulfill conflicting demands and obligations of work and family and to live up to the high expectations they have set for themselves. Although many parents are basically confident in their abilities and view themselves as generally good parents, they also have many questions and concerns about child development and parenting practices, as shown in Figs 2 and 3.

- Just 8% rated themselves as "outstanding" and say they do not feel a need to improve; all others indicate that they would like to improve their parenting performance.

- Close to half (45%) said they definitely want to improve in several areas. Chief among these is the "time crunch" they face in trying to be available for their young children.

- Almost two in five parents (37%) cited not spending enough quality time with their children as a main reason they feel they may need to improve as parents.

- Fully half of all parents said they end most days feeling that they spent less time than they wanted to with their young children – whether a lot (20%) or a little (27%).

Although parents seem well aware of the importance of the love and time they give their infants and toddlers, they feel that they need to do a better job of understanding and responding to their children. For example, parents felt they needed to improve because they:

- Find it hard to understand their children's feelings and needs (19%)

- Do not know how to handle difficult situations with their child (19%)

- Lack confidence in their overall parenting skills (10%)

Fig 2. Parents' response to the question:

How would you rate yourself as a parent so far?

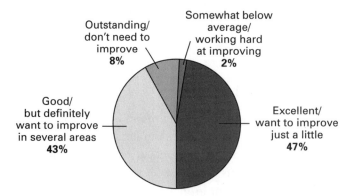

Only a handful of parents feel they have no need to improve –
Most parents feel good about themselves as parents,
but want to improve in key areas.

Ref: ZERO TO THREE, Key findings from a Nationwide Survey Among Parents of Zero-to-Three Year-Olds. Washington, DC: ZERO TO THREE and Peter D. Hart Research Associates; 1997.

Fig 3. Areas in which parents feel the need to improve.

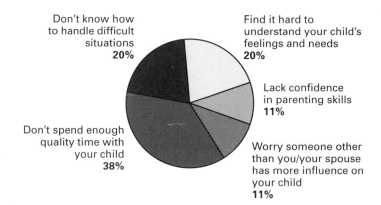

Don't know how
to handle difficult
situations
20%

Find it hard to
understand your child's
feelings and needs
20%

Lack confidence
in parenting skills
11%

Don't spend enough
quality time with
your child
38%

Worry someone other
than you/your spouse
has more influence on
your child
11%

Ref: ZERO TO THREE, Key findings from a Nationwide Survey Among Parents of Zero-to-Three Year-Olds. Washington, DC: ZERO TO THREE and Peter D. Hart Research Associates; 1997.

Parents' desires to obtain information on how they can best support their children's development are strongest *before* their first child is born. A majority (70%) of respondents said they did at least a moderate amount of work to get ready for their first experience as parents – either by reading, or talking to others to get information or advice.

Parents are more likely to seek information very early in their children's lives (from birth to 8 months) than later. This suggests that it is important to get information on child development to new – and expectant – parents as early as possible. Our focus groups confirmed that parents are more receptive to guidance before they have children or when their babies are very young, because they feel that they are learning about child development *on the job,* through their parenting experiences.

By reaching parents early, one avoids provoking guilt or anxiety among parents whose children are past 2 or 3 years old, who may perceive messages that emphasize the critical importance of development in the first 3 years of life as telling them that it is too late to enhance their children's development. As one mother in a Richmond, Virginia focus group put it, "I feel that … when she was born I was just so new at everything, and I'm hoping I get better and better day by day, month by month, and year by year. It scares me to death thinking that in a year, that's it, my time is up."

Parental Socioeconomic Differences

Parental attitudes and actions regarding advance preparations varied greatly according to socioeconomic status, with low-income parents reporting having done less advance preparation than did other parents. Thirty percent of low-income parents said they basically just wanted to "see what it was like" first. This is in striking contrast to 18% of parents overall who chose to "wait and see."

Despite these advance efforts, relatively few parents of young children say they felt totally prepared for parenthood when they had their first children. Those who felt least prepared included younger parents, lower-income parents, and single parents. Low-income and single parents also are more likely than others to have felt that they lacked emotional support.

These data are important, because our survey found that preparation is correlated with a positive parenting experience. Those who begin parenthood thinking they are ill-prepared are far more likely than those who think they are well-prepared to feel

- stressed and worn out (59% of less-prepared vs 31% of well-prepared parents)

- afraid of doing something wrong (48% vs 27%)

- afraid of not being good parents (43% vs 23%)

- unsure about what to do a lot of the time (39% vs 18%)

Sources of Parent Information and Support

Parents of infants and toddlers seem thirsty for information and advice on how to understand and respond to their own children's unique needs, changes, and behaviors, and to promote their emotional, intellectual, and social development. Parents can be overwhelmed by the sheer volume of questions that arise in their day-to-day lives, since, as one mother in a Boston focus group put it, "Babies don't have instructions."

When parents of young children seek information or advice on children and parenting, they tend to rely on informal networks. Even in these days of geographic mobility and long distances between family members, parents turn most frequently to their own families, as shown in Figs 4 and 5.

- Two in five say they call their mothers or mothers-in-law, and about the same proportion seek other relatives' help.

- Friends and neighbors are a source of help for one in five parents of infants and toddlers.

   This underscores the fact that parents place greatest value on information that is provided in the context of a familiar relationship.

Beyond the realm of family and friends, pediatricians are the professionals that parents consult most (15%) when they feel they need advice. The news media are also an important source of supplemental information on infants, toddlers, and parenting: Nearly half (46%) of all parents indicate that they pay significant attention to newspaper articles and news reports on these topics; 36% look for information in magazines; and 39% pick up literature in their pediatricians' offices on a regular basis.

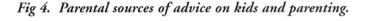

Fig 4. Parental sources of advice on kids and parenting.

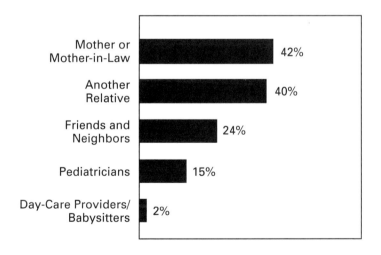

Ref: ZERO TO THREE, Key findings from a Nationwide Survey Among Parents of Zero-to-Three Year-Olds. Washington, DC: ZERO TO THREE and Peter D. Hart Research Associates; 1997.

Fig 5. Other sources of parent information.

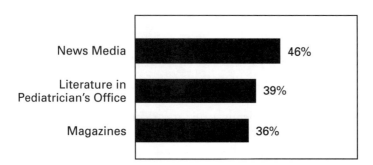

Ref: ZERO TO THREE, Key findings from a Nationwide Survey Among Parents of Zero-to-Three Year-Olds. Washington, DC: ZERO TO THREE and Peter D. Hart Research Associates; 1997.

Indeed, concern for the serious problems facing families has prompted an explosion of information and advice about child-rearing in mass media. Child-development and parenting education has become an increasingly prominent topic in print media and for initiatives within electronic media – including public, cable, and network television, as well as the Internet. Today's parents, who are time-pressed, isolated from other information sources, and well-accustomed to acquiring information via "sound bites," are increasingly likely to look to the media as a parenting resource.[8]

Relevance of Findings for Scientists and Professionals

Our data clearly demonstrate that many parents today lack vital information and support for their child-rearing efforts. This heightened need crosses lines of culture, race, ethnicity, and socioeconomic status. Who can know with certainty how to ensure that their children will survive and thrive in the 21st century? Who knows how to give young children a solid foundation in their own family and community values (which, these days, may represent an amalgam of several traditions) while preparing them to function in wider worlds? Though some parents may assert that "the way my parents raised me is good enough for my kids," many other parents – and grandparents – wonder what lessons from the past remain useful in an anxious new world.

Role of Mass Media and Experts

In their search for answers, parents turn in part to mass media sources and to "expert opinion." The widespread availability and influence of mass media communications channels present the scientific/professional community with a great opportunity to reach and inform parents, as well as a strong imperative to do so in a proactive, strategic way.

First, the opportunity. Researchers have found that knowledge of child development can significantly influence parents' interaction with children and children's cognitive development.[9,10] Mass media gives us the ability to reach enormous numbers of parents. A recent study of parenting education and the media found that almost every parent is exposed to printed information about parenting, and many are repeatedly exposed. The ubiquity of television is well documented. Media experts who track the children's Internet market project that the number of families with Internet access will almost triple by the year 2002, to 55%.[8]

We also know (from theory, research, and professional opinion) that information conveyed via mass media can and does have a significant impact on parents' attitudes and parenting behaviors and hence also on child outcomes.[8] Stern points out that today, the media provide powerful representations of who the baby and mother are and ideally ought to be, and what constitutes competence, age appropriateness, and so on.[11]

Second, the imperative. Given that so much information about early childhood development and parenting is being disseminated via various mass media, professionals from all disciplines who work with infants, toddlers, and families have a responsibility to engage with researchers **and** with the media concerning communications to families and front-line caregivers.

Parents' responses to our survey and focus group questions pose several key challenges that members of the scientific and professional communities must address to be most effective when talking about early childhood development and parenting.

Parents say they want simple, concrete messages but complain that parenting "tips" don't fit their own babies and circumstances.

What kind of information do parents want and need? ZERO TO THREE's research found that parents have many uncertainties about how they can promote healthy emotional, social, and intellectual development. To address this gap, parents first need clear explanations of what scientists understand about typical development in the earliest years of life. Rather than using complex terminology which parents report is an immediate "turn-off," our descriptions must depict the story of development using concrete examples drawn from everyday experiences and behaviors. This story must make clear the interplay between nature and nurture – and particularly help parents to understand the powerful influence their own actions and reactions have on their children's growth and development (eg, When you talk with your baby, you help her... When you share in your baby's excitement, she learns that...). Such basic, authoritative information provides parents with a context in which to understand and react more appropriately to their own children's individual needs, behaviors, and cues. It also helps them gain a fuller appreciation of the extent to which their shared everyday moments build a strong foundation for healthy development.

We must take this a step further, however, and go beyond providing general information. An often-heard criticism from parents is that suggestions offered in parenting resources often are not meaningful to them and their own babies. Over and over, parents in ZERO TO THREE's research (and those who comment in our website guest book) asked for specific, easy-to-understand guidance on parenting. For example, parents in our focus groups said they would appreciate "tips" on how to understand their babies' unique preverbal communications and behaviors, so they could be more responsive to their needs.

As we know, there are no "tips" or shortcuts to effective parenting. Learning to read a baby and becoming attuned to him require a great deal of time, careful attention, trial and error, reflection, and so on. Moreover, our field research indicates that parenting advice should not be prescriptive. Effective communication with parents requires a tough balancing act. On one hand, parents crave specifics on what they can do to promote their children's development. On the other hand, detailed "how-to's" are likely to be rejected by many parents as irrelevant to their children's and family's unique needs.

At ZERO TO THREE, we have struggled with this challenge a great deal – and have devised a promising solution. Guided by our field research, we have developed a communication approach designed to provide parents with valuable empirical, generic knowledge about not only the course of early development but also the role that caregivers and the environment play in shaping development. Of particular importance, our communications also seek to give parents basic tools of careful observation and thoughtful reflection that will enable them to adapt that knowledge to their own children, families, and circumstances and to operationalize that wisdom in their everyday lives.

What I am really suggesting here is that intermediaries between scientists and front-line caregivers can join with parents as coinvestigators. As such, we can encourage them to look at and understand their children and themselves, give them the tools to guide their observations and analysis, and support their efforts to solve the mystery of their children's behaviors and to develop the most appropriate ways to parent their children. For example, in helping parents learn how to read their children's cues, one might use vignettes to illustrate ways of *observing and thinking about their children's cues and behaviors* (pointing out that similar cues might mean different things for different children) to determine what responses would be most appropriate. While the scenarios presented in these vignettes may or may not be directly relevant to a given parent and child, our intent is to describe a process of observation, reflection, and response that *will* have broad meaning. This should help parents work through many other interactions with their children and find optimal solutions for their families.

Parents are most receptive to messages that are positive, not overwhelming or prescriptive. At the same time, communication efforts must acknowledge parents' everyday realities.

Parents are more receptive to information designed to engage and excite them about the great *opportunities of early childhood* than to messages that scare, overwhelm, or make them feel guilty. Similarly, overloading parents who are already feeling anxious, burdened, or inadequate with prescriptive instructions and lists of "shoulds" and "shouldn'ts" can be counterproductive, serving to increase stress and further undermine parents' confidence. This was clear when parents in our focus groups were asked how the following statement made them feel:

> "What happens to a baby from birth to its third birthday has enormous, long-lasting, lifetime impact on development – emotional, social, intellectual, and physical. This is a window of opportunity for parents to have a positive impact on all those areas of a baby's development."

This comment evoked a steady stream of anxious commentary, including:

- Complete skepticism: "How can you even prove that's true?"

- Anxious self-doubt: "It makes me paranoid...even though I'm trying, I do the best I can, like if I do one thing wrong...I'm an idiot...So, I think you always question yourself, even though you do the best that you can for them."

- Fear: "I find it overwhelming. My anxiety level is up to here as it is. I think it's scary to think about that. Yes, it's important, but at the same time, it's very intimidating."

- Indignant denial: "I've got to go to work, I just have to live with the fact, have to live life, I can't just...revolve around my daughter and be paranoid 24 hours a day, 7 days a week."

- Pragmatic: "I think you definitely want to do your best to expose them to things, but all this emphasis on between the ages of 0 and 3...You have to do everything you possibly can or you ruin the rest of their lives – it's really out of whack...My parents, they didn't do any of that."

In our educational material, we offer parents positive, affirming messages (such as "You can learn to read your baby" or "You can understand your child's temperament") along with specific tools for achieving such goals. Examples of empowering messages include:

- "How you are is as important as what you do." The way you act with your child, and the way you interpret and then respond to her behavior, will strongly influence what she learns from those interactions. Understanding who you are as a parent requires self-awareness about your attitudes and expectations and about your own temperament and way of approaching and relating to the world.

- "Don't just do something, stand there." Unless it is an emergency, you do not need to react immediately. Taking a few moments to observe and think about what is happening may lead to a more effective response.

- "Parenting is a lifelong learning process." When something you do does not create the desired or intended effect, it should not be seen as a failure. You are learning something new about your baby that will guide you in trying something different.

Messages such as these are particularly affirming, because they connect with parents' everyday lives. ZERO TO THREE's research made clear that communication efforts must acknowledge the realities of parenthood. If they do not – if we present recommended, ideal strategies that seem irrelevant to them – parents are likely to disregard that information. For example, a father with two jobs vehemently rejected the suggestion that he and his wife spend 30 minutes of uninterrupted "floor time" each day watching their baby and letting him explore, etc (a suggestion that other parents found quite appealing), saying: "My wife and I are very busy people. Kids can be as well developed without it. I don't like that statement, it's unrealistic. When you put a child in unrealistic settings, you're not really preparing them for the reality of the world we live in."

One key message from ZERO TO THREE to parents who feel overwhelmed by their responsibilities is that "Everyday moments are times of greatest learning for you and your baby." Parents who lack the time or interest to follow a specific infant stimulation routine usually want to learn how they can make the most of interactions during daily activities – diapering, feeding, dressing – to teach their young children that they are loved, cared for, safe, and secure. Such parents typically are delighted to hear how these common interchanges can actually serve as opportunities to learn important things about their children – such as their likes and dislikes and how they respond to different sensory experiences. Thus, by building on what parents already know and do with their children, we can help parents feel affirmed and in so doing offer them meaningful strategies to stimulate their children's development.

Communication efforts must acknowledge that parents know their children best – and recognize and respect ethnic and cultural differences.

Our research confirmed that many parents mistrust "experts." They are most receptive to information provided by professionals in the context of a trusting relationship that truly honors parents' primary role as chief mediators of their children's development and caregiving environments. As one focus group father put it, "Basically, I don't think someone can tell you about your own kid . . . I'm with my child every day. This so-called expert doesn't live with me, doesn't see what's going on . . . . [Their degree] is all paperwork."[11]

Implicit in developing positive, supportive partnerships with parents is the need to understand and respect ethnic and cultural differences. As our focus group of African-American fathers made clear, cultural differences are important. They can sometimes put parents in direct opposition to professional views many hold as "proven facts" about what is best for young children. In these cases, professionals must be careful to recognize that such divergent views stem from different cultural experiences rather than from a lack of knowledge on the part of parents.

This was evident in the focus group's discussion of social development, in which it became clear that fathers perceived their children's exposure to multiple caregivers – an unavoidable fact of life for all of the group's participants – as a positive experience, which they characterized as putting their children "ahead of white children." As one father bluntly put it, "We're African-Americans.... We're not white or rich, we don't have a nanny, or we don't have a wife who can sit home all day long. We have to go to work, we have to make ends meet, so we have to have that baby with a third or a fourth person. So they have to socialize much earlier than the average white child." This man went on to assert that this was very beneficial for the children, "...because they're learning to deal with other individuals besides Mommy and Daddy."

Front-line practitioners have reported similar observations concerning class/cultural differences in parents' perspectives on young children's exposure to multiple caregivers. For example, mothers in a focus group of Early Head Start participants in the Grand Boulevard neighborhood of Chicago, Illinois said that they believe it is important for their infants and toddlers to learn to relate to many different caregivers.[12]

When they stated they would completely reject advice from someone who was not African-American, our group of fathers made it clear that cultural sensitivity and shared cultural identity/experiences are essential prerequisites for effective communication about parenting.

> *Father:* "If that person wasn't a brother or a sister, I'd certainly be looking at them from an angle like, 'What can you tell me about raising a black child?'"

> *Moderator:* "Right off the bat, if they're not black, they're out of your comfort zone?"

Father: "I'd be more comfortable if they were black, because then at least I'd know that person was raised in a black household. I don't like the fact of being under a magnifying glass with somebody else's set of rules that I don't know."

ZERO TO THREE's field research and one-on-one communication efforts with parents of young children have taught us that a powerful strategy for minimizing obstacles posed by differences of race and class is to begin discussions by finding out parents' own goals for their children and approach interactions with parents as opportunities to join with them in a respectful partnership that helps them find ways to meet their goals.

An example of appropriate communication. Through a new partnership with Kellogg's, ZERO TO THREE has developed educational messages for parents of young children and other caregivers that over the next few months will be featured on the back panels of 22 million boxes of Rice Krispies cereal.

At first glance, the language on these cereal boxes might seem like something a competent copywriter could turn out in an hour or so. In fact, a group of ZERO TO THREE board members, our Director of Communications, and a copywriter debated for several weeks about just which words to choose for this very limited but very visible space. No, "Snap, Crackle and Pop" have not been renamed "Watch, Wait, and Wonder," or even "Snap, Crackle, and Attune." The text "speaks through the baby," for example:

- We say, "Talk **with** me," not "Talk **to** me."

- We say, "Share a book with me," not "Read to me for 15 minutes a day."

- We say, "Share in my excitement," not "Praise my achievements."

- We talk about the process of building a loving relationship: "... Sharing pictures and stories ... **makes me feel close to you**." "... I learn that you'll take care of me. **This helps me feel secure**."

We encourage the parent to observe, and we offer clues, rather than tips – for example, **Watch and listen to me.** Give me time to respond. My eyes, expressions, and body language tell you things even before I say my first word. When I turn away, I may be telling you, "I've had enough." A big smile may mean, "Let's talk more," or "I like what you are doing, keep it up!" The pleasure of our give-and-take encourages me to communicate, speak, and learn words.

Talking With Parents One-on-One: Innovative Strategies in Primary Pediatrics

As ZERO TO THREE's market research makes clear, parents are heavily invested in learning how they can contribute to their children's growth and development. Although today's parents are interested in the latest research findings and recommendations from "expert" sources, and, as we've discussed, mass communications vehicles can address these needs to some degree, *our research confirms that parents want information and guidance specific to their own children and families, provided by authoritative sources in the context of a trusting relationship.* How, then, can child health and development professionals partner with parents of young children to address this need?

Operationalizing Bright Futures: A New Movement in Pediatric Practice to Expand Support for Child/Family Development

One compelling answer is the pediatric primary healthcare setting, the most universally available and often-used source of professional support for families with children under age 3.[3,13] This cutting-edge vision, described in *Bright Futures: Guidelines for Health Supervision of Infants, Children and Adolescents,* calls for an expansion of pediatric practice beyond its present focus on physical health, to fulfill a vital prevention and health-promotion role by monitoring child development, promoting positive parent-child relationships, and boosting parents' knowledge, confidence, and competence.[3]

We have strong evidence that such child health and development services would find a ready and willing clientele among parents of infants and toddlers. Indeed, parents surveyed by ZERO TO THREE say their pediatricians are the professionals they rely on most for advice on child development and child rearing. These parents, however, are not fully satisfied with the quantity or quality of information they presently receive from this source. Forty percent of parents reported that their pediatricians never (or only occasionally) talk to them about their children's social, emotional, and intellectual development – the areas about which parents have the least information and the most questions. When asked if they would be interested in having their pediatricians facilitate helping them to understand their children, answer questions, and provide guidance on their children's development, two thirds (65%) felt such services would be very important, and another 19% saw them as fairly important.

This confirms a similar desire expressed by parents polled in The Commonwealth Fund's 1996 *Survey of Parents with Young Children,* which found that parents want more information, services, and attention from physicians on how to help their children thrive during their first years. A majority of parents said they would be willing to pay a modest fee for supplemental pediatric services such as home visits and a telephone advice line.[14]

In fact, such services have become available for selected families with young children in demonstration sites across the country. A range of initiatives, launched in the past few years, are testing model approaches to promoting all domains of children's development and building positive relationships with parents. Model initiatives include:

- The dissemination of *Bright Futures: Guidelines for Health Supervision of Infants, Children and Adolescents,* developed by leading national pediatric experts and supported by the federal Maternal and Child Health Bureau of the Department of Health and Human Services

- The *Healthy Steps for Young Children* initiative, currently operating in 15 evaluation and 6 affiliate sites across the country, which offers a core set of services, including developmental screening, home visiting, and parent groups that together restructure the way pediatric care is offered to children from birth to 3 years

- ZERO TO THREE's *Developmental Specialist in Pediatric Practice Project,* which provided for children with developmental or emotional problems: developmental screening, early identification, short-term intervention, timely referral and follow-up; for their parents: anticipatory guidance and support

- The *Pediatric Pathways to Success* model of enhanced pediatric primary care for low-income families at Boston Medical Center

- T. Berry Brazelton's *Touchpoints Project,* which emphasizes developmental and relational aspects of well-baby/child care and local service-delivery organizations

While data from formal evaluations will not be available for some time, early evidence from these initiatives strongly suggests that enhanced pediatric services *give parents meaningful guidance and support, and advance healthy infant/toddler development in cost-effective ways.* For example:

- A stable, trusting relationship with a child-development specialist provides a context for identification and remediation of emerging problems in parent-child relationships. The specialist also offers personalized, relevant, meaningful information and support, which can strengthen parents' knowledge, confidence, and competence in stimulating their young children's social, emotional, and intellectual development.

- Regular developmental monitoring in the context of well baby/child care leads to prompt identification of health and developmental problems. This permits appropriate early intervention and eliminates or reduces the need for more costly rehabilitative efforts later in life.

- Low-income families who feel connected to a dedicated advocate are better able to make appropriate use of primary pediatric care. This makes them less likely to inappropriately use costly services such as emergency room and inpatient hospital care.

ZERO TO THREE's Developmental Specialists in Pediatric Practice (DSPP) Project

ZERO TO THREE's DSPP Project (funded by the Bureau of Maternal and Child Health and private donors) was designed to explore the feasibility of broadening the scope of primary pediatric care by adding a nonmedical Developmental Specialist (DS), who could provide a range of services to support the development of infants, toddlers, and their mothers and fathers.

For 2 years beginning in July 1995, two Masters' level infant/family professionals – an early childhood educator and a clinical social worker – served as DSs in two pediatric sites in the metropolitan Washington, DC area. They provided developmental screening, early identification, short-term intervention, and timely referral and follow-up for children with emotional or developmental problems. They also provided parents with anticipatory guidance and support to strengthen their effectiveness in nurturing their children. The part-time DSs saw a total of 636 children: the majority (65%) were under 12 months of age; 19% were between 12 and 24 months; 11% between 24 and 36 months: and 5% were 36 months and older.

Key outcomes/lessons learned. The DSPP Project evaluation included detailed documentation of key decision points and activities related to the services of the Developmental Specialists, periodic interviews with pediatric staff, and a survey of parents who used the DS services.

By all indicators, the DSPP approach was effective. It provided vital individualized support for parents to help them form healthy, strong attachments with their children. The program also helped them foster their young children's emotional and overall development.

By forming mutually respectful, trusting alliances with parents and medical colleagues, the Developmental Specialists engaged families in meaningful personalized discussions of growth and development. Through these relationships, the DSs were able to:

- Strengthen parents' understanding and responsiveness to their children's developmental needs

- Assuage parents' anxieties about normal parenting challenges, build confidence, and develop parenting skills

- Identify children's developmental difficulties and begin early treatment

- Provide short-term interventions that enabled parents to address specific crises or behavioral, emotional, or relational problems

- Promote access to specialized services for families with special challenges

- Increase the capacity of the primary care setting to provide comprehensive support for infant/family development

The Developmental Specialists also strengthened the overall pediatric team's understanding of emotional development. In the words of one pediatrician, the DS's participation enriched his own ability to engage with families by encouraging him to "get down on the floor" with babies and toddlers.

Other factors that contributed to the Developmental Specialists' ability to build effective alliances with parents included:

- ***Commitment to approaching each parent as an individual.*** Just as they talked about each baby as unique, the DSs respected each family as unique and joined them "where they were." The DS often spent the first visit asking how parents were doing, how they were feeling about their new roles, and what support they felt they needed. By attending to parents first, the DS let them know that she was interested in them as well as in their child. This was particularly important when dealing with teen mothers, many of whom stated that one of the most painful parenting experiences was seeing the baby "get all the attention" and feeling ignored.

- *Attention to "professional use of self."* A trusting open relationship between the DS and parents was essential to mutually understanding the baby's unique profile and discovering meaningful ways to foster the baby's development. The DSs found that talking about their own struggles as parents helped build connections and overcome potential obstacles posed by differences in professional status, race, or ethnicity.

- *Reframing.* Helping families give new meaning to their children's behavior was a simple but powerful tool to strengthen parent-child relationships. On many occasions, after empathizing with parents' exhaustion in dealing with their very mobile, energetic infant, the DSs introduced the idea that the child was in fact very smart and developing well, rather than being "bad" or "hyperactive" or "out to drive them crazy." Reframing also provided the basis for helping many parents understand and provide appropriate nurturing for their children in areas of vulnerability. For example, one mother was troubled by her boisterous 2-year-old's tendency to give his peers "hard hugs" and to "lose it" around tactile activities such as toothbrushing or dressing. The DS helped her understand these incidents as self-protective maneuvers against tactile intrusions, rather than as "bad" behavior, which she and her husband had been punishing. This mother was extremely grateful for what she called a "gift" – an invaluable insight about her son and strategies to help him cope with this sensitivity – which she received in less than 30 minutes, during a routine visit to her pediatrician.

- *Empathy for parents' feelings and experience.* There was often a parallel process between Developmental Specialist and parent, and parent and baby: As the DSs became more engaged and understanding with parents, parents became more engaged, patient, and accepting of their own children. For example, by empathizing with one mother's feelings of rejection and personal inadequacy at her infant's excessive crying and avoidance, the DS was able to help her understand that her child was not being "fussy" or manipulative but was oversensitive to sound and touch. Engaging this mother in this way helped end a pattern of misunderstanding and misattuned caregiving that surely would have caused this mother-and-child relationship to deteriorate further over time.

The DSs' services filled a critical void for many parents, who reported that they greatly valued this unique opportunity to share, within a supportive, nonthreatening setting, their concerns and questions about how to do the best possible job of nurturing their babies and toddlers. Responses to parent surveys confirmed parents' highly positive feelings about these expanded pediatric services. Parents wholeheartedly endorsed the DSs' work and were able to articulate several specific benefits to them and their children of this comprehensive, integrated approach to well-baby care.

The vast majority of parent respondents reported that they had had a chance to discuss specific concerns about their children and learn something about their children's behavior and how to handle it. They felt they could understand more about how to help their child learn as a result of their contact with the DS and thought it would be very helpful to be able to talk to the DS on a regular basis. Parents' voluntary comments reveal that their encounters with the DS had a strong, positive effect: "I thank God for people like her"; "She is very supportive in helping me understand my son better – please keep her here"; "I love being able to take my daughter to her." These favorable responses are of potentially great interest to managed care providers and insurers who seek to gain a competitive edge in attracting subscribers.

Medical staff at both sites also clearly valued DS services – for their families, themselves, and their overall practice. Pediatric clinicians recognized the DS's special ability to approach, communicate with, and engage parents as partners. Practitioners at each site noted that significant benefits resulted from having someone with the time, interest, and knowledge to respond to parent concerns. As the lead pediatrician at the Kaiser HMO facility wrote in a memorandum requesting the use of pediatric department funds to support the DS's salary:

> [The DS] provides immeasurable good will and a necessary service for Kaiser through her ability to delve into areas and problems the providers don't have the time for, may not know how to handle, and would almost certainly refer out. If she didn't do these things, the patients would be asking the providers, and probably getting "no" or "I don't know" for an answer, taking valuable provider time, and making members dissatisfied. She has been with us about 18 months, and we have found her services invaluable.

Challenges to Sustaining/Expanding Developmentally Oriented Pediatric Services

Given the considerable benefits associated with integrating DS services into primary pediatric care settings, how do we "scale up" this model and make this vital support available to more families with young children?

The principal challenge to achieving this goal is developing stable financing that can sustain these services beyond finite periods of public and private grant support. In ZERO TO THREE's DSPP Project, notwithstanding strong commitment from leaders in both pilot sites, efforts to move financial responsibility to the practices themselves proved unsuccessful. Medical staff already besieged by a barrage of cost-containment measures were unwilling to increase practice costs by adding a DS whose services were not likely to be reimbursed by insurers. An attempt to fund her services through a parent-paid fee-for-service arrangement did not generate sufficient revenue to cover her full salary. Finding strategies to finance enhanced pediatric services independent of short-term grant funding is also a concern of the Healthy Steps for Young Children Initiative.[15]

Here again, effective communication by leaders in the professional and scientific communities can play a key role in helping realize this important goal. By working to communicate our knowledge of the lifelong consequences of early emotional development and healthy parent-child interactions, we can help convince insurers, managed care providers, healthcare purchasers, providers, and other stakeholders to invest in this model of expanded pediatric care.

Conclusions

Although we know that parents and caregivers who provide strong positive emotional relationships and appropriate stimulation create the foundation for proper intellectual, social, emotional, and physical development, many parents lack the time, resources, and information to provide appropriate nurturing to their young children. These parents are hungry for specific information about *their* children and *their* lives to help them do a better job of parenting. The scientific/professional community has a clear responsibility to play an active role in addressing this need.

Primary pediatrics offers a unique opportunity for medical and nonmedical professionals to form partnerships with parents on behalf of infant/toddler health and development. As the DSPP Project, Healthy Steps, and other initiatives show, such alliances can be effective in boosting parental confidence, knowledge, and competence; promoting positive parent-child relationships; and closely monitoring infant/toddler development.

The confluence of several factors – including growing public and political interest in the years from birth to age 3, the steady rise of barriers to effective parenting, the burgeoning of scientific knowledge about early development, and the emergence of successful models for outreach and support to parents – make this an ideal time for professionals to reach out and offer support to mothers and fathers as they struggle to promote their young children's healthy emotional development. Such support might take the form of enhanced pediatric services, coordinated mass-communication efforts, or other strategies to provide families with vital knowledge and resources to support effective child-rearing. I suggest that it is the responsibility of professionals from all disciplines who work with infants and toddlers to:

- Read and understand child development research

- Put research findings into a meaningful context for families and front-line caregivers

- Enlist parents as "coinvestigators" of their infants' and toddlers' development, using the same basic tools of careful observation, rigorous data analysis, and thoughtful reflection as would any researcher

We all must play a part in these efforts. I encourage you to consider how you and your colleagues can contribute to this exciting national movement.

References

1. Schor E. Measurable development in parents: a goal in effective primary care. *Zero to Three*. 1997;17:41-43.
2. Olds D, Kitzman H, Cole R, Robinson J. Theoretical foundations of a program of home visitation for pregnant women and parents of young children. *Journal of Community Psychology*. 1997;25:9-25.
3. Green M, ed. *Bright Futures: Guidelines for Health Supervision of Infants, Children and Adolescents*. Arlington, VA: National Center for Education in Maternal and Child Health; 1994.
4. Erickson MF, Korfmacher J, Egeland BR. Attachments past and present: implications for therapeutic intervention with mother-infant dyads. *Development and Psychopathology*. 1992;4:495-507.
5. Lally JR, Mangione PL, Honig AS, Wittmer DS. More pride, less delinquency: findings from the ten-year follow-up study of the Syracuse University Family Development Research Program. *Zero to Three*. 1988;4:13-18.
6. Werner E. Individual differences, universal needs: a 30-year study of resilient high risk infants. *Zero to Three*. 1988;8:1-5.
7. Seitz V, Rosenbaum LK, Apfel NH. Effects of family support intervention: a ten-year follow-up. *Child Development*. 1985;56:376-391.
8. Simpson R. *The Role of the Mass Media in Parenting Education*. Boston, MA: Center for Health Communication, Harvard School of Public Health; 1997.
9. Tinsley B, Lees N. Health promotion for parents. In: Bornstein MH, ed. *Handbook of Parenting, Vol 4, Applied and Practical Parenting*. Mahwah, NJ: Lawrence Erlbaum; 1995:187-204.

10. Okagaki L, Divecha D. Development of parental beliefs. In: Luster T, Okagaki L, eds. *Parenting: An Ecological Perspective*. Hillsdale, NJ: Lawrence Erlbaum; 1993:35-67.

11. Stern D. *The Motherhood Constellation*. New York, NY: Basic Books; 1997.

12. Gilkerson L, Stott F. Listening to the voices of families: learning through caregiving consensus groups. *Zero to Three*. 1997;18:9-16.

13. Kaplan-Sanoff M, Brown T, Zuckerman B. Enhancing pediatric primary care for low-income families: cost lessons learned from pediatric pathways to success. *Zero to Three*. 1997;17:34-36.

14. Young K, Davis K, Shoen C. *The Commonwealth Fund Survey of Parents with Young Children*. New York, NY: Commonwealth Fund; 1996.

15. Zuckerman B, Kaplan-Sanoff M, Parker S, Young K. The healthy steps for young children program. *Zero to Three*. 1997;17:20-25.

International Perspectives in Early Emotional Development

Robert J. Haggerty, MD

Introduction

The World Health Organization's definition of health as the optimal state of physical, emotional, and social well-being clearly involves early emotional development. The field of early emotional development grows more important daily because of changes in the prevalence of childhood illness, and the influx of new information on early childhood development (Tables 1, 2). In addition, it is clear that one cannot separate physical, emotional, and social well-being; children present a seamless whole of interaction among these various factors. The goal of child healthcare remains to provide technically competent and empathic care for the child and her/his family to ensure optimal well-being.

Table 1. Twentieth-century trends in pediatric morbidity[1]

Classic Pediatric Morbidity (1900-1955)
- Infectious diseases
- High infant-mortality rates
- Poor nutrition
- Few cures for chronic diseases
- Diseases of overcrowding
- Epidemics, eg, influenza, polio

The New Morbidity (1955-1990s)
- Family dysfunction
- Learning disabilities
- Coordination of care
- Emotional disorders
- Functional distress
- Educational needs

Beyond the New Morbidity (1990s and onward)
- Social disarray
- Political ennui
- New epidemics, eg, violence, AIDS, cocaine
- Increased survivorship
- High-technology care

Table 2. Factors changing pediatrics[2]

- Diversity, multiculturalism, and a world view
  - Increased travel   - Gender roles
  - Immigration   - Mobility
- Technology
- Economic, educational disparity
- Environmental issues

The International Perspective

The needs of children differ in each country, and so, too, will the services they require. The global view of health has generally been limited to concern about exotic diseases coming into the United States, and the treatment of these diseases in patients overseas. However, there is another significant aspect of a global view: We can learn from other cultures.

In the past decade, at least two important innovations from the developing world are being practiced in the developed world: oral rehydration for children with diarrhea, and the presence of a doula during childbirth. The impact of a doula on reducing the duration and complications of labor was first recognized by Drs Kennell and Klaus in Guatemala – their findings have since been confirmed in nearly one dozen controlled trials.

The Child Development Program in Thailand

An exceedingly interesting program in early child development that may benefit children all over the world is being implemented in Thailand. The Thai Community-Based Child Development Program is predicated on the same neurodevelopmental research indicating that early infant stimulation is crucial in helping children achieve their full potential. In this integrated, multidisciplinary family-based child health program, child developmental elements have been incorporated into the backbone of the service. The elements (Table 3) emphasize intersectorial collaboration and bring together health, education, community economic development, social welfare, and nongovernmental organizations with community volunteers to empower families to provide better care for their children (Fig 1).

Table 3. Community-based child development

Program Elements
    Theoretical basis – neurodevelopmental research
    Intersectorial integration – health, education, community development,
    social welfare, community volunteers
Support
    Thai government
    UNICEF
    Save the Children
Ages
    Birth to 5 years
Community Volunteers
    Women with children
    1-week training (principles of child development)
    Each visits 5 families in their homes
        Assess by HOME method
        Teach mother use of toys & stimulation
        Nutrition advice

The center of the service program is a community volunteer, usually a woman who has raised children and who, after short introductory training, is assigned five families who are expecting new babies. She makes a home visit shortly after the birth of the baby, assesses the home using an adaptation of the HOME assessment instrument,[3] and evaluates the mother's capacity to care for and adequately stimulate her baby. She then instructs the mother in a variety of early infant-stimulation techniques, including talking, touching, holding, playing, and the use of appropriate toys. The program has been supported by UNICEF, Save The Children, and the Royal Thai Government. From 1990 to 1996, the program was implemented in 16 provinces in Thailand. The program evaluation (Table 4) demonstrates that in villages where the program has been implemented, developmental characteristics (such as IQ) were better than in comparison villages. In addition to these IQ scores, children in the program villages weighed more and had a reduction in second-degree malnutrition. This success motivated the Thai government to fund and implement the program in all 75 provinces, and to increase the age from preschool up to and through 18 years.

Fig 1. Thailand's Family Development Program.

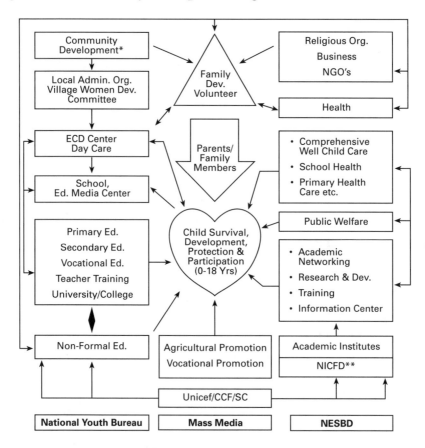

*Coordinating agency for program implementation.

**Coordinating agency for academic and technical support.

Source: Personal communication; Nittaya J. Kotchabhakdi, MD, Mahidol University, Bangkok, Thailand

Table 4. Results of Thailand Program Evaluation

	Experimental	Control
Mean IQ pretest	85.8	89.5
Mean IQ posttest	94.0	90.7
Posttest children with IQ = 100	18.3%	13.8%
Posttest children with IQ > 100	8.3%	3.0%
HOME Scores +	80%	68%

Table 5. Recommendations of International Pediatric Association workshop

Develop a comprehensive service package

Referral and feedback for those with developmental problems

Educate students from all sectors

Child development includes family function

Make parents first-line developmental resources

In the fall of 1997, an International Pediatric Association workshop was held in Thailand. The participants went to program villages, made home visits, studied the data, and made a series of recommendations that are important for early child-development programs (Table 5).

First, there is a need for a simple but comprehensive well-child service package, including developmental assessment, to help instruct care providers. This is needed because one of the limiting factors in early child-development programs is lack of protocols or service packages to guide nonprofessional workers.

Second, a referral system is necessary for those with developmental and behavioral problems, with effective feedback to community-level workers.

Third, students of medicine and other health-related fields should be involved in these programs. In particular, health students should learn to work collaboratively with other sectors, such as education and economic development.

Fourth, perhaps most important, the concept of child development should be expanded to include family function. All too often, child development is looked on as an assessment of physical milestones. This approach, characteristic of the developmental-disabilities field, has serious limitations in terms of optimizing the broad development of children.

Fifth, all personnel must realize that parents are the first line of child-development assessment and intervention. Health workers need to teach parents the developmental and interactional skills necessary for healthy infants.

United States Programs

Two programs in the United States have incorporated some of these principles into an effective early intervention. These are the Nurse Home Visiting Program of David Olds, and the Healthy Steps Program, now being implemented through the Commonwealth Fund. Neither of these programs is as broad as the Thailand Community-Based Child Development Program; they do not involve multiple sectors in the community, and the Healthy Steps Program does not begin during pregnancy. A concept more akin to the Thailand program is the proposal by Robert Chamberlin to "put it all together," which means involving multiple sectors to deal with the whole family and community, as well as with the individual child, and carrying out rigorous evaluation. The Thailand Community-Based Child Development Program offers much for those of us in the developed world to emulate.

References

1. Palfrey JS. *Community Child Health: An Action Plan for Today.* Westport, CT: Prager Press; 1994.
2. Noggerty RJ. Child Health 2000: new pediatrics in the changing environment of children's needs in the 21st century. *Pediatrics.* 1995;96:804-812.
3. Caldwell B, Bradley R. *Home Observation for Measurement of the Environment.* Little Rock, AR: University of Arkansas; 1979.

Section 6:
Discussion

Section 6.
Discussion

Discussions during the Pediatric Round Table covered the spectrum of issues relating to the importance of early emotional development. The consensus of those exchanges is presented in this final chapter.

The faculty of the *1998 Johnson & Johnson Pediatric Round Table: New Perspectives in Early Emotional Development* are among the world's leaders in the field of infant development. Each brought to the table years of experience from a variety of disciplines. The salient points of their discussions are summarized in the following chapter.

Communication Is Important

Emotional development in infants and children has life-long effects, and everyone caring for them – pediatricians, child health professionals, families, and caregivers – has an important role in the growth and development of unique and healthy human individuals. A common theme to facilitate optimal infant development, advanced by all participants in this *Pediatric Round Table,* is the need for excellent communication and cooperation among all individuals who influence young lives.

On one level, improved communication between researchers and clinicians will get meaningful new information into practice where it can be used effectively. This process will be even more effective if professionals from both disciplines, in the interests of cross-fertilization, exchange ideas and observations early and frequently. In many ways, round-table meetings such as this one break new ground and establish the foundation of productive alliances.

On another level, communication between professionals and parents, grandparents, and day-to-day caregivers must have an appropriate tone and content to actually deliver meaningful effective messages. It is often important to step back from years of professional training to think in parent terms. What do parents have to know to have the greatest positive effect on their baby? What do I have to avoid saying so that I don't add to their uncertainty, anxiety, or frustration? One often-repeated example of the latter dealt with explaining why the first years of life were important in the child's later health and well-being. All too often this knowledge made parents worry that even the tiniest mistake would destroy the baby's opportunity for a happy, healthy, and productive life.

The answer to this dilemma is that there is no simple answer. Every baby, every family, every environment is unique. Each is the product of a diverse genetic, cultural, and religious heritage. The pediatrician must embrace this complexity, yet communicate with simplicity.

Major Messages for Professionals and Parents

But what is new, valid, and meaningful to professionals and parents?

Emotional development is important. A basic tenet is that early emotional development is as important as early physical development. Talking about physical development is always somewhat easier, because well-established milestones for growth and physical skills have been known for years. Discussing emotional and behavioral milestones is more complex because they are less well-defined; and there may be a danger in proscribing clear-cut "emotional milestones" because each infant is unique and develops at his or her own pace.

Early life is a crucial time in a person's development. At a young age, the brain is growing, developing, and open in special ways to visual, tactile, olfactory, and auditory stimulation. The combination of these stimuli, the way people interact with infants, and the total environment in which infants live all influence long-term behavior and intellectual development. For example, development of emotional attachment between a mother and her new baby is important within hours and days of birth. In cultures where mother and baby are kept apart, the rates of infant abandonment and abuse are high; these rates plummet when mother and baby are provided maximum contact with each other. In this case, by allowing emotional development to occur fully and naturally, a healthy maternal-infant dyad is formed, a baby is cared for by his mother, and society benefits on all fronts.

Discussing and evaluating emotional development. Addressing emotional development requires professionals who are sensitive and emotionally avail-

able. Helping parents and infants through emotional or behavioral problems is not the same as treating otitis media. Practitioners need to "be there"
for their patients, not just physically, but emotionally. This involves using
your own emotions to appreciate the uniqueness and individuality of those
you care for. Your emotions help you understand your patients' feelings of
interest and surprise, struggle and suffering, or anxiety and depression. Your
emotions are a window into your patients' lives, and antennae for receiving
their behavioral cues and concerns.

Considering this new dimension of clinical practice prompted a discussion
that focused on the role pediatricians and pediatric nurses play in emotional
and behavioral development. In the current environment of managed health
care, what exactly are pediatric specialists, and what should they do? A concern was that emotional issues, although important, are not generally considered billable items within managed health systems. Therefore there is little
incentive to devote time and resources to them. Bringing a developmental
specialist into a group practice has certain advantages, but the issue of funding is once again a problem. But perhaps more important was the observation that when parents come to a pediatrician, they want to see a *pediatrician*.
There are, for better or worse, expectations and privileged relations that exist
only between physicians and nurses and their patients. Although other
trained health professionals contribute immensely, the pediatric specialists
are often the first point of contact and should take the lead in emotional
assessment.

Because this is not often the case, there is a need to motivate, influence,
and educate medical professionals in the skills of emotional and behavioral
assessment. Quite naturally, these skills need to be applied in clinical practice. Once again, communication among peers is important in making others
aware of early emotional development. Continuing Medical Education
programs, journal articles, symposia, conferences, and just *talking* to one's
colleagues are all valid methods to increase awareness of development. For
medical students and pediatric residents, more training should be available
in infant development and behavior.

The role of family and environment. Infants exist in complex settings
involving parents, relatives, caregivers, religious beliefs, and ethnic practices,
as well as the physical environment. These create a tapestry within which
the infant's life is woven; each thread leads to and from the infant in ways

that professionals should understand. With that understanding, opportunities are created to form therapeutic alliances for the benefit of the infant.

The infant's overall environment was cited as crucial – the number of risk factors correlates inversely with later success. Infants with multiple risk factors are more likely to be developmentally and intellectually compromised compared to those with few or no risk factors. The pervading role of the environment complicates interventions or research that address only one or two variables when many risk factors may be present. Therefore, it may be beneficial for professionals to take a step back and examine the whole picture before diagnosing or intervening in developmental problems.

Yet within this tapestry, the birth of a baby provides an entry point for positively affecting with development in a familial context. Because birth is a time of reorganization and redefinition for the mother and family, professionals have an unmatched opportunity to get involved. At or around birth, there is an openness that enables you to learn about parental expectations, ghosts, or potential problems in the caregiving environment. Learning of these situations makes it possible to reassure parents, and when needed, to embark on more extensive interventions.

It is also important to remember that mothers are not the only caregivers intimately involved with newborns and children. Fathers make important, tangible contributions to infant development. Professionals are encouraged to include the role of fathers in their own context of infant development, and consequently encourage fathers themselves to actively participate in their babies' lives.

Similarly, nonparental caregivers can have considerable impact on infant development. An emerging concern for this group is how to provide them with appropriate developmental information. In light of the focus first on mothers, then on fathers, caregivers (who may be with the infant as much or more than the parents) could certainly benefit from additional consideration. In the absence of more concrete plans, communication once again is important – professionals need to talk with parents, and parents with caregivers, to ensure that infants are getting all they need to develop optimally.

The Need for More Research

Early emotional development is a field rich in opportunities to further the understanding of fundamental processes that shape the lives of infants and families. At the biological level, much can still be learned about the chemical, physiological, and structural relations between the developing human brain and behavior. This exploration should include expanded study of normal baseline behavior, as well as examples of abnormal development, pathology, and trauma.

In examining behavior itself, better descriptions are needed for a variety of clinical syndromes and emotions; any such description would then be subject to empirical verification. Also worth studying is the possible identification of hierarchical emotional milestones in development – on the other hand, such milestones may be absent, and research will reveal the importance of individual variability in emotional development.

The richest areas for research will flow from the collaboration of professionals with different, yet complementary skills and experience. Cooperation among neurologists, psychologists, developmental biologists, pediatricians, and nurses can lead to improved study design and more definitive data for virtually all issues in early development. Working together will help everyone appreciate the complexity and contextualized nature of emotions, and help create new tools to capture and understand that complexity.

And finally, research is needed to discover the best ways to deliver information about early emotional and behavioral development to parents and caregivers. Although it can be anticipated that optimal communication will involve a variety of techniques and approaches, helping parents understand their infants and themselves is at the heart of many intervention strategies. By sharing our new perspectives in early emotional development in the most effective ways, we can make a lasting positive impact on the healthy development of infants and their families throughout the world.